Introduction to the Theory of Knowledge

Introduction to the Theory of Knowledge

D. J. O'CONNOR

Emeritus Professor of Philosophy, University of Exeter

and

BRIAN CARR

Lecturer in Philosophy, University of Exeter

UNIVERSITY OF MINNESOTA PRESS

Published by the University of Minnesota Press,
2037 University Avenue Southeast, Minneapolis MN 55414

Printed in Great Britain

Library of Congress Cataloging in Publication Data
O'Connor, D.J.
   Introduction to the theory of knowledge.
   Bibliography.
   Includes index.
   1. Knowledge, theory of.   I. Carr, Brian.
   II. Title.
   BD161.C347   121   82-2057
   ISBN 0-8166-1132-7   AACR2
   ISBN 0-8166-1133-5 (pbk)

The University of Minnesota
is an equal-opportunity
educator and employer.

CONTENTS

PREFACE

The theory of knowledge – 'epistemology' as it has been traditionally called – has an intimate connection with other branches of the philosophical enterprise, and it has from earliest times had a central place within the enterprise as a whole. Plato's Theory of Forms was an early theory of the nature of knowledge and at the same time a metaphysical theory – that is, an attempt to describe the constitution and structure of reality. (It is indeed reasonable to expect that a theory of knowledge should be developed hand in hand with a metaphysical theory, that an account of *how* we know should come with one of *what* we know.) Most strikingly the major divide among philosophies of the seventeenth and eighteenth centuries was that between rationalism and empiricism, and that was essentially an epistemological divide.

But epistemology is connected with other branches of philosophy as well. For example, philosophical psychology (also known as the philosophy of mind) deals with the nature of the mental side of man, and the old problem of the relation between mind and body. Epistemology is closely relevant here, for it treats of the knowledge which we have of mental events: the much used notion of the 'privacy of mental states' in philosophical psychology is, in one of its guises, an epistemological notion. Epistemology is closely relevant to the philosophy of religion also, since the nature of faith needs to be elucidated in terms of its relation to rational belief, and this notion is one of the most basic in our enquiry. Religion introduces a special interest, what is more, in that kind of knowledge which is knowledge on authority. A further connection exists between epistemology and the philosophy of science, which seeks to elucidate that peculiar institutionalised form of empirical knowledge; and which indeed many empiricists look upon as epitomising rationality in belief. And the

vii

philosophy of science has a special interest, from the predictive and retrodictive import of the theories of science, in the nature and very possibility of knowledge of the future and the past.

What is more, epistemology has close connections with the philosophies of all those disciplines which seek to attain knowledge of one sort or another, though remaining of more general scope and broader concern than any of them, such as the philosophy of psychology, of physics, of sociology, or of history. Some would argue that the importance of epistemology lies precisely in its connection with such weighty concerns as physics and sociology, realising that any serious consideration of these enterprises leads quickly to basic questions about the nature of knowledge, its relation to interpersonal criteria of evidence, and so on. Epistemology is of course important for that reason; the history of thought testifies on the other hand to a persistent and central interest in the nature of knowledge as such. It is an essential step in understanding the nature of man and the nature of the world he inhabits to ask how they interrelate. The fundamental status of this question is witnessed by the frequency with which epistemological matters force themselves forward in philosophical investigations generally.

This book is primarily designed as a text for students who already possess some grounding in philosophy. Such students should be better placed to appreciate the detail of our presentation, and not lose sight of the wood while scrutinising the trees. On the other hand we have tried to keep very much in mind that the theory of knowledge is ideally suited as a way into philosophy generally, and we hope that the book can find a place as a general introduction for students who have had no previous acquaintance with the subject. Given this second intended audience the rather severe limitations which present costs enforce on book publishers is not so regrettable: we have been forced to select what we see as the central and most important issues, and suppress the natural instinct of philosophers to pursue all intricacies of argument and variety of opinions.

We have tried, within the space permitted, to integrate contemporary with historical material, so that a correct sense of continuity of problems and preoccupations comes over to the reader. We have also tried to introduce whenever possible material from psychology and physiology, so that the philosophy does not seem totally divorced from other intellectual pursuits. We have also taken pains to use technical vocabulary only when strictly necessary and have always spelt out the meaning of such terms.

Philosophy is the paradigm of a rational activity, and we have always placed great emphasis on the *arguments* for or against the views we discuss. It is hoped that the student will be encouraged by this example to look to the arguments in philosophical debates and not just the positions adopted – and we would hope further that the student will improve his philosophical skills by trying to find the faults (as surely there must be such) in the arguments presented here. If the teacher finds inadequate coverage of his favourite topics, or insensitive and unfair treatment of his favourite arguments, this can readily offer an ideal opportunity to begin the task of constructive critical thinking with his or her students.

We have tried in this book to present the most basic issues which arise in epistemology from as non-partisan a position as possible, and in such a way that the reader can move easily from the text to books and journals in which current issues are being vigorously pursued. This latter aim has made it sometimes necessary to leave the level of the purely introductory, and follow a topic some way into the complexities of its ramifications. Light, we hope, is nevertheless thrown thereby onto areas of current research which would otherwise be forbidding and impenetrable to the reader.

We would like to express our appreciation of the comments and advice given on various parts of the book by our colleagues at Exeter University, Ron Atkinson, Geoffry Keene, Glenn Landford, and Betty Powell. We would like also to thank Margaret Boden of Sussex University, and Editor of the Harvester Studies in Philosophy, for her warm encouragement of this project and continuing support against successive failures to meet deadlines.

Sections of Chapter I are based, in part, on a paper which appeared in *Philosophical Inquiry*, Vol. I, No. 3, 1979, under the title 'The Grounds of Uncertainty'.

CHAPTER I

SCEPTICISM AND CERTAINTY

Introduction

Epistemology, the theory of knowledge, is concerned with knowledge in a number of ways. First and foremost it seeks to give an account of the nature of *knowing* in general, that is, to provide an analysis of the concept of knowing which will adequately handle its use in all the varied contexts in which we apply it; and it seeks to give accounts of the important related concepts such as belief, certainty, and truth. The tendency throughout the history of philosophy, and a tendency which has been very apparent during the present century, has been to provide such an account of knowledge by setting out the conditions under which the proposition 'A (the subject) knows that P (the proposition)' is true, but such a truth condition analysis can be supplemented by other forms; in particular the conditions under which it is *reasonable to say* (perhaps falsely) 'I know that P' – that is to *claim* to know that P – throws light on the nature of knowing.[1]

A second concern of epistemology is with the *sources* of knowledge, with the investigation of the nature and variety of *modes of acquiring* knowledge. By far the most obvious and undeniable mode is perception, though this is not the only candidate which has presented itself. It has been commonplace up to the present century for philosophers to suggest that a second (and on many accounts a superior) mode is that of intellect or reason, particularly where it was hoped to show that knowledge is attainable of realms transcending the experienced world, whether of the 'real' world hidden behind the phenomena, or of God. Among such philosophers probably the most influential were René Descartes and Immanuel Kant, and during the nineteenth century F. H. Bradley, in England. Often it has been thought that there are further modes of knowing, dubbed 'intuition', for example a moral sense by which we acquire knowledge of moral truths, or a sense through which we acquire knowledge of aesthetic truths, or even one through which we discover mathematical truths. However, the twentieth century has been very much the era of empiricism which denies that knowledge can be acquired via reason or intuition, and so it is no accident that the greatest concentration of attention recently has been on the analysis of sense-perception. Bertrand Russell is probably the best known exponent of this philosophical tradition, with A. J. Ayer carrying the torch in England of the logical empiricist school of Vienna.

The third concern, with the *scope* of knowledge, is clearly closely related to the other two. The world of physical objects is within its scope (though some philosophers have denied even this), but the correct account of our knowledge of it has been much disputed, and the expression 'the external world' indicates the presupposition of our lack of direct contact with it which is made by most philosophical accounts – and which possibly creates most of the problem. There is also knowledge of the mental life of ourselves and others, of which an account is needed. The past (known through memory) and the future seem to many to fall easily within the scope of knowledge, but many philosophers would also have extended it further to embrace an ultimate mind-independent reality, some very general necessary truths about reality or the world of experience, and of course moral, aesthetic, and mathematical truths. An empiricist's commitment to an austere view of the sources of knowledge must be expected to result in a limited scope for knowledge as well.

The fourth concern of epistemology has been, and for many still is, to defend our criteria for knowledge against the attack of *scepticism*. This has been undoubtedly epistemology's most striking feature, the problems and pre-occupations of philosophers in this field being concerned to a very great extent with the sceptical possibility that we have *no* knowledge in this or that area – of the future, the past, the external world, of God and so on – and with ways of trying to answer the sceptic's challenge. Once more it is apparent that this concern is closely linked with the others, and it is again no surprise that the empiricist has not only defended knowledge gained from the senses against scepticism, but has himself proposed the sceptical thesis for knowledge of greater scope or from a different source. (Indeed Russell and Ayer are probably best known for their sceptical views.) An easy and attractive way of dealing with the sceptic who claims we have no knowledge whatsoever, is to point out that he is convicted out of his own mouth, for his positive thesis has sufficient scope to encompass itself: this hardly provides, however, anything like a conclusive victory for the defender of our standardly accepted criteria for knowledge, for (as the empiricist's case makes plain) a sceptic can easily limit his attack to a more narrowly circumscribed area. More importantly, the positive thesis that we can have no knowledge is interesting only because of the reasons advanced in its favour, and much is to be learnt from a consideration of the variety of such reasons which have at one time or another been advanced. Scepticism raises legitimate questions which any theory of knowledge must answer.

Descartes and Hume

The two major figures in the history of scepticism, having had the greatest influence on the kind of sceptical problems considered and the basic approach to answering those problems, were René Descartes in the seventeenth century and David Hume in the eighteenth. Descartes was not himself a sceptic; on the contrary he presented his philosoohy as the answer to sceptical tendencies which had been rife in the intellectual world since the Renaissance: it is nevertheless true that his problems and his solutions had a major influence on subsequent discussions of scepticism. Hume, on the other hand, was a self-professed sceptic, though he recognised man's inability to maintain himself in a state of total disbelief except in his most philosophical moments. Leibniz, Bayle, Voltaire, and Kant all found themselves within an intellectual problem situation handed down from one or both of these major figures. Mill, Mach, James, Russell, Moore and Wittgenstein all deal with problems which can be traced back to Descartes and Hume.

The thesis that we have no knowledge in this or that 'area of enquiry' – if we may use such a grand term to distinguish mental from physical states-of-affairs for example, or past from future – is typically put forward on the basis of the critical rejection of whatever knowledge criteria we commonly use in that area. It is as well to be clear at the outset just what these criteria are with which the sceptic finds fault. As will be seen in Chapter III, there are a limited number of conditions commonly recognised by philosophers which have to obtain before knowledge itself can properly be ascribed to someone; these include (1) that the proposition P in question is true; (2) that the subject to whom knowledge is being ascribed believes that P is true; and (3) that P is indubitable, in the sense that it is not reasonable to withhold assent to P and it is reasonable *not* to doubt that P. Unless such conditions obtain we would not accept the claim 'A (the subject) knows that P', and those conditions are indeed naturally referred to as 'knowledge criteria'. Such criteria are, however, obviously of very general application, being conditions required for knowledge in all areas of enquiry, and are not themselves typically subjected to critical scrutiny by the sceptic. What on the other hand *is* specific to a particular area of enquiry is the sort of consideration taken account of in deciding whether some proposition in that area is indubitable, and it is this criterion which the sceptic disputes. Knowledge criteria in this sense, *standards*, or *criteria of certainty*, vary from one area to another, though there are undoubtedly some similarities across the various boundaries.

The objections raised by Descartes and Hume to the prevailing standards of certainty are importantly different, and both can be seen reflected in the persistent problems of epistemology: Descartes' reservations concerning the current criteria for indubitability can be characterised as the objection that they provide no complete *guarantee* of the truth of the propositions which they warrant; Hume's that they are not themselves provided with an independent foundation which would justify their application. It is worthwhile considering both of these positions in some detail.[2]

Descartes' *Meditations on First Philosophy* (1641) 'Wherein are demonstrated the Existence of God and the Distinction of Soul and Body' is a classic work in both epistemology and metaphysics, purporting to establish a system of knowledge which is immune from sceptical criticism in being founded on a correct understanding and knowledge of God. The *Meditations* are presented as a series of reflections on the foundations of knowledge, and the first of them expounds a set of searching sceptical arguments against prevailing criteria. Descartes aims to seek out one or more propositions which will prove totally immune from sceptical objections, and which will provide the foundation for a system of knowledge more secure than the one it replaces. To accomplish this end Descartes adopts the principle of withholding assent 'no less carefully from what is not plainly certain and indubitable than from what is obviously false'.

The arguments against the standard criteria for certainty are as follows: a great deal of what we commonly consider to be knowledge has been acquired from, or by means of, the senses, but it need only be pointed out that the senses have sometimes deceived us to realise that what they indicate is not certain and indubitable. Secondly, if we consider only those cases of perception which are least likely to be mistaken, concerning objects which are neither minute nor remote, it can be seen that even here mistakes are possible: for example, in dreaming we have been misled into thinking we are experiencing the real world, and 'there is no certain mark by which to distinguish sleeping from waking experiences'.[3] We cannot be certain therefore that what we are experiencing is not simply a dream. Such criticisms, however, have no application to knowledge which neither asserts nor implies the existence of objects in the world of public experience, knowledge, for example, of propositions of arithmetic or (pure) geometry any of which could be just as true as they are now even were there no physical world to experience, so the indubitability of such propositions is so far unassailed: as Descartes writes, 'whether I am awake or asleep, two and three add up to five, and a square has only four sides; and it seems impossible for such obvious truths to fall under a suspicion of being false'. There is nevertheless reason to withhold assent from even these propositions: 'I judge that other men sometimes go wrong over what they think they know perfectly well; may not God likewise make me go wrong, whenever I add two and three, or count the sides of a square?' If the hypothesis of a deceiving God is thought to be offensive we can suppose 'an evil spirit who is supremely powerful and intelligent, and does his utmost to deceive me'. There seems to be no reason why such a powerful and malevolent being could not exist and deceive me on all such simple non-empirical propositions.

We should note that in these arguments Descartes has not set out at all clearly the knowledge criteria he is attacking, resting content instead with the briefest indication of the types of knowledge he finds defective – these are the perceptual, as in 'I am wearing a cloak, sitting by the fire', and the area which he calls that of 'obvious truths' such as '2 + 2 = 4' or 'A square has four sides'. (This division is hardly exhaustive, and it is interesting that he has not included knowledge of one's own state of mind or intentions.) Descartes' point can briefly be put as the claim that the standard criteria (whatever they are) which warrant certainty are defective. Secondly, we can note that there are two different kinds of consideration indicated in Descartes' three arguments, one of which is more legitimate than the other. Commentators on Descartes' *Meditations* are fond of pointing out that his arguments for scepticism sometimes rest on actual cases where we have been misled, and it is clearly illegitimate to argue that from knowledge of such mistakes which would involve having established what *were* the facts, to a general scepticism covering all such knowledge claims. Undoubtedly Descartes' charge against the standard criteria is fundamentally that they provide no watertight *guarantee* of the truth of whatever they warrant. This is clear from his reliance on the *possibility* of an evil demon, and the absence of a certain mark to distinguish waking experiences: the standard criteria do not suffice to rule out such possibilities. (Actual mistakes in relying on the standard criteria also point to their fallibility.) It is obvious that Descartes will be satisfied only with a criterion of indubitability which is infallible.

In the *Second Meditation*, Descartes produces a proposition about which he claims there can be no doubt whatsoever. Considering the hypothesis of an evil demon he proclaims: 'Let him deceive me as much as he may, he will never bring it about that, at the time of thinking that I am something, I am in fact nothing . . . This proposition "I am", "I exist", whenever I utter it or conceive it in my mind, is necessarily true.' The proposition 'I exist' is indubitable, not simply in the sense that our standard criteria warrant its acceptance without hesitation, but in a stronger sense. It is again obviously more than a reference to our psychological inability to doubt our own existence (if that is indeed the case), but its correct identification and description is somewhat confounded by the bewildering variety of formulations Descartes gives of his 'primary truth' which he apparently takes to be equivalent. He formulates it as 'I think', 'I exist', 'I am a thinking thing', and even

as 'Cogito ergo sum', which is presumably equivalent to the compound proposition 'I think, and my thinking implies my existing'.[4] It is reasonably clear that there is a need to give the proposition 'I exist' a position unassailable by the evil demon, yet some
have seen this as a consequence of the peculiar degeneracy of the
words as a vehicle of information: in as much as these words
convey no information to myself (and very little to my hearers) it
is not surprising that the demon cannot mislead me on the matter.[5] Such an interpretation is perhaps a little unfair, for in the
first place the proposition 'I exist' asserts a state of affairs which
could have been otherwise and hence conveys *some* (factual)
information, and in the second place its immunity from doubt is
rather (at least in part) a consequence of the fundamentality of
the proposition – it is not something for which I could possibly be
required to provide *evidence*.

Whatever may be the correct explanation of the immunity of 'I
exist' from the kind of scepticism propounded in the *First Meditation* there is every reason to think that Descartes himself failed to
grasp its nature. For he believed that his 'primary truth' provided
the new criterion of certainty which we was seeking: 'I am certain
that I am a conscious being. Surely then I also know what is
required for my being certain about anything? In this primary
knowledge all I need is a clear and distinct perception of what I
assert . . . It looks as though I could lay down the general rule:
whatever I perceive very clearly and distinctly is true.' (*Third
Meditation*) Now the proposition 'I think' is *not* indubitable
because it is clearly and distinctly perceived. This is seen from the
fact that Descartes rejected propositions of simple arithmetic (e.g.
'2 + 2 = 4') or geometry in the *First Meditation* as not indubitable,
although they are perceived clearly and distinctly, the evil demon
argument being used precisely at this point. Secondly, it is plain
enough from any natural sense of 'clearly and distinctly perceived
to be so' that 'I think' is not indubitable for that reason. Descartes
is mistaken therefore in his identification of his new criterion.

Could clarity and distinctness nevertheless serve as the criterion Descartes was seeking? It could do so only if it provided an
infallible guide to truth, for this, as we have seen, is just what our
standard criteria fail to offer. Now on the face of it clarity and
distinctness is indeed infallible, for what sense can we make of the
statement 'I see clearly and distinctly that P (e.g. there are four

sides to a square), but perhaps it is not so'?[6] There immediately arises the new problem for Descartes that in that case we may simply *think* we are clearly and distinctly perceiving some truth when we are not doing so, and Descartes would have to look for another criterion to decide when clarity and distinctness occur.

It is plain, however, that Descartes did not understand 'clarity and distinctness' in this sense, such that 'I see clearly and distinctly that P' implies *logically* that P, for he immediately asks how the general rule of clarity and distinctness is to be validated, and he certainly does not treat it as a logical truth. He sees no need for a criterion to decide when we *are* clearly and distinctly perceiving something – this is something over which the evil demon is apparently assumed to be powerless, and suggests that all that pertains to a clear and distinct perception is wholly contained within consciousness. Descartes' validation of the criterion was denounced as circular by his contemporaries and it is, to say the least, difficult to defend it against that charge. He argues, by steps which can only have been accepted because of their clarity and distinctness, to the existence of God and to His non-deceitfulness; then to the claim that God is the author of our clear and distinct ideas, and hence to the indubitable truth of those ideas. In explanation of our actually making mistakes in some of our judgements, notwithstanding a non-deceitful God as our creator, Descartes offers the theory that it is the exercise of our freedom of will in choosing to believe propositions which are not clear and distinct which is to blame; as long as we choose to believe propositions which we clearly and distinctly perceive to be true we are *guaranteed* success by God's benevolence. The criterion is infallible.

Descartes is the first major figure in modern rationalism, a philosophical position which has seldom found favour with British philosophers who, by and large, have taken their stand on some version of empiricism. Rationalism essentially involves the belief in the possibility of knowledge of substantial truths *a priori*, or independently of experience, and we have seen how Descartes ascribes such a status to the propositions 'God exists' and 'God is not a deceiver' among many others. These *a priori* truths are substantial and not trivial ones, concerning the fundamental nature of reality and our knowledge relationship to it, and are *a priori* because known by the 'light of reason'. Descartes' own position, as we have seen, is that such truths become available to us via the criterion of clarity and distinctness, but other rationalists have other explanations of such knowledge which apparently evade the need of such criteria: Plato thought our *a priori* knowledge was the result of an immediate acquaintance in a previous disembodied state with the relevant truths; Leibniz, that such knowledge was 'innate', in some sense possessed from birth. Empiricists deny that any knowledge other than that of trivial tautological truths is possible *a priori*, all knowledge worthy of the name being achieved by the use of the senses, so no substantial truths are innate possessions or acquired by rational intuition or by a Cartesian criterion. David Hume was a proponent of empiricism, rejecting the metaphysical speculations of rationalism in this famous passage in his *Enquiry*:

> If we take in our hand any volume – of divinity or school metaphysics, for instance – let us ask, Does it contain any abstract reasoning concerning quantity or number? No. Does it contain any experimental reasoning concerning matters of fact and existence? No. Commit it then to the flames, for it can contain nothing but sophistry and illusion.[7]

A second feature of rationalism is a consequence of the first: its central claim implies a commitment to ideas or concepts – those which occur in judgements expressing *a priori* knowledge – which are themselves not acquired from sense experience. The standard account is that these are also innate (implanted in the mind by God, on Descartes' version) and much effort was expended by Locke in the seventeenth century and Hume in the eighteenth in rebutting this claim. (It is at this point that empiricism, which essentially concerns possible kinds of knowledge, becomes closely allied to positivism, a theory of meaning which severely restricts the realm of the meaningful to sense experience from which alone on that view can arise ideas or concepts.) A third feature of rationalism is the strongly systematic character it ascribes to knowledge, as we have seen illustrated by Descartes' development of his metaphysics. The 'light of reason' reveals a set of closely interrelating truths which form a hierarchical system, some few standing as the foundation stones of the rest of the structure. Mathematical knowledge is quite clearly the paradigm form of knowledge which rationalists have in mind, even though they do not always present their systems in a formally rigorous guise. In the eighteenth century the rationalist Spinoza very explicitly adopted this form of presentation, with clearly identified (and numbered) axioms, and an indication of the method of deriving the resulting theorems: few rationalists however have developed their systems in quite the manner of Spinoza's *Ethics*.

Hume was not only the major proponent of British empiricism in the eighteenth century, he was at one and the same time a major critic of the only kinds of knowledge forms which that philosophy recognised, and particularly of knowledge gained through the use of the senses. In his *Treatise of Human Nature* (1739) and *Enquiry Concerning Human Understanding* (1748), he presents arguments against rationalism (including arguments against the claims of religion in the second work) but also a perceptive critical discussion of empirical knowledge. At first sight this leaves no scope for knowledge of *any* form but some areas actually escape his criticism, both a limited range of *a priori* knowledge of various kinds which we know by immediate intuition and something which can, by stretching the term, be called 'empirical', namely the class of propositions describing the immediate deliverances of the senses. (The members of this class are usually called 'incorrigible' propositions.) It is indeed a curious feature of empiricism in most versions since Hume's that the greater part of empirical knowledge is not recognised as such, and this is true even of twentieth-century versions. Hume tries to lessen the impression of austerity given by his empirical scepticism, the result of his critical analysis, by insisting that his philosophical results will have and should have no effect on what we take to be the facts in ordinary experience. Although there is no *rational* justification for the judgements we make, they are nevertheless the product of the unalterable nature of the human mind. 'Nature by an absolute and uncontrollable necessity has determined us to judge as well as to breathe and feel,' he writes.[8] Such claims can however only lessen the psychological impact of Hume's scepticism and not the logical import of his critical argument, and this 'mitigated scepticism' has removed any right we may have thought we had for claiming indubitability for propositions about the physical world.

Hume's discussion of empirical knowledge begins with a distinction between 'matters of fact' and 'relations of ideas', a distinction between two kinds of truths and consequently between two kinds of propositions. Propositions expressing relations of ideas, for example those found in arithmetic such as '3 × 5 = 15', 'are discoverable by the mere operation of thought, without dependence on what is anywhere existent in the universe'.[9] In contrast to these *a priori* truths, matters of fact cannot be established by thought alone: 'The contrary of every matter of fact is still possible, because it can never imply a contradiction and is conceived by the mind with the same facility and distinction as if ever so conformable to reality.'[10] Hume's second move is to distinguish between a direct and an indirect way of establishing these truths. In the case of *a priori* truths, the distinction is between *intuition* and *demonstration*: some *a priori* propositions are so simple that we can see them to be true by mere inspection, others require that we derive them from propositions known by intuition. Similarly there are propositions expressing matters of fact which can be established immediately from observation, those propositions which directly report our impressions, and others which require reasoning – 'moral' reasoning Hume calls it, to distinguish it from demonstration which establishes *a priori* truths alone – and it is of course the nature of this moral reasoning with which Hume is here concerned.

With these distinctions understood, Hume looks for the 'foundation' of all moral reasoning, and discovers this in the principle 'that instances, of which we have no experience, must resemble those, of which we have had experience, and that the course of nature continues always uniformly the same'.[11] This uniformity principle is, Hume suggests, what would be needed as a major premiss in any argument from experience to a conclusion ascribing similar characteristics to the unobserved areas of the world. To be fair to Hume, we must note that he is talking here of a simple form of argument from experience, that which predicts effects from observed events where we have had previous experience of such connections; on the other hand, Hume has singled this type of argument out for special consideration because he regards it as the fundamental type of reasoning from experience, all our (non-observational) knowledge of matters of fact being founded on our knowledge of cause-effect relations.[12] We can therefore take it that Hume's uniformity principle is supposed to have a necessary place as a premiss in any 'moral' reasoning from experience.

The Humean objection to moral reasoning emerges from a consideration of the epistemological status of the uniformity principle. What kind of knowledge can we possibly have of this proposition? It is clearly not known to us by intuition, for that would require that it can be established *a priori*, and by the same token it cannot be shown to be true by demonstration. 'It implies no contradiction that the course of nature may change and that an object, seemingly like those which we have experienced, may be attended with different or contrary effects.'[13] It is of course also not known by observation, for it hardly reports present impressions of the senses, so the only remaining possibility is that it is established from experience by means of moral reasoning. It will be clear however that such an argument would be viciously circular, for all moral reasoning, on the above analysis, has to assume the uniformity principle as a major premiss. Hume's criticism is complete: the uniformity principle has no foundation and hence reasoning from experience rests on unjustified premisses. As we have seen, Hume looked to the nature of the mind to explain the inferences we do make from experience: 'After the constant conjunction of two objects, heat and flame, for instance, weight and solidity, we are determined by custom alone to expect the one from the appearance of the other . . . All inferences from experience, therefore, are effects of custom not of reasoning.'[14] But whether we follow Hume's example and say we do not reason from experience, or whether we say we reason on the basis of unjustified assumptions, the upshot is the same: the inferences we make from experience are unwarranted, and empirical scepticism is the only rational conclusion.

Hume's analysis can be found wanting on a number of counts. We may note that the notion of 'demonstrative reasoning' with which the argument proceeds appears peculiarly narrower than we normally allow; for 'demonstrative' is normally taken as coextensive with 'deductive', where an argument is deductive (or 'deductively valid') if the premises logically necessitate the conclusion. This wider notion of a demonstrative argument allows both propositions expressing relations of ideas *and* those expressing matters of fact to appear as premises or conclusion whereas Hume's notion allows only the former to do so. This is very closely connected with Hume's construal of 'moral reasoning' from experience as deductive, with the uniformity principle as a major premiss. Clearly the *form* of the argument is the same for Hume whether reason or experience is providing the grounds, and the demonstrative-moral distinction is one of content alone. What is more, the uniformity principle, which Hume suggests would be needed as a major premiss in arguments from experience, is on the face of it totally false. Nature does *not* continue always uniformly the same, and it requires a great deal of effort to discover in what ways it does, and in what it does not. This strongly suggests that such a principle is not in fact used, at least in such an unconditional form.

Hume's analysis is not for these reasons without value, however, for a reconstruction can easily be made which again provides a strong challenge to empirical knowledge. First we have to distinguish inductive from deductive inferences, where in the former the conclusions do not follow logically from the premisses; rather, premisses provide support for, or give grounds for, believing the conclusion. There are many kinds of inductive inference, one kind being the sort of causal prediction made central by Hume, and of course just as there are valid and invalid deductive inferences so there are acceptable and unacceptable inductive ones. Within the class of acceptable inferences we can discriminate those which provide greater support for their conclusions from those providing less, and the discipline called inductive logic is responsible for analysing the factors on which such strength of support depends. What is more there are inductive arguments which are taken to provide not just some good, or even *very* good, grounds for their conclusions, but *full* support or conclusive grounds: such arguments permit us to accept as true the proposition so established, for they make it indubitable: the principles which permit such judgements are indeed just those criteria of certainty or indubitability which have so far formed our main topic of interest. Now if we ask how these 'principles of acceptance' are to be justified it is plain that the position is very similar to that which Hume described in respect of the uniformity principle. The propositions expressing the principles are anything but necessary truths, for those principles of acceptance which *are* expressed by necessary truths are rules of *demonstrative* inference, not inductive – to say that an inference has such a form, that if its premisses are true then its conclusion must be true, is to say that its conclusion is deducible from its premisses. It cannot then be possible to establish inductive principles of acceptance by direct intuition or by demonstration from propositions known by direct intuition. And as they are not direct reports of observations the alternative would appear to be that they are established by inductive arguments from experience. This is clearly not a viable alternative, for an unacceptable circularity would in that case arise; and the conclusion can only be that the propositions expressing inductive principles of acceptance cannot be established in any way. In other words criteria of certainty lack any justification, either from logic or from experience, and we are not justified in our reliance on them. Empirical scepticism is again the inevitable result.

This Humean scepticism has been presented in a very general form, as indeed was intended by Hume in his own version, and more specific versions of it can easily be produced for any limited area of empirical knowledge. Hume's own example suggests immediate application to the criteria we have for assessing propositions about the future course of events, and the major 'problem of induction' is thereby generated, but it can and has found expression in problems concerning the class of propositions about the past, the external world of public experience, and about the mental states of other people. In each case it is possible to identify criteria which are used to warrant belief, and Humean scepticism demands we forfeit the right to believe true any such propositions.

Hume's scepticism differs radically from the Cartesian objection on the basis of fallibility, although both can be seen as a consequence of the fact that standard criteria of certainty warrant belief in propositions which do not follow logically from the grounds in their favour. In neither case however is the argument simply that reasoning on the basis of these criteria is not demonstrative and is therefore unacceptable.[15] In Hume's case the argument is rather that non-demonstrative reasoning lacks a rationale, and it is for that reason that demonstrative reasoning alone is acceptable. A question which must be left for later discussion is whether demonstrative reasoning itself can in fact be provided with a rationale.

The Appeal to Ordinary Language

Although Descartes and Hume presented the most influential forms of attack on criteria of certainty it is clear that other forms are also possible. One would be the claim that some particular criteria in a given field of knowledge are not just fallible in the Cartesian sense, but *practically* fallible in that they actually in practice lead us astray, by and large: such criticism might be raised against predicting future events by consulting the oracle or reading tea leaves, and clearly such criticism, if true, could reasonably be expected to lead to scepticism or replacement by other criteria. Another kind of criticism would be that some criteria are unwarranted in the non-Humean sense that there are positive reasons for thinking that they are not to be trusted, for example reliance on the Church's authority for an account of the structure and constituents of the physical universe. Another kind again would be the claim that our criteria of certainty are in some way logically incoherent, perhaps for logical reasons unsatisfiable by anything. It is however reasonably clear just what would be needed to answer satisfactorily any such sceptical charge, for example by showing that no such logical incoherence exists, though the task might well be a difficult one. The same cannot be said of the Cartesian and Humean arguments and there is even now no consensus of opinion on how these are to be met. There has nevertheless emerged in the present century a fairly wide-spread conviction, originating from the work of such philosophers as Wittgenstein, Austin and Ryle, that the correct approach in epistemology lies in appealing to the ordinary use of the terms of epistemic appraisal. It should immediately be said that there are major differences between the philosophers just mentioned and also between those philosophers who have taken most seriously their ideas, yet it is possible to illustrate the general kind of reply which scepticism would receive from 'ordinary language' philosophers. Norman Malcolm's discussion[16] of a common contemporary argument will prove an illuminating example of this approach.

The view that no empirical proposition is ever certain, and that therefore we cannot properly claim to know the truth of any such proposition, has commonly been advocated by empiricists since Hume. It may seem an odd claim for this particular group of philosophers to make, but of course the class of empirical propositions is taken to exclude the 'incorrigible' ones, and so to include only those contingent propositions which assert or imply the existence of occupants of the public physical world. ('Incorrigible' propositions are so-called because statements expressing them are not refutable or open to amendment by other people.) The propositions that there is a tree in my garden, and that I see a table in front of me, are typical members of the intended class. However, though empiricists have made an exception of incorrigible propositions, their thesis severely limits the range of legitimate claims to knowledge of the world and deserves careful scrutiny.

What the empiricist has in mind is that all empirical propositions strictly go beyond the immediate evidence which we have for them, evidence that only concerns how things *look, appear* or *seem* to the observer. For example, the presence of a physical table which I see in front of me is established by what I *seem* to see (what there *seems to me* to be), and in a strict sense the presence of a real physical table is more than I am warranted to claim on the basis of such evidence. This can be clearly brought out by pointing to the fact that, unlike propositions about how the world seems to be, a proposition such as 'There is a table in front of me' (or 'I see a table in front of me' which implies that there is a table there) has implications about what will happen under a variety of circumstances, and any of these implications might well turn out false. It is possible that when I reach out to touch the object it scuttles away into the corner, or my hand passes straight through it, and if something like this happens we have to say that there was no real table there after all. The fact that these things are *possible*, that they cannot therefore with certainty be ruled out, clearly shows the inconclusiveness of the evidence which we have for empirical propositions.

There is more than one point here on which the ordinary language approach could fasten and Malcolm concentrates on the use made of the notion of possibility. Let us call G the proposition 'There appears to be a table in front of me'. Now the proposition 'There is a table in front of me' (S) implies 'If I reach out I shall feel a hard surface' (P); however, on the empiricists' argument, it is possible that not-P, and hence it is not certain that P, therefore we cannot know that S on the strength of G. Malcolm distinguishes the following senses of the proposition 'It is possible that not-P':

    I   'P is false' is not self-contradictory, i.e. P is contingent
    II   P is not entailed by our grounds for S (G), i.e. 'G and not-P' is contingent
    III   There is some reason to believe that not-P
    IV   There is no reason to believe that P
    V   Our grounds for P are not conclusive.

Now in the evidential circumstances envisaged it obviously cannot be denied that not-P is possible, as long as this is understood to mean I or II; clearly P is contingent and does not follow logically from G. The argument claims however that the possibility of not-P implies that it is not *certain* that P, and with sense I or II this is just not the case. With senses III, IV, and V the implication does hold, yet on the one hand neither I nor II implies any of III to V, and on the other hand in the envisaged evidential circumstances III to V are all false.

Malcolm does not claim to have made an exhaustive list of all the things we could mean by 'possible' so is not open to criticism on that count. Even more, the point would be missed by any empiricist who claimed that his use of terms was incorrectly represented by Malcolm's list – this would simply underline Malcolm's general position that the empiricists' argument only carries if it departs from ordinary usage. Our ordinary understanding of terms like 'possible', 'conclusive', 'reason for believing' and so on just do not warrant the particular sort of argument offered in support of the claim that empirical propositions are never certain.

Malcolm's choice of the term 'possible' for consideration is in fact warranted not just by the particular argument under consideration but even more so by the fact that the notion of certainty appearing in the empiricists' claim is understood by them in terms of the wrong notion of possibility. This point is indeed of quite general importance for though the modern empiricists' understanding of certainty is peculiar, it is not theirs alone but has been shared by other philosophers (including Hume) who adopted versions of scepticism. The difference between this and the ordinary understanding of certainty can be registered as follows:

'It is certain that P'

can be given the sense

(A) P is beyond all (logically) possible doubt

where this means that P is entailed by G, G being the grounds for P (i.e. given G it is not possible that not-P), or alternatively the sense

(B) P is beyond all reasonable doubt.

(A) is a technical definition of 'certainty' which is meant to capture the usage common to the empiricist and other sceptics. ('Doubt' being a psychological noun we can justify its use in this definition by pointing out that if some proposition P is seen to follow logically from another G which is taken to be true, then one cannot consistently doubt P.) (B) however is meant to capture the sense of 'certainty' operating in ordinary language in the sort of context which we are discussing, and can be elucidated further: what is needed for this kind of certainty is that G is such as we would normally regard as sufficient to warrant unhesitating, non-tentative acceptance of P, and this warrant is not at all undermined by logical *possibilities* (such as that of an evil demon) which are consistent with G but which are *merely* possibilities. (If reason is given for believing such a possibility to be actualised, the warrant is undermined and P is no longer certain.) Whenever P is seen to satisfy these conditions it is of course reasonable *not* to doubt its truth, and equally unreasonable to do so. Clearly another way of making this distinction between senses of certainty is to talk, as we have done already, of the different criteria of certainty (or indubitability) demanded by ordinary usage and by philosophical tradition; and we have seen how Hume fits into this tradition, and how Descartes makes a similar demand in terms of infallibility.

To illustrate these points in relation to our example, it is obvious first, that the proposition 'If I reach out my hand will not contact something solid' is not inconsistent, and, secondly, that it is not contradicted by 'There seems to be a table in front of me'. The empiricist is perfectly correct in insisting that the proposition 'There is a table' is not certain beyond all possible doubt in the above sense for quite clearly it is not entailed by the evidence.

However it *is* certain beyond all reasonable doubt for all the evidence points in its favour and is sufficient to warrant unhesitating belief. Indeed one can claim to know that it is true, and would be perfectly justified in doing so.

Now Malcolm's rebuttal of the sceptic's reasoning and conclusion, by appealing to our ordinary use of the key terms in the argument and pointing out the sceptic's departure from that use, is perfectly legitimate. The sceptic has supported his conclusion with an argument which is invalid on any ordinary interpretation of his terms, and in the absence of (1) an indication that he intends his words in a new sense, and (2) a defence of his innovations, it is perfectly legitimate to reject his argument. There are other arguments, apart from the empiricists' argument outlined above, which establish sceptical conclusions in an equally unacceptable manner, and the appeal to ordinary language has therefore an important and undeniable role to play in discussions of scepticism. Unfortunately ordinary language cannot be taken as the *final* court of appeal in epistemology, unless it can be supported by considerations showing that any departure from ordinary language, any refusal to use terms like 'knowledge', 'certainty', 'good grounds' and so on in their usual application, is to be ruled out as senseless or otherwise unacceptable. In other words what the appeal to ordinary language needs if it is to be regarded as a serious obstacle to scepticism in general is some proof that ordinary language cannot be discarded. It is just not the case that all arguments for scepticism are based on a failure to grasp our ordinary concepts of knowledge and certainty, or an illegitimate unsignalled replacement of our concepts by others – we have indeed seen how the scepticism of Descartes and Hume is quite properly based on a recognition of actual features of our concepts. Cartesian and Humean scepticism can only be met by an appeal to ordinary language if ordinary language is itself provided with a defence.

Intimately connected with the use of ordinary language to refute scepticism is the appeal to common sense, as instanced in a number of papers by G. E. Moore. Whether the two appeals are at root identical depends on what the common sense view of the world is taken to involve; Moore's papers contain a number of criteria for identifying the contents of this view, including those of universal or common acceptance and our compulsive acceptance of a proposition which do not obviously identify the same class, nor warrant our equating these appeals. Nevertheless Moore's examples in his paper 'Defence of Common Sense'[17] – propositions expressing the existence and duration of a variety of physical objects, some of them being human bodies, and of many different experiences related in systematic ways to these bodies, and other propositions of the same generality and level – give good grounds for equating them. Our concept of knowledge has, we have assumed, a range of criteria associated with it covering a variety of classes of propositions, which allow us unhesitatingly to accept as true various members of these classes; such criteria can be regarded as part of the concept of knowledge or certainty, and are incorporated into distinctions and classifications we make in ordinary language. Acceptance of ordinary language is therefore tantamount to acceptance of those propositions warranted by the relevant criteria of certainty, and such appear to be the propositions which Moore intends as comprising the common sense view of the world. To be more accurate, we should say that there is an intimate connection between the 'known' propositions of ordinary language and Moore's common sense propositions, for Moore's propositions are more general than the others: a proposition such as 'There are physical objects some of which are human bodies' asserts the truth of some of a range of propositions concerning the existence of human beings at various times and places which are certified as 'known' by ordinary language. The connection is clear and intimate, nevertheless, and enables us to equate the appeals to ordinary language and common sense.

Moore's defence of common sense is therefore of central interest for scepticism, but unfortunately puts up no insuperable hurdles. His strongest case appears to be that the standard presentations of scepticism involve a peculiar sort of inconsistency: of the propositions of common sense he writes:

> If we know that they are features in the 'Common Sense view of the world', it follows that they are true: it is self-contradictory to maintain that *we* know them to be features in the Common Sense view, and that yet they are not true; since to say that *we* know this, is to say that they are true. And many of them also have the further peculiar property that, if they are features in the Common Sense view of the world (whether 'we' know this or not), it follows that they are true.[18]

At most this puts limitations on the forms in which scepticism can be presented, and has no force against Cartesian or Humean scepticism. Neither were presented as denials of the truth of the propositions concerned, only as denials of our right to assert their truth with certainty. And although sceptics are prohibited from ascribing with certainty any view to common sense, they can legitimately find fault with, and offer alternatives to, our knowledge criteria.

Some ordinary language philosophers have looked to the 'paradigm case argument' to provide the required underpinning. What this argument claims is that it is undeniable, in the sense that the denial would be unintelligible, that at least some epistemic[19] situations which we describe as knowledge are indeed so, for it is precisely in terms of these paradigm cases of knowledge that we are taught the concept. These cases are what give sense to the terms 'knowledge' and 'certainty' so it is literally nonsense to deny that they are correctly so called. This form of argument involves a number of questionable assumptions, one of them being the thesis that our acquisition of concepts is through the presentation of cases which instantiate those concepts, and this clearly does not hold for all concepts. Many of them are acquired via their logical relationships with others we already possess, and there is no obvious reason why the concept of knowledge should not be one of them. What is more, even when a concept is acquired through the presentation of instances, as for example simple colour concepts may well be, it is still the case that a conceptual setting is given in terms of which the concept can be placed: for example, in being taught the concept *red* we have to know that our attention is being directed to a certain type of feature of a physical object which it possibly has in common with other physical objects and for that matter with purely visual objects (such as after images) also.

The paradigm case argument is also committed to another closely connected thesis, that the meaning of an expression is the object or situation which the expression names, or if not to quite such a stark form of 'the naming theory of meaning' then at least to the thesis that meaning is a matter of definition in terms of paradigms. If we did learn a concept (such as *red*) via some instance of it the connection between concept and instance would not be so close that we could not question if it was really such a good instance after all – and we might well do so when we understand more of its logical connections with other concepts. But the major objection to the argument is this, that even were these theories of learning and meaning correct, it is still not the case that we cannot ask whether we ought to have the concepts we do have. All that would be true is that, given *this* understanding of some concept C, it is undeniable that such and such instances (through which the concept is defined) *are* instances: we can still ask for a 'deduction' of the concept (to use Kant's term), a proof of our right to the use of the concept.

J. O. Urmson in 'Some Questions Concerning Validity'[20], though (wrongly) accepting the paradigm case argument as valid for *descriptive* terms, i.e. those whose only function appears to be to describe features of the world, rejects it for *evaluative* ones. He argues that a term like 'good' or 'valid' – where 'valid' is taken to refer for example to those arguments which our criteria of certainty take as warranting acceptance of a proposition – have both a descriptive and an evaluative aspect: like ordinary descriptive terms, their use involves the recognition of certain identifiable features of the situation described, yet they also have an evaluative force of commending the object. Our use of an evaluative term involves the recognition of standards which objects must satisfy to earn the commendation:

> The straightforward use of such terms as 'good' in a given field presupposes a set of agreed standards of goodness in that field amongst those who use it; giving reasons for or against a thing being good is to show that it conforms to these standards. Thus in a given circle the standards for goodness in apples may be a certain taste, size, shape, keeping qualities, absence of worm-holes, etc.[21]

But, and this is his crucial point, though there is this close logical connection between an evaluative expression and the accepted standards for its appropriate use, 'this cannot be identity of meaning, for no evaluation can be identical in meaning with a description'.[22] Applying this to the term 'valid' – or 'certainty' and 'knowledge', for what are in question are the criteria we have for assessing the epistemic standing and hence acceptability of propositions – the point is that the criteria or standards for its use have a close logical connection which yet does not amount to identity of meaning with the evaluative term. Because of this, when we have identified the standards of validity which we share there still remains a perfectly legitimate question: what good reason can be given for evaluating arguments in this way? And of course the sceptic takes himself to have given good reasons for not doing so.

Urmson identifies an argument of P. F. Strawson's (from his *Introduction to Logical Theory*, pp. 256–7) as one version of the paradigm case argument, which however it is not, for Strawson does not commit himself to the theories of learning and meaning of that argument. Nevertheless, Urmson's discussion does meet Strawson's argument for the illegitimacy of the question 'Is induction a *rational* or *reasonable* procedure?' Strawson is particularly interested in the limited form of inductive argument concerning inference from past observations to a generalisation predicting similar occurrences, but his point can easily be generalised to cover all knowledge criteria. He writes:

> It is an analytic proposition that [A] it is reasonable to have a degree of belief in a statement which is proportional to the strength of the evidence in its favour; and it is an analytic proposition . . . that [B] other things being equal, the evidence for a generalisation is strong in proportion as the number of favourable instances, and the variety of circumstances in which they have been found, is great.[23]

In so far as [B] identifies the criteria we use in such inferences, Urmson's claim is that it cannot be analytic, and so we can ask whether these criteria really ought to be accepted. In just the same way we can question the criteria for saying a generalisation is established, acceptable without hesitation. Strawson does indeed add a second point: just as we can ask whether some action is legal and appeal to the legal system for an answer and yet we cannot ask whether the legal system itself is legal for there are no legal standards to appeal to in that case; so we can ask of particular beliefs whether they are justified and appeal to the standards of inductive inference, but we cannot sensibly ask the same question of our application of inductive standards itself. There are no standards in terms of which we can provide an answer, so the question is senseless. This analogy with legality is however unacceptable for, apart from emotive uses of the term, legality is something which is purely defined by the legal system operative in a given community whereas a proposition's being certain is more than its evidential support conforming to given standards: it implies the worthiness of the proposition to be accepted unhesitatingly. (When 'legality' is used emotively by critics of the legal system a similar kind of implication is being introduced.) If we cannot answer the question 'Are our standards worthy of acceptance?' because we have nothing to appeal to this does not in itself make the question senseless, and after all the sceptic has alternative standards in mind by contrast with which ours are found wanting. We can add that even though our standards of inference are basic in Strawson's sense there might yet be considerations which could be adduced for the use of just those standards rather than others.

What kind of defence could reasonably be offered for the criteria which are embodied in ordinary language? A partial defence would point out how these criteria have evolved over a period of time against rival criteria which have been discarded, no doubt for a variety of reasons including some which were epistemologically disreputable, but importantly because they have been replaced by criteria proving more reliable or because some positive reasons have emerged to discredit them. Whatever causes may be indicated for change of knowledge criteria it cannot be denied that intellectual considerations have also been operative and that current criteria enjoy positive merits lacking in alternatives. Such a consideration is indeed merely a partial defence of these criteria simply because it says nothing to meet the criticisms of Descartes and Hume, but it can be developed into a more satisfactory defence. We have admitted Descartes' charge that our criteria are not infallible, but what would be the result of replacing them by the only one which clearly is, that of logical implication? The only propositions which in that case would be certain (and so about which we could justifiably be certain) would form a very limited class, including only the *a priori* propositions known 'immediately' (as Hume would say), those 'incorrigible' observational propositions describing our immediate experiences and thoughts, feelings, and intentions (in so far as we are indeed aware of them directly and not through inferring them from our behaviour), together with whatever we can be allowed to intuit by some other faculty if such exists, and of course anything we can deduce from these. The class would not include anything concerning the external world, the future or the past, or other people. It is obvious that acceptance of the sceptic's criterion would severely restrict our body of knowledge. Such was obvious to the Greeks, as was equally the need to accept *some* beliefs concerning these areas, a further point which is central to the defence. Knowledge does not exist solely in and for itself but is required in all deliberation, decision, and action, and we have therefore a very pressing reason to advance beyond the sceptic's boundaries. If this point is taken with that above a justification of a kind emerges for our particular criteria.

Such a pragmatic argument differs from the limited kinds considered explicitly by Hume but it is unfortunately not clear that it evades the force of Hume's argument completely, for it apparently falls foul of the reconstructed version of Hume's dilemma; it is after all an argument which rests on contingent facts about human needs which would have to be accepted on logically inconclusive grounds, and moreover aims to justify continued use in the future of our current criteria on the basis of past success. The impression will remain therefore that the argument cannot properly meet the fundamental criticism of Humean scepticism and something again remains to be added. A final line of defence for ordinary language criteria might be to raise this question: Why accept the sceptic's own reasoning? Why accept that because our criteria are not infallible, providing no *guarantee* of truth, or because no justification is ultimately forthcoming which makes no use of the criteria in question, we therefore ought not to use them? These arguments are clearly not warranted by ordinary language criteria, nor logically could they be, and it is difficult to see how they could be defended by the sceptic. In other words, for a sceptic to argue that because the grounds for some proposition P are logically inconclusive, or in accordance with criteria which are ultimate and unsupportable for that reason, we therefore do not know that P – that we are not in a position justifiably to claim that P – is to depart from ordinary usage and in effect to offer another in its place. The sceptic's position in its turn demands a justification, and in the face of what was said about the evolution of criteria and the need for some criteria such as we now use, it looks as though the sceptic must finally give way.

The Grounds of Uncertainty

In order to distinguish the traditional epistemologists' conception of justified knowledge claims from that of ordinary language a distinction was made between 'certainty beyond all possible doubt' and 'certainty beyond all reasonable doubt', when it was suggested that conclusive reasons for believing, in ordinary usage, are indeed *logically* inconclusive. There is a second distinction between kinds of certainty which is needed to clarify problems in epistemology, *viz.* between the sort of certainty which is applicable to people and that which is applicable to propositions. For example, many people are certain that God exists though fewer would say that the proposition 'God exists' *is* certain. We may use the terms 'subjective' and 'objective' to denote, respectively, these two kinds of certainty. The distinction has much wider application than to examples of faith of course, although there is a tendency for it to be masked in ordinary language by a frequent interchangeability of sorts between 'I am certain that P' and 'It is certain that P'. Reference, though covert, was previously made to the subjective notion of certainty in the definitions of certainty beyond logical and reasonable doubt, both in the use of the notion of doubt and also that of unhesitating belief. Objective certainty has, furthermore, a connection with subjective certainty via the notion of rationality, a connection which is substantiated by the previous definition of certainty beyond all reasonable doubt: a man is rational if he is certain only about those propositions which *are* certain. (To demand however that he also be certain about *all* propositions which are certain is to go further than that definition, and would be to demand more than is reasonable.) This is part of the reason why in ordinary cases the distinction is not always apparent.[24]

In order to further the task of giving an account of our use of the concepts of knowledge and certainty, we can now profitably consider a bold but mistaken thesis propounded by Malcolm,[25] namely that not only *do* we take an immovable stand on the truth of some propositions concerning the public physical world but that this is a non-contingent matter demanded by our concepts of knowledge, proof, grounds, and so forth. What is in essence the same thesis is suggested in Wittgenstein's last philosophical notes (published in 1969 under the title *On Certainty*) – Malcolm acknowledges a debt to conversations with Wittgenstein on this subject[26] – although Wittgenstein would have had reservations about the form of Malcolm's presentation. The thesis has important consequences for scepticism and can be regarded as one version of the appeal to the workings of ordinary language. Malcolm's paper is both compact and clearly argued, qualities which have helped to make it a classic presentation of this tradition.

Malcolm argues first that ordinary usage contains both a strong and a weak sense of 'know', and he offers examples of the use of each. It is used in its strong sense 'when a person's statement "I know that P is true" implies that the person who makes the statement would look upon nothing whatever as evidence that P is false'.[27] As an example of this use Malcolm instances the natural reply to someone who produces a clever 'proof' to show that $2 + 2$ does not equal 4: 'I can't see what is wrong with your proof; but it *is* wrong, because I *know* that $2 + 2 = 4$.' We do not admit that any argument or any future development in mathematics could show that it is false that $2 + 2 = 4$. In contrast the weak sense is used in the case where, having calculated that $92 \times 16 = 1472$ and subsequently having been asked if I am sure that 1472 is correct, I answer 'I *know* that it is; but I will calculate it again to *make sure*'. Though I claim to know that $92 \times 16 = 1472$ I am nevertheless willing to *confirm* it, and in so doing I allow for the possibility of a refutation. Summarising the difference between these cases Malcolm writes:

> When I use 'know' in the weak sense I am prepared to let an investigation (demonstration, calculation) determine whether the something that I claim to know is true or false. When I use 'know' in the strong sense I am not prepared to look upon anything as an *investigation*; I do not concede that anything whatsoever could prove me mistaken.[28]

(Wittgenstein, though agreeing with the spirit of Malcolm's distinction, would not wish to speak of two senses of 'know': he suggests that the expression 'I know' makes sense only in application to propositions which we *can* call into question, doubt, check up on and so on.[29] All occurrences of 'know' are therefore occurrences of Malcolm's weak sense.) The distinction is applicable to empirical as well as arithmetical cases, and Malcolm offers an example of the use of both the strong and the weak sense in that area. The former is provided by the case where, sitting in normal circumstances in front of a desk with an ink-bottle on top of it, and presented with the declaration by others that there is no ink-bottle, I am prepared to question their sincerity or eyesight with 'I *know* there is an ink-bottle here – I can *see* it'. 'There is nothing whatever,' writes Malcolm, 'that could happen in the next moment or the next year that would by me be called evidence that there is not an ink-bottle here now.'[30] It is easy to think of cases where our use of 'know' does not involve such a strong commitment, and one of Malcolm's is this: we would be prepared to accept (though we would be surprised to learn) that astronomers had unfortunately made a great error in the observations and calculations which led them to the belief that the sun is about ninety million miles from the earth and that the true figure is twenty million, and yet we nevertheless want to claim 'I *know* that ninety million is the correct figure'.

The second part of Malcolm's thesis is that this duality of use is not an isolated feature of ordinary language which philosophers may comment on and deplore as lax or unreasonable, but reflects a logical point concerning our common concepts of evidence, proof, and disproof. The crux of his argument is this: 'In order for it to be possible that any statements about physical things should *turn out to be false* it is necessary that some statements about physical things *cannot* turn out to be false.'[31] Precisely the same point applies to the arithmetical examples, and in this respect some *a priori* statements and some empirical statements possess the same logical status. Summarising the conceptual point, Malcolm writes:

> The statements that $5 \times 5 = 25$ and that here is an ink-bottle both lie beyond the reach of doubt. On both, my judgement and reasoning *rests*. If you could somehow undermine my confidence in either, you would not teach me *caution*. You would fill my mind with chaos.[32]

It is only because we take the strong, uncompromising stand on some propositions of arithmetic or concerning the observable world that we can meaningfully talk of 'making sure' that other propositions are true, others 'turning out to be false', others being doubtful. (Wittgenstein writes: 'If I want the door to turn, the hinges must stay put.'[33])

Malcolm's argument is interesting on a number of counts, not the least being that he explicitly developed it in an attempt to elucidate the element of truth contained in a frequently held misapprehension concerning the nature of knowledge, namely that knowledge and belief are two states of mind which differ in their intrinsic qualities and which we can distinguish by introspection. On that view we can discover whether we know something or merely believe it by reflecting on our mental state, a thesis which it would be difficult to defend seriously. The proof that this is so follows from the fact that knowledge requires the truth of what is known and the overwhelming majority of things which we know have nothing whatever to do with any mental state which we might be in while we know. In order to discover whether A knows that P, where P is a proposition stating something about the world independent of the content of A's mind, it is obviously insufficient to consider solely A's mental state. To put this another way, if A has knowledge of some fact and if (as is commonly the case) this knowing by A is considered to be A's having some mental state representing the fact, that his mental state does indeed represent the fact is not ascertained by inspecting the state alone. It is only by perversely equating knowledge with a state of being certain that P and H. A. Prichard[34] could defend the contrary thesis, for reflecting on one's state of mind seems a reasonable way of deciding whether one is or is not certain about what one believes. Malcolm's thesis allows the development of a claim which bears a superficial resemblance to Prichard's, namely that reflection can make us realise that we are using 'know' in the strong or weak sense in a particular case. This resemblance is however only superficial, for the truth of P never follows from the fact that someone claims to know that P using the strong sense – otherwise we could, for example, produce an elegantly simple proof of God's existence[35] – and furthermore Malcolm's notion of reflection is not Prichard's notion of introspection. What we reflect on, according to Malcolm, is 'what we should think if certain things were to happen'.

Failure to provide a defence of Prichard need not mean that Malcolm's thesis is trivial, for it has two interesting consequences for scepticism about the public world. First, acceptance of this thesis would entail rejecting the empiricists' location of certainty solely in incorrigible propositions concerning the immediate contents of sense, for as Malcolm emphasises our talk of making sure of empirical propositions, of checking up on and doubting them, requires that some *empirical* propositions are held beyond doubt's reach. As Wittgenstein wrote, 'The truth of certain empirical propositions belongs to our frame of reference.'[36] The foundations of knowledge are not to be sought in propositions of the form 'There seems to be an A', but within the class of propositions about the public world itself. Acceptance of Malcolm's thesis would, secondly, have the consequence that an all-embracing doubt of the sort envisaged by philosophers such as Descartes (in the *First Meditation*) should be recognised as unintelligible in terms of what we normally mean by 'doubt'. This arises from the second part of the argument, which asserts that doubt is something set against the background of firm beliefs and consequently is limited by some unquestioned propositions. To the common assumption of the need for a firm basis for the rest of the superstructure of knowledge Malcolm has added that this is equally a basis for conjecture and doubt.

To see how Malcolm's argument fails, we need first to realise that there does indeed exist an objective difference in the status of the propositions which he says we can strongly or weakly claim to know. (The case of arithmetic raises problems concerning the nature of basic knowledge and of our acceptance of arithmetical truths which must be left for a later chapter, so we can concentrate here on the examples about the physical world.) Now even if in the end we reject Malcolm's way of drawing the distinction and his grounds for it, there nevertheless exists a difference here worth noting. It is tempting but wrong to try to fit the examples onto our distinction between the two kinds of objective certainty, so that the 'strong' cases are taken to be certain beyond all possible doubt, and the 'weak' cases only beyond all reasonable doubt. This will not work for clearly 'Here is an ink-bottle' is not in the envisaged circumstances *logically entailed* by the grounds in its favour. It does in fact share with the proposition about the sun's distance a logical (deductive) gap from the evidence or grounds in its favour. So much indeed was argued by Descartes in his *First Meditation* and since accepted by many, including Malcolm. The distinction in question is rather one which can be elucidated in terms of certainty beyond reasonable doubt alone.

Remembering the sense assigned to this notion, it should be clear that within the envisaged circumstances – in good light, and in conditions which one has no reason to believe abnormal – the proposition 'Here is an ink-bottle' *is* beyond reasonable doubt: one would be perfectly warranted in unhesitatingly accepting this proposition as true. It is also clear that the proposition 'The sun is about ninety million miles from the earth' demands a very much more complex procedure for its establishment; the gap between proposition and evidence is in a sense even greater than in the ink-bottle case, and until the relevant procedure has been painstakingly completed the proposition will not be certain. Circumstances are easily envisaged therefore in which propositions like 'Here is an ink-bottle', which state observable facts about the physical world, can be certain beyond reasonable doubt yet other propositions which express ascertainable facts of a more recondite kind cannot. This essentially simple point must be carefully distinguished from Malcolm's distinction between strengths of the term 'know': it does not imply such a distinction for in the circumstances in question the proposition about the sun's distance, not being certain, is not known to be true. What is more there is absolutely no reason why this proposition cannot itself become certain, for all that this requires is for the relevant procedures to be followed through. This in itself is an important fact about objective certainty, that it is not simply a function of what evidence lies waiting to be discovered but involves also our coming to see this evidence as warranting our acceptance of the proposition.

Malcolm draws his distinction between the strong and weak senses of 'know' essentially in terms of the notion of subjective certainty, for what is peculiar to the propositions which we strongly claim to know is the steadfastness with which apparently problematic experiences are rejected as hallucinatory or otherwise misleading. It is essential to realise just how strong a commitment is involved in this attitude, this kind of subjective certainty being a totally uncompromising one, and the question arises whether such an attitude could ever be supposed *reasonable* if taken to any empirical proposition. A case could perhaps be made for saying that it would be reasonable in respect of propositions having (objective) certainty beyond all *possible* doubt in as much as such propositions follow logically from their grounds, for no circumstance could ever then arise to negate the force of these grounds. (Even so it would be reasonable only to the extent that it was already warranted in the case of the grounds themselves, for only then could one say that nothing will go against the truth of that for which they are grounds.) This attitude would appear on the face of it much too strong to take towards propositions which are merely certain beyond all reasonable doubt, for the non-demonstrative nature of the step from grounds to these propositions lays open the possibility of some circumstance arising which should persuade us to reconsider our position. It seems foolhardy for someone to say that no circumstances whatsoever would or should convince him that no ink-bottle exists after all. Rationality apparently demands that you change your mind when the evidence goes against you.

Malcolm's thesis that we do and should remain steadfast on some empirical propositions is supported by the observation that our concepts of evidence, proof and disproof demand it: that unless some propositions about the physical world are totally beyond revision no other propositions about that world can turn out to be false, confirmed, or even doubtful. This is the conceptual point on which everything rests. Wittgenstein uses the same argument – which we can call 'the relativity argument' – to establish the need for fundamental propositions which are beyond doubt. For example he writes: 'The *questions* that we raise and our *doubts* depend on the fact that some propositions are exempt from doubt, are as it were like hinges on which those turn. That is to say, it belongs to the logic of our scientific investigations that certain things are *in deed* not doubted.'[37]

This relativity argument is, however, misguided. Its refutation follows from the conjunction of the following two facts: (1) that the criteria of certainty with which we work provide for the *quite reasonable* acceptance of propositions, propositions which are only certain beyond all reasonable doubt and which we may need to revise in the face of further unfavourable evidence; (2) that the warrant provided by those criteria of certainty extends to our *use* of these propositions precisely in the way required by the relativity argument. If we have quite reasonably accepted as true a proposition P which is beyond reasonable doubt we are thereby, and by the same token, warranted in using P as a platform from which to make epistemic appraisals of other propositions as doubtful, probably, and disproved. The acceptance of P goes hand in hand with the rejection of not-P and anything which entails not-P, and (for example) in judging doubtful any proposition Q which *is* doubtful given the truth of P. If it is indeed the case, as the relativity argument in part suggests, that epistemic judgements are properly made against a background of accepted propositions, such a background can quite satisfactorily be provided by propositions which we are ultimately willing to revise. The further claim which the relativity argument makes for totally unrevisable beliefs cannot be accepted. We must therefore conclude that the second part of Malcolm's compound thesis is misguided. Moreover, since this relativity argument constitutes the only *a priori* consideration put forward for the division of the meaning of 'know' into a strong and a weak sense the existence of such a division can only be established on the basis of an empirical investigation into common usage. The apparent objective difference between Malcolm's cases, as we have argued above, can be accounted for without introducing two senses of 'know' and Malcolm's compound thesis must therefore be rejected.

Is it not, however, the case that we can argue along these lines only because at a deeper level there are unshakeable propositions to be found, which constitute the foundation on which other propositions can be said to be certain beyond reasonable doubt? In other words, though these 'certain' propositions can be used to assess others in the relevant way, they are themselves based on propositions which are totally beyond revision. Well, in the first place, there is no obvious reason to restrict the scope of the above argument so that the epistemic judgement that P is certain needs a special kind of basis: propositions which we have quite reasonably accepted can as well be used to provide the grounds for the further appraisal that other propositions are or are not certain in the same sense. In the second place it must be remembered that Malcolm and Wittgenstein are both arguing for the existence of unshakeable *empirical* propositions and no independent reason – independent, that is, of the relativity argument itself – has been provided for looking for the bedrock of justification in the realm of empirical propositions rather than that of propositions concerning immediate experience. What is more, no independent reason has been provided for thinking that there has to be a bedrock at all.

But are we not in any case inevitably committed to accepting a specific system of rules for judgements of certainty (a system of *criteria* of certainty), and has not Wittgenstein shown in *On Certainty* that such a system is in part *constituted* by propositions which are not up for revision in any circumstances? Undeniably, Wittgenstein added much to the characterisation which Malcolm provided of the propositions which are supposedly beyond question, particularly in placing their acceptance in a social setting with his insistence that agreement on such foundational propositions is part of the agreement in form of life underlying our 'language games'. The acceptability of Wittgenstein's developed account must be judged in terms of its contributions to his overall account of language; what we have argued here is that the thesis of unrevisable propositions, if judged in terms of the one *a priori* argument which is offered by Malcolm and Wittgenstein, is unacceptable. Whether there are other pressures to accept Wittgenstein's description of the foundations of our language use is another matter.

Part of the interest of Malcolm's paper, as noted above, is its implications for scepticism and the empiricists' attempt to locate certainty in propositions about the immediate contents of sensory awareness. Malcolm's failure to prove his main thesis must not be taken as removing the whole force of his attack on scepticism for a more limited thesis suggested by his argument, that certainty *beyond reasonable doubt* serves as a basis on which other epistemic judgements can be formed, has much the same force. Judgements of certainty do indeed provide a basis or underpinning of our various epistemic assessments and traditional empiricism was therefore digging too deeply to discover the foundations. What of the second implication of Malcolm's thesis for scepticism, namely that an all-embracing doubt is logically impossible because doubt needs a basis in firm conviction? This thesis is a perfectly acceptable one, as long as we are careful to relate it to certainty beyond *reasonable* doubt.

The point must however be argued; doubt is after all a psychological attitude and *prima facie* there would seem to be no reason why it could not be totally extensive over all propositions. There is indeed no reason why someone, in the spirit of Descartes, should not doubt any and every proposition, and he would have the advantage of consistency over his opposite number who was certain about each and every proposition. This is not to say however that we would take him for a rational man.

We must, to begin with, distinguish two notions of doubt, just as we did with certainty, the one applicable to people and being a psychological attitude and the other applicable to propositions, these being instanced in judgements of the form 'I doubt that (whether) P' and 'It is doubtful that (whether) P': we can call these the subjective and objective notions of doubt respectively. It is not at all surprising that doubt should parallel certainty in this respect, for they operate in the same dimension and indicate alternative attitudes which people may have or alternatives in the status of propositions. Secondly, just as we suggested earlier that subjective certainty is warranted only in those cases where objective certainty exists, so we can lay down a condition of rationality in relation to doubt which relates the two notions just distinguished: a man is rational if he doubts only those propositions which *are* doubtful. Now just as our criteria for certainty indicate the conditions which a proposition should satisfy to be certain, and so to warrant certainty on the part of the believer, they also, and by the same token, indicate when a proposition is to be taken as doubtful; there may well be freedom to choose when and why to doubt, but this freedom no more protects the doubter from the accusation of neuroticism than the same freedom in the case of certainty protects the believer from the charge of foolhardiness. To substantiate the thesis of the relativity of doubt, it need only be pointed out that criteria for the doubtfulness of propositions can be most simply (and schematically) stated thus: doubt is warranted in respect of some proposition P if there are either reasons *against* the truth of P (i.e. in favour of some alternative Q implying not-P) or if there are no reasons *for* P (i.e. no choice between P or Q is justified). Doubt is therefore, just as much as certainty, properly seen against a propositional basis. That furthermore this basis is one of firm – but not totally unyielding – conviction appears to be a fact about our epistemic attitudes.

Basic Knowledge

Our discussion of knowledge and certainty has been mainly concerned with the status of propositions accepted on the basis of others, and we have shown how the sceptical arguments of Descartes and Hume led to the demand that the evidential relationship warranting belief (and hence providing a basis for knowledge) be a very strong one. Descartes saw this connection bet-ween our clear and distinct idea of P and P itself as provided by God's goodness; most philosophers have followed Hume in requiring the logical relationship of entailment or deducibility. We encapsulated the difference between this traditional criterion of indubitability and that of ordinary usage with the two defini-tions of certainty 'beyond all logically possible doubt' and 'beyond all reasonable doubt'. We also looked at attempts to defend our use of the latter notion and considered the kind of defence with which an ordinary language approach in epistemology might reasonably be provided.

We have nevertheless had occasion to refer to the idea that, apart from beliefs held on the basis of other beliefs, there are beliefs of a more fundamental sort which do not have this kind of backing; moreover such beliefs can constitute knowledge and indeed, on the traditional view, must constitute knowledge in as much as they provide the ultimate grounds on which all other propositions are accepted. The very existence of beliefs of the evidentially based kind ('non-basic' beliefs) seems to demand that there be basic beliefs on pain of circularity or infinite regress in the justifications of those beliefs, for if every belief were accepted on the basis of others these would be the only alternatives. We are required therefore to recognise a dichotomy of basic and non-basic beliefs, and in consequence one of basic and non-basic knowledge. The writings of Descartes and Hume, as well as those of most other philosophers through to the present century, clearly exhibit this view, usually in a form which ascribes a hierar-chical structure to our system of knowledge. Whole classes of propositions are candidates for one or other of these types of knowledge, and even on the non-basic side there is a stratification of propositions in terms of the evidential relationship. Twentieth-century empiricism, for example, takes the basic beliefs which constitute basic or 'direct' knowledge to include what we directly perceive – how the world appears to us through our five senses – and erected on these are non-basic beliefs con-cerning the public physical world, and on these in their turn are beliefs concerning the mental lives of other people. This is clearly traceable to Hume's distinction between propositions concerning 'the present testimony of our senses or the records of our mem-ory'[38] known directly by observation, and propositions which are known only indirectly through 'moral' inferences. Descartes' basic knowledge is provided by propositions proclaiming *that* we clearly and distinctly perceive that P, Q, or R, and the next stage in the hierarchy of knowledge by the propositions P, Q, R and so on themselves; finally these are used as axioms from which Descartes draws out the rest of his system.

The major question we must now face is in what sense certainty can be ascribed to basic beliefs. Certainty, as so far defined, in terms of logically possible and reasonable doubt, clearly applies only to non-basic beliefs, so we have yet to characterise the kind of certainty which philosophers have traditionally ascribed to basic beliefs. It does in fact transpire once more that a clear disparity exists between this sense of certainty and that which really does apply to basic beliefs; the import of scepticism has been thought to be that basic beliefs must be absolutely beyond all question if such beliefs are to be warranted, and if they are to provide an adequate basis for the warranted acceptance of other beliefs.

The empiricists' basic propositions we have previously termed 'incorrigible' (following their practice), meaning that they are not open to amendment or refutation by other people. These propositions report a variety of things, not only thoughts, feelings and intentions but also (what is more indicative of the nature of the world beyond the subject's mental life) what the subject seems to remember and how the subject is appeared to by the external world. These latter propositions can be variously complex, from the very simple 'Red, here, now' type of proposition to the more sophisticated 'It looks to me as if there is an X' (a table, a hand, etc.) or 'I seem to see a Y'. Since our knowledge of the external world has been of primary interest to empiricists the greatest emphasis has been on such 'seems' propositions as candidates for basic knowledge; the kind of consideration relevant to these incorrigible propositions is however relevant to the others also. Descartes' basic propositions, to the effect that I have a clear and distinct perception that P, can also be called incorrigible in the intended sense, for they share the relevant immunity from refutation or amendment. It is worth stating that incorrigibility does not necessarily imply that the statement cannot be revised later by the person to whom it pertains, only that we must be the authority on how the world seems (or seemed) to him. In this sense he has 'privileged access' to these mental occurrences.[39]

Such then are the candidates for basic knowledge. The term 'incorrigible' has also been used with a much stronger implication to characterise the certainty that applies to such basic propositions, meaning now that we logically cannot be mistaken about them. It is of course clearly possible for me to be mistaken in believing that *you* are appeared to in a certain way, or have a particular clear and distinct idea, but then these propositions are not incorrigible for me in the original sense. What is being claimed is that the person for whom a basic proposition is basic logically cannot be wrong about that proposition. For him they are in a sense self-justifying, in that their truth is a logical consequence of his believing them. We have already seen how Descartes' first truth has this characteristic, and the question is why it should be thought that all members of the wider class of basic propositions have it also. Except in so far as the kind of inference which Hume called 'moral' does not apply to basic propositions by definition, this position is rather assumed than argued for. Argument is however required, for the absence of inference alone does not guarantee that the relevant experiences have been correctly described, the incorrigibility (in the strong sense) of basic propositions clearly ruling out this possibility of misdescription.

The explanation of philosophers taking this position is their failure to distinguish having from knowing about experiences, intentions, feelings, and so on. This conflation is most tempting in the case of feelings, for being in pain and feeling a pain have an apparent identity, and feeling a pain is surely being aware of that mental occurrence. But on the contrary, however we interpret the latter notion of feeling a pain, we must distinguish the occurrence of the feeling itself from any cognitive awareness which might accompany it, if only because there enters into the latter a conceptual element lacking from the former. Having a pain demands on the face of it no conceptual ability on the part of the subject, but knowing that you have a pain involves an awareness of the self and its mental attributes which requires the possession and application of relevant concepts. Similarly we must distinguish between having some experience X, for example its seeming or looking to you as if there is a table in front of you, from your being aware that you have experience X. The latter involves a new conceptual dimension. It follows from this that we can indicate a logically possible error even in basic beliefs concerning how the world appears in direct experience, namely the misdescription of the experience in question. Ayer at one time argued that such a 'misdescription' could be no more than a simple misuse of language, a verbal mistake which essentially involved no factual error.[40] His latest position disowns such a view on the grounds that the distinction between verbal and factual mistakes is not easy to draw.[41] It is clear however that more is at stake in our envisaged error than a slip of the tongue or accidental use of the wrong word, for no correct belief is identifiable independently of the terms actually applied in the description. The experience is wrongly described in the sense that the wrong concepts are used in its description. We must conclude that basic propositions are not incorrigible in that they are not immune from all doubt.

We cannot by the way accuse Descartes of quite the same mistaken conflation of having and knowing one's mental states, for he held an explicit thesis to the effect that mental states are self-intimating so we cannot fail to attribute to ourselves whatever is contained in our consciousness.[42] Such a theory is unfortunately most implausible, and has been rejected in the case of beliefs and intentions, as well as desires, by much of recent psychology. We should also note that, even were Descartes' thesis correct, or even were the conflation of knowing and having experiences allowable, the possibility of some kind of error would still remain: error could arise within the experience itself. If it seems to me as if there is a table, I am involved in concept application, as I am even in the simpler case of 'Red, here, now', and the possibility of misapplying concepts must be allowed. Error is therefore possible within the experience as well as within the description of it.

What kind of certainty can basic beliefs be ascribed? As in the case of our non-basic beliefs we may talk of their being certain 'beyond all reasonable doubt'. Now we clearly cannot understand this expression in exactly the sense previously assigned to it, for we are now talking of basic beliefs in support of which no evidence or grounds are forthcoming; we can nevertheless understand it in a sense which is sufficiently close to the previous one to justify using the same form of words. Circumstances are easily imagined in which it would be perfectly reasonable for someone to accept unhesitatingly the proposition that he has such-and-such an experience: though error may arise in more than one way the possibility of error alone is insufficient to undermine the warrant he has for his belief. Conceptual error is always possible as a consequence of some peculiar temporary disability or confusion, or incompetence when faced with experiences that are new or relatively so, but in the absence of specific reasons to believe it has actually occurred we allow him his beliefs about his experience. Nevertheless, circumstances are also imaginable in which this warrant can be undermined and others can cast doubt on his competence to make judgements about his experiences for it is in general true that we share the same experiences in the same circumstances. Under normal conditions something red will appear red to those who have the conceptual competence which we call the possession of the concept *red*, and in normal circumstances the presence of a table will be responsible for its looking as if there were a table to those who have the relevant concepts. In so far as we share concepts we share experiences also, and it is therefore possible to have reason for questioning someone's assessment of his own experiences. We could, in other words, have good reason to think him confused or temporarily disabled in making such assessments and revise his judgements accordingly. Not only are basic propositions not beyond all possible doubt, they fail to be incorrigible in the original sense as well: they are after all open to amendment or refutation by other people.

Basic beliefs retain their defining characteristic of not being accepted on the basis of other beliefs and so retain a kind of fundamental status in our corpus of knowledge. The present consideration has nevertheless introduced a demand for coherence between individual judgements made by different subjects about their experiences and ultimately also judgements made about how the world actually is 'beyond the appearances'. Just as a knowledge of how things normally appear to people will enable me to revise someone else's judgements of appearance, a general grasp of how the world appears in certain circumstances – how for example green things appear in red light – will be reflected in my own decisions about what experiences I am having, and in the original conceptualisations which comprise these experiences. The kind of axiomatic fundamentality placed by traditional theories of knowledge in basic beliefs is refuted by this need for such beliefs to fit with others, both basic and non-basic.

CHAPTER II

BELIEF

It is the central task of epistemology to provide an account of knowledge and of such related concepts as belief, truth and evidence; and an account which shows how these concepts are related. Our discussion of scepticism in Chapter I advanced a little in that direction, though admittedly the proposals made were few and unsystematic. Nevertheless they do indicate the direction in which a fuller understanding of the concept of knowledge is to be sought: one suggestion, for example, was that a proposition of the form 'A knows that P' requires the truth of P itself – only propositions which are true can be known, or, as we may say, truth is a necessary condition of knowledge – and we shall therefore need to look closely at that claim (Chapter III). Many other conditions have been suggested by philosophers as necessary or sufficient for knowledge, and an account of some of the major ones will be provided in Chapter III, as well as a discussion of the very enterprise of analysing knowledge. We shall concentrate in the present chapter on the concept of belief.

Theories of Belief

An elementary distinction is that between the actual believing of P and the proposition P itself, which in another usage is also spoken of as 'the belief that P'. The nature of propositions is a subject for later discussion but we can assume for the moment that it is an unproblematic concept; it is certainly the case that in ordinary usage we make the distinction just mentioned using 'belief' to refer to either the believing or to what we may call the 'object' of the believing, *what* is believed, and the philosophical term 'proposition' is used for the latter. Our interest here will be concen-

41

trated on belief in its former sense, the sense in which we can say things like 'His belief that she would honour her promise lasted only five minutes', or 'His belief in Christianity is a consequence of his upbringing'.

A second fundamental point is that beliefs can be assessed as true or false. In this they differ from other mental attitudes which can take the same objects: just as we can believe that P, so we may regret that P, hope that P, wish that P, and so on, but it is only with belief that truth and falsity is the appropriate dimension of assessment. Many other attitudes no doubt contain belief within them – and regret would be one such case – so truth and falsity do indeed have relevance to such attitudes, yet clearly only to the belief component itself. It is interesting to note in passing that belief, as well as such other attitudes as fear and desire, may take objects of more familiar kinds, namely persons, causes, or other things: for we may believe in X, have fear of X, or desire X; where X may be God, liberty, long walks, or something of that kind. The extent to which belief in this kind of object may be reduced to belief *that* some propositions are true is a question of some controversy, and we may take our primary interest in knowledge as excusing us from doing more than mention it here.

A third feature of belief is that we talk quite happily both of beliefs as being held for such-and-such *reasons*, and as being the result of such-and-such *causal* factors, again this being something which belief has in common with fear, desire, hope, and other mental attitudes. A related problem concerns the extent to which a belief (or fear, etc.) for which we can indicate causes can also be, at one and the same time, the product of reasons, for there is often an implied lack of rationality in the ascription of causes for people's beliefs (or fears, etc.). There is however no *a priori* argument clearly connecting this common implication of causal ascriptions with a fundamental incompatibility of reasons and causes, and we can perhaps look to A's having the belief that Q (which is his reason for believing P) as the (or a) major *causal* factor in his belief that P wherever a reason is in fact operative.

Mention must also be made of a difficult question of great contemporary interest, namely whether it is possible to ascribe beliefs to non-language users. Of factors responsible for the strong temptation to take a negative position on this question one of the major ones must be the practice of linguistic philosophy itself, for in this tradition philosophers have concentrated on linguistic expressions as indicative of features of our conceptual scheme and thereby have closely associated thought and language. Were we however to make the contrary assumption that concentration on language is, as concentration on behaviour was for methodological behaviourists in psychology, solely a means of approaching the thought behind it, other hurdles would yet present themselves for such ascriptions of belief. An influential one for example is presented by Wittgenstein's so-called Private Language Argument[1] which denies the possibility of possessing concepts not shared by others, language offering the means whereby this is effected. Another follows from the fact that any such ascription would of necessity concern beliefs having a far simpler form than the complex beliefs achievable by language users, for in the absence of a shared language there can be no complex conceptual inheritance of the kind familiar to us; but even this is not the end of the matter, for such beliefs would need to be classed alongside the beliefs of language users which are neither linguistically expressed nor made conscious to the believer, finding expression only in our non-linguistic behaviour. This last objection, even if not putting up an insuperable obstacle for such belief ascriptions, does have the merit of bringing out the disparate nature of what we classify as beliefs even in the case of language users, and this is a timely warning that we may have difficulty in identifying more than 'family resemblances' (to use Wittgenstein's phrase) between beliefs of different kinds. That said, there is perhaps no harm in pointing out that the considerations advanced against the indiscriminate ascription of beliefs all make the assumption that beliefs are possessed only by those creatures which possess concepts, our hesitation to ascribe the former being consequent on our hesitation to ascribe the latter.

We may turn now to the two theories of belief which have traditionally competed for the philosopher's favour, one of which views belief as a mental occurrence or act on the part of the believer, and the other equates believing with behavioural dispositions which the believer exhibits. The dispositional account has had its greatest following among philosophers of the present century, who were no doubt influenced by the emergence of the psychology of behaviourism with its stimulus-response model of animal and human behaviour; it was also seen as a more viable account than the older mentalistic theory and does have some clear advantages over it.

Belief as Mental Act

An early version of the mentalistic theory can be found in Hume's *Treatise*, within his discussion of inference from cause to effect. In Section VII of Book I, Part II, he asks 'Wherein consists the difference betwixt incredulity and belief?'; where by 'incredulity' he means to include both alternatives to believing P, namely disbelieving P and (in traditional jargon) 'barely entertaining P' without believing or disbelieving it. Hume's question is for that which differentiates belief from these other positions: his answer is that an opinion or a belief 'may be most accurately defin'd, a lively idea related to or associated with a present impression'. To understand this we need to remember that Hume is primarily involved with the question of how we get from the perception of some present thing or event to an expectation of some future thing or event which will be a consequence of the former. To generalise the account by relaxing this connection to a particular form of inference, Hume is defining belief simply as a 'lively idea'. The fact that on any literal interpretation of the expression 'lively idea' the definition works at best only for the limited kind of belief Hume had in mind – and not for general beliefs (belief in general propositions such as 'All men are mortal' in contrast to 'Socrates is mortal') or belief in logically true propositions – must be supposed an important shortcoming.

What is more it is fairly easy to see how Hume is forced into his account by his philosophy of mind, which construes thought as the presence of discrete ideas to consciousness (a view shared, by the way, by Descartes) and which further regards this consciousness of ideas as very similar to ordinary perception. Now ideas on Hume's theory can be varied in only two ways, either by the addition of other ideas or by varying their degree of 'force or vivacity' (thus Hume continues the perceptual analogy), and as he thinks belief adds no further idea to the idea which is entertained it can only be a matter of superior liveliness. Belief is therefore a lively idea.

Aside from the inevitable vagueness of the account resulting from Hume's use of this perceptual model, it suffers from two major defects. One is that it makes no allowance for the fact that we can talk of people believing things when they are asleep, or unconscious, or simply not thinking of those things at all. There are very many things which each of us believes at all times during our lives even though we may only have occasion to think of a few of them over any period of time, and what is more we hardly cease to believe them when we fall asleep. The trouble with identifying belief with an introspectible mental occurrence such as a lively idea is that this possibility is thereby precluded, and we only believe what we have in mind at the time. Clearly the solution is to recognise a dispositional use of the term 'belief' when we are talking of the beliefs of people which they are not conscious of at the time, and at the very least a mentalistic account must be supplemented in this direction. It could be claimed however that the spirit of the mentalistic account is not necessarily lost by such supplementation as the non-dispositional sense of 'belief' might be the 'primary' sense: what we must make room for, so it might be argued, is a disposition to have the mental occurrence – Hume's lively idea – in those cases where we *are* conscious of our beliefs, and this is all that the disposition comprises. The mentalistic theory could be saved in this way, and whether we allow the move must depend on the other shortcomings of the theory. An argument which might seem to support the revised account is that the existence of beliefs in a dispositional sense surely requires beliefs in an occurrent sense, just as fragility is parasitic on things actually breaking; but on reflection it should be plain that there is no reason why the occurrences which manifest the disposition should themselves be beliefs in any sense, as we shall see from the dispositional accounts of Ryle and Braithwaite to be considered later.

The second major defect of the mentalistic account is its misconstrual of our grounds for *belief ascriptions*. In the case of ascribing beliefs to other people, the theory apparently requires that we establish the presence of a lively idea in the subject's mind, but on the contrary we base our belief ascriptions on what the subject says and does (and in the case of his perceptual beliefs we depend to a large extent on what we can see to be the case ourselves). The value of this consideration can perhaps be disputed on the basis of a direct comparison with the ascription of other mental occurrences such as being in pain, it being obvious that here we must distinguish the *grounds for* such ascriptions from their *meanings*. The case is however totally different when we consider self-ascriptions of belief, that is the ascription of beliefs to oneself. This Humean mentalistic theory is clearly committed to saying it is done on the basis of an awareness of the relevant lively idea, and this is just not the way we do it. Our knowledge of our own beliefs is not the result of introspective discovery of Humean lively ideas, and we must look therefore for an alternative account of belief. Yet it would be premature to reject all mentalistic theories on the basis of Hume's failure, particularly in the absence of any viable alternative account of self-ascription of belief, and it is perhaps possible that Hume's downfall here was again simply the result of his perceptual model of thinking. We must look first at a more sophisticated account of belief as a mental occurrence.

Such a theory was proposed by Cook Wilson, and adopted with modifications by H. H. Price in his paper 'Some Considerations about Belief'.[2] Belief is said to comprise a conjunction of two separate acts, (1) the *entertaining* of the proposition P, and (2) the *assenting to* or *adopting of* that proposition. Assenting to P has two elements, a volitional and an emotional one: the former is the preferring of P to alternatives Q, R, S and so on; the latter is the feeling of a certain degree of confidence with regard to P. Price illustrates the analysis as follows:

> Suppose we have lost the cat. We entertain the propositions that the cat is in the cupboard, that it is in the coal scuttle . . . Presently we hear a noise from the direction of the cupboard, and forthwith we *assent to* or *adopt* the proposition that the cat is in the cupboard.[3]

Belief on this analysis is 'reasoned assent to the proposition'. Cook Wilson did however recognise the existence of another kind of occurrence which we also call belief, and which we described as 'being under the impression that P'. Price calls it 'mere acceptance' and illustrates it with the example of seeing a man with something of the dress and appearance of an acquaintance Smith, and 'without weighing of evidence or any consideration of alternatives' we straightaway jump to the conclusion that it *is* Smith. 'Mere acceptance' is 'the unreasoned absence of dissent', in Price's words. To Cook Wilson's two kinds of belief Price adds a third which he calls 'reasonable assurance', illustrated by the sort of belief one may have in one's friend's veracity which is the product not so much of conscious consideration of alternatives and deciding evidence, but of a protracted acquaintance with his behaviour. Reasonable assurance is defined as 'a progressive disinclination to doubt an entertained proposition, where the disinclination is caused by a series of experiences which are in fact, but are not noticed to be, such as they would be if the proposition were true'.[4] Reasonable assurance is therefore supposed to stand between reasoned assent and mere acceptance, with the latter as its lower limit.

We should discuss briefly the use made by the theory of 'entertaining a proposition'. Undoubtedly there are occasions on which we consider the evidence for and against some proposition and, deciding that the balance is neither in the favour of the proposition nor against it, we refuse to commit ourselves either way – such is a fairly sophisticated attitude to reach which is itself the product of thought. Here we have arrived at an attitude which is neither believing P nor disbelieving P, but remaining neutral on the matter. This might at first sight be just what Cook Wilson and Price meant by 'entertaining P without believing or disbelieving it' (and Hume referred to as 'conceiving the ideas according to the proposition'). That it is not follows from the requirement that entertaining is a mental act which can occur either in total separation from any more complex attitude to a proposition, and also as part of such attitudes as believing, doubting, questioning, supposing, and so on. On this usage a proposition must be entertained *before* we can arrive at the sophisticated refusal to believe or doubt P: it is as though before we can do anything to P we have to have it in mind, and entertaining it is this having in mind. Now in a sense this is quite acceptable, if we are careful not to read it as requiring that P be 'entertained' *temporally* before, or as a *separate* act from, questioning or supposing or believing and so on. There is an acceptable alternative philosophical usage which sees such cognitive attitudes as 'modes' of entertaining a proposition, as also are various emotional and volitional attitudes such as fearing, desiring, and hoping; with this tradition we can have no quarrel. An act of entertaining in Cook Wilson's sense is very different and the need for it most questionable. Price indeed finds an adequate description of the supposed phenomenon most elusive. In his early (1934) paper he calls it 'the most mental thing we do', 'the basic intellectual phenomenon', and says that 'there is something ultimate and unanalysable here, which can only be indicated and not explained'. He does however suggest that it is equivalent to 'knowing what it would be like for P to be true', unhappily because this is the same as understanding P which is hardly an identifiable mental act but instead a lasting ability of language users. (In the only sense in which understanding might be a mental act, where it is equivalent to coming to grasp the meaning of a sentence, it is hardly something which we have to do each time we return to the proposition.) In *Belief* (1969)[5] he questions whether considering or realising what it would be like for P to be true can be the correct account, but rejects both as suggesting too much time and thoughtfulness. Finally he comes up with this not very enlightening suggestion: 'When we entertain a proposition our capacity for considering or realising what it would be like for a certain sentence to describe something is always subactivated.'[6] It would appear best to try to do without this separate act of entertaining in a theory of belief.

Turning now to the rest of the Cook Wilsonian analysis, it must be realised just how little it really says about belief as such. The theory rather says a good deal about the various ways in which we arrive at our beliefs, for this is essentially what distinguishes rational assent from mere acceptance and reasonable assurance; and even then it is hardly exhaustive in its characterisation of these routes. Beliefs can be acquired in ways which could not qualify as rational in the sense in which all beliefs recognised by the theory do, as a result for example of brainwashing, propaganda, or simply of logically fallacious reasoning. Now the various routes to belief can fairly be held to throw *some* light on the nature of the end result, but the conceptual connection between belief and routes to it is hardly as close as that which holds in the case of knowledge. If a man can properly be said to know that P then he must have arrived at his knowledge by one of a few accredited routes, be it by direct perception or on authority or in a way which satisfies the standard criteria of knowledge; beliefs may be held for a wide variety of reasons, some reasons being respectable and others not, or even for no reason at all.

The end result of these routes is therefore the major question at issue and Cook Wilson's theory is surprisingly uninformative about this: according to the route involved, belief is described as (1) assenting to P, which is the preference of P to Q, R, etc.; (2) not dissenting from P; or (3) being disinclined to doubt P. Not surprisingly these are very near equivalents and hardly informative as definitions of 'believing'. What is more, no reason is given for saying that different routes produce different end results, a thesis clearly contained in Price's choice of three different phrases. Why cannot the end result be the same?

How does the theory fare against our criticisms of Hume? Does this version of the mentalistic thesis make allowance for a dispositional use of the term 'belief'? One reason for saying not is that all three cases recognised by the theory involve entertaining P, which is a mental act or occurrence taking place at some moment in time and of which we can be introspectively aware. Furthermore, the definition of assent clearly makes this an episode in the conscious life of the believer, so in the case of beliefs arrived at by conscious reasoning no room is left for a dispositional use. Mere acceptance also (we can surmise on the basis of Price's example) is episodic, but reasonable assurance is not by definition something happening at a moment. Where Price's theory fails to account for dispositional ascriptions of beliefs it might seem that its modification in that direction could easily be accomplished, just as Hume's theory was supplemented by a secondary sense of 'belief'. It is not clear, however, just how Price's account of reasoned assent could be retained in its essence, for what would the dispositional beliefs be dispositions to do? It is implausible to see a dispositional belief as a disposition to assent to P, to prefer P to alternatives, on each occasion P is thought of – for why should a *renewed* act of assent be necessary?

Moving to the question of the theory's account of belief ascriptions once more, we must say that for many of our beliefs, if not all, we have no need to introspect a mental act of assenting to discover a basis for ascribing those beliefs to ourselves. Perhaps this is most clear with beliefs which have *not* been rationally arrived at, so that no assent in Cook Wilson's sense took place, and yet which we express most readily – 'assent to' in the non-Cook Wilsonian sense of publicly expressing one's commitment to the proposition – when the occasion arises. Indeed, many of our most cherished beliefs concerning our personal relationships, for example, are of this nature and we can obviously have no need to refer to a non-existent act of assenting before informing others where we stand on these matters. Concerning mere acceptance and reasonable assurance – both cases of rationally-based belief –

in as much as we must remain unclear just what the believer is supposed to be doing, it is difficult to say precisely what if anything the believer must introspect before he can ascribe these beliefs to himself; perhaps if we need to admit the introspection of some assenting act in the case of beliefs which are painstakingly arrived at we could allow an introspective basis for those other beliefs also. But do we need to suppose introspection of assenting in Cook Wilson's 'belief proper'? On the contrary, even where we hold a belief as the result of careful consideration it is not necessary to peer inwardly to discover a mental act of assenting before we can answer the question 'Do you believe that P?'; it rather appears that we have, in some sense, a *direct* access to the belief itself independently of any mental act on our part, so that we can 'tell right off' whether we believe that P. This is not necessarily to say that we *never* 'introspect an assent act' when asked 'Do you believe that P?', and we shall try to suggest later an interpretation of this phrase which makes it a reasonable thesis. To offer this interpretation is, however, to go beyond the letter of Hume's and Price's theories.

Belief as Behavioural Disposition

We turn now to the dispositional theory of belief. The traditional rival to a mental occurrence account, this was in fact hinted at by Hume in an appendix to the *Treatise*: he wrote that belief 'is something felt by the mind, which distinguishes the ideas of the judgement from the fictions of the imagination . . . and renders them the governing principles of all our actions'.[7] A less hybrid position was adopted by Alexander Bain in *The Emotions and The Will* (1859): 'Belief has no meaning, except in reference to our actions'; and in *Mental and Moral Sciences* (1868) he writes: 'The difference between mere conceiving or imagining, with or without strong feeling, and belief, is acting, or being prepared to act, when the occasion arises.' C. S. Peirce was attracted to this view also, as were many twentieth-century logical positivists such as Hans Reichenbach and Rudolf Carnap, and the English philosophers Richard Braithwaite and Gilbert Ryle. According to the version presented by Braithwaite – in his paper 'The Nature of Believing'[8] – the sentence 'I believe that P' is said to mean the conjunction of two propositions: (1) I entertain P, and (2) I have a disposition to act as if P were true. Not all versions of this theory would include entertaining as Braithwaite's does – presumably because he wishes to suggest that we should have been aware of the proposition believed at least once, as of course we would be when ascribing this belief to ourselves. Ryle's account[9] makes no such mentalistic concession.

This approach to belief promises some clear advantages. A disposition, for one thing, is a property which an object can possess at times when it is not being manifested, or indeed which need never be manifested: a pane of glass is fragile at all times up to its actual breaking, and a rubber band can be elastic without ever being stretched, and lose its elasticity after prolonged exposure to sunlight. There is therefore no objection to ascribing beliefs which are not being manifested at the time, or which are never exhibited in the behaviour of the subject. (On the other side, by way of contrast with the attribution of dispositional properties in science, it should be noted that these are thought to reflect non-dispositional properties of the microscopic particles of matter.) On the question of knowledge of beliefs there are also benefits, for we do in fact know of other people's beliefs from their behaviour (including what they say); and we can even come to know of our own beliefs by reflecting on our own behaviour, this being sometimes the only way we can become aware of those ill-considered and unreasonable opinions which we all harbour. The apparent weakness of the dispositional approach in this respect is that it is committed to the claim that all knowledge of beliefs is in this way indirect, so denying the fact that self-ascriptions are very often not based on behaviour. Braithwaite recognises only three routes to self knowledge:

(1) A direct induction from my knowledge of my behaviour in the past to knowledge of my behaviour in the future. (2) By means of *Gedankenexperimente*: I may consider how I shall act in the future in a given situation, and infer that I shall act in the way I think I shall act. (3) By relying on my feelings: I may have a feeling of conviction towards the proposition entertained, and infer that I shall act upon it.[10]

Each of these routes is indirect, and Braithwaite's theory fails to provide for the undeniably direct access we have to many of our beliefs.

There is however a move open to the theory which would seem to provide for this, and which is certainly within the spirit of the theory. One such version was indeed suggested by Rudolf Carnap[11] (though not specifically to meet the present objection) and it has certain *prima facie* advantages. This is simply to extend the notion of 'being disposed to act as if P is true' to include, as well as the non-verbal bodily actions envisaged by Braithwaite's sort of theory, such verbal actions as saying 'I believe that P' or simply 'P' or answering 'Yes' whenever the relevant circumstances arise, such as being asked 'Is it the case that P?' Our beliefs are, after all, often expressed in a verbal form and the dispositional theory ought therefore to encompass such responses. It could then be argued that what we have referred to as 'the self-ascription of beliefs' is just such a situation as this, rather than a careful inward investigation of our mental activities or outward monitoring of our own behaviour. What is more the verbal behaviour is tied to the belief as one manifestation of the disposition, and what could be more direct than that? Self-ascription can therefore easily be construed as having a direct connection with the belief disposition without going outside the dispositional theory.

Now such an extension has the merit of connecting our verbal behaviour with our beliefs, and reminding us how spontaneous our reports of our beliefs are, but such an extended dispositional theory is not without difficulties. To begin with, what we say and what we do are not always consistent, so that no clear disposition emerges from the totality of our behaviour. This might be resolved, as we sometimes actually do resolve such a lack of harmony in our sayings and doings, in terms of the idea of weakness of will, placing emphasis on the saying rather than the doing; alternatively the doing could be taken as the proper indicator of belief on the principle that 'actions speak louder than words'.[12] (This problem is not, of course, peculiar to the extended dispositional theory, for our non-verbal behaviour is not always explicable in terms of a consistent set of beliefs.) Secondly, this account of belief ascription is at most an account of the public self-ascription of beliefs for other people's benefit, and fails to account for the private self-ascription which can go on unspoken for nobody's benefit but one's own. It does, however, naturally suggest an extension whereby such private acts are construed as 'saying to oneself' that one believes that P, where this constitutes another manifestation of the disposition; what it does not suggest is what might take the part of the stimulus for the response provided in the social setting. A third and particularly damning criticism arises as follows. The suggestion is that the belief disposition be construed as including among its manifestations 'assenting to P' in one form or another, and that this is what constitutes self-ascription. Now this assenting to P might indeed be a way of manifesting the belief, but it has still to be construed as a reporting of the belief. Assenting to P cannot be understood simply as an unthinking utterance of words which is a mere motor response to a stimulus – although the connection of the theory with behavioural psychology explains a tendency of the theory to so construe it – but is rather the expressing of the belief that P, informing the hearer where you stand. Not only does this present a major problem of circularity for the attempt to define belief in terms of assenting – the notion of belief being itself required to explain the latter notion – but it leaves the problem of self-ascription unresolved. If there is a disposition to assent to P in the relevant ways, it is a disposition to inform others that one holds the belief. To include such an expression of the belief among the modes of manifesting the disposition hardly explains how it can come about, nor in particular how it can be based on a direct knowledge of that belief.

We come now to assess the general approach of the dispositional theory in either of its versions. The major question is whether the central phrase 'being disposed to act as if P were true' (or 'in a manner appropriate to the truth of P') can be spelt out in a satisfactory manner. Obviously if reference to belief has to be made in a full definition of this expression the dispositional theory is involved in a crippling circularity. The phrase in question lacks an immediately clear sense, but Braithwaite illustrates it with a perfectly ordinary example which brings out the intention.[13] He writes:

> Thus my disposition to act as if strawberries gave me indigestion means that, under relevant external circumstances (my being offered strawberries) and my needs being to preserve my health, I shall behave in a manner appropriate to the indigestibility of strawberries, namely, I shall refuse them. Under similar external circumstances, if my need is to have indigestion . . . I shall accept the strawberries.[14]

The statement 'I have a disposition to act as if P were true' therefore asserts a relationship between four things or sets of things:

> (1) My present and future actions, (2) the external circumstances originating the actions, (3) the relevant internal circumstances of my body and my mind, which I shall call my 'needs', and (4) the proposition itself.[15]

It is necessary, however, for Braithwaite to give a general characterisation of the phrase in question, as well as this illustrative example, and he believes (as he must) that such need make no reference either to the belief that P or belief in general:

> The appropriateness of my action consists in its satisfying my needs, and the satisfaction of needs is something into which no element of belief . . . need enter. It is something of which I do not despair of a naturalistic explanation, though I am unable to provide anything more definite than to talk of a state of comparative quiescence following a period of complicated activity.[16]

It is easy to see that such a definition requires major modification. Whether or not some action results in the satisfaction of my needs depends on the circumstances in which the action takes place: I shall of course hold beliefs about these circumstances and the appropriateness of my action to the truth of P must make reference to these other beliefs. It would, in other words, be possible for some action to *fail* to satisfy my needs (even though the proposition on which I act is true) simply because of some purely fortuitous occurrence, and we would not want for that reason to rule out the action as inappropriate. In the same way the action might *satisfy* my needs because of some purely fortuitous occurrence and it could not be called appropriate for *that* reason. This difficulty is clearly illustrated by Chisholm's example of a man who drives along a particular road in order to keep an appointment with a friend but has an accident along the way that results in a failure to satisfy either this intention or the rest of his needs. The action was nevertheless appropriate. Similarly, someone on the way to the bank might discover a wallet full of money, his needs therefore being met: we would not wish to say his action of going towards the bank was appropriate for *that* reason.[17]

There is a sense therefore in which the satisfaction of my needs must be non-accidental, namely that my other beliefs about the circumstances of the action should be correct. We can revise Braithwaite's definition accordingly and say that 'Action A is appropriate to the truth of P' means that 'A will, given the truth of all my other (relevant) beliefs, satisfy my needs if P is true'.

This is even now not an adequate account, and requires one more modification. Among my other beliefs there will be some concerning the consequences of action A which can be expected, in particular the belief that A *will* satisfy my needs if P is true. There is a good case for saying that *this* belief need not in fact be true at all for my action to be appropriate; if I do *believe* that A will result in the satisfaction of my needs then this is sufficient for its appropriateness. The definition should therefore be revised as follows: 'Action A is appropriate to the truth of P' means that 'I *believe* that A will, given the truth of all my other (relevant) beliefs, satisfy my needs if P is true'. We have now arrived at a much more plausible account, but unfortunately the definition of appropriateness twice makes use of the very notion of belief which appropriateness was introduced to explain. The dispositional theory must therefore be rejected as an adequate account of belief.

It should be clear from this discussion of 'acting as if P were true' that the belief that P cannot be equated with a disposition to one specific form of action, and herein lies another major problem for the theory. In presenting his own dispositional account, Ryle makes a distinction between single-track and multi-track dispositions, contrasting belief with such dispositions as brittleness the manifestations of which are of one kind. Belief is described as a multi-track disposition which can be actualised in an indefinitely heterogeneous range of activity.[18] Now this in itself might make belief dispositions suspect in contrast to the standard kind of disposition treated in the sciences, though many of these latter dispositions (e.g. being magnetic) have more than one way of exhibiting themselves. The situation is in fact worse than Ryle suggests, for in the case of belief the disposition could be exhibited in more than just a wide range of actions but in a boundless range, including inaction itself. The point is that anything might count as acting in a manner appropriate to the truth of P, for this essentially depends on all the other relevant beliefs, motives and wants of the believer. What might constitute the range of actions appropriate to 'Today is Monday'? It is easy to concoct a whole range of situations in which diverse and conflicting actions would be appropriate, and we can give no limited disjunctive list of such actions. This point is not refuted by the fact that we may sometimes be able to specify a narrow range of actions which someone who held a particular belief would in normal circumstances take: such would be the case for the man who believed that strawberries are indigestible, or that exercise prolongs one's active life. We know what kinds of thing consitute holding these beliefs because we assume a definite set of motives and needs, and a certain general view of the nature of the world on the part of the believer. We cannot however simply equate such a limited range with acting as if P were true for any such P, for the simple reason that in some circumstance a man might hold the relevant belief and yet not exhibit this particular disposition. What if I wanted you to think that I was of the opposite opinion? By the same token, doing one or more of the standard things which the range includes might not be a result of holding the belief in question: think of the belief that the glorious dictator of one's country is God's gift to an undeserving populace. We must conclude that to ascribe a belief is not to ascribe any specific behavioural disposition. Given the difficulty of finding a non-circular account of the appropriateness of an action to the truth of a proposition, this really signals the downfall of this theory of belief.

One final problem: The theory construes the belief that P as a disposition which is manifested in circumstance C by action A. What explanation can be given of the believer taking this action? Normally we would look to his wants and his belief that P to provide the explanation, but if his belief is *equated* with doing A in circumstance C it can hardly provide part of the explanation. Action A therefore lacks an explanation on the dispositional theory.[19]

This discussion can be ended on a more positive note. Believing that P must not be equated with having a disposition to behave as if P were true. This must not be understood, however, as implying that no connection whatever can be found between belief and action; it is consistent with the discussion so far to claim that your believing normally makes a difference to your behavioural dispositions. What you do, it has been already claimed above, is a function of the complex of your beliefs and wants and so the acquisition of a new belief is in the usual case followed by some modification of your behaviour. And although we cannot equate believing that P with having a specific behavioural disposition, for many propositions (e.g. that exercise prolongs active life) we can nevertheless predict just what you will do if you believe them. We can do this, as noted above, because we assume a definite set of motives and a certain view of the world on your part.

Belief as Mental State

We have found reason to reject the two traditional theories of belief, but it is not too difficult to see that they each contain a grain of truth. Belief is not a mental act, yet the *acquisition* of a belief often is. We frequently come to our beliefs by a process of deliberation and finally a decision, and this decision is a dateable mental occurrence.[20] Again, belief cannot be equated with a behavioural disposition, yet clearly belief is closely related to behaviour. Why do we have beliefs at all? Many of them serve to guide our actions and this can be seen as their *raison d'être*. It would not be correct however to view belief simply as a guide to action, for that would overlook the important area of theory construction, the intellectual and non-practical activity which is most clearly expressed in the work of scientists but is common to all. We do acquire beliefs which have little if any relevance to anything we do – beliefs about the distant past or the distant future, such as that our sun will eventually become a dead star, might serve as examples – and although it could be argued that they might conceivably have such relevance, it is false that they are in general acquired for that reason.

An adaptation of Ramsey's idea that a belief is 'a map by which we steer' will provide a useful analogy.[21] We can think of our beliefs as conjoined to form an account of the world for us, a map of reality, and to add or take away a belief is to add or subtract a feature of that map. Ramsey subscribed to the dispositional theory and we must part company with him by noting that we only steer by this map sometimes, that it is valued often for itself as well as for its practical applications. As for the mental act account, this analogy improves on it by offering at least a metaphor for the act of 'assenting' to P: we add P to our map of the world, an act which is part of our theory building activity and can have further consequences, both intellectual and practical.

To regard believing that P as having P on one's mental map is to regard believing as a mental state, a continuing attribute of one's mental existence. Such a view escapes the criticisms made of mental act and occurrence accounts concerning the persistence of beliefs generally. Such a view shares with dispositional theories the benefit that beliefs need not be manifested in any actual behaviour. And even better, it advances on dispositional theories by keeping beliefs and behavioural consequences separate, so allowing beliefs to provide explanations for what people do.

Recently D. M. Armstrong has developed a mental state theory in some detail[22] which tries to expand Ramsey's dictum while remaining closer to Ramsey's intent. First belief maps, unlike mere thought maps, are maps by which we steer, so Armstrong retains this behavioural aspect. Secondly Armstrong equates his map with a physical state, following his general materialist view of man whereby mental attributes generally are contingently identical with physical ones. Most importantly Armstrong's theory differs from ours in construing particular beliefs – rather than just the corpus of beliefs as a whole – as maps, a theory which demands a strong structural parallel between thought and reality. Such a picture theory was held by Wittgenstein and Russell early this century, but has since found little favour.

Does our sketch of a mental state theory offer hope for a better account of the self-ascription of beliefs than those already discussed? We saw that our response to the question 'Do you believe that P?' is frequently based neither on introspection of a mental act or other occurrence, nor on inspection of our behavioural responses. The map analogy allows room for two intuitively attractive schemas. In the first place, our response is based sometimes on a more or less protracted deliberation of the matter of P, which we can construe as considering whether to extend or alter our map to incorporate this proposition. (Such may be offered, indeed, as a plausible account of 'introspecting a mental act of assenting'.) In the second place we frequently respond without this process, which was called above 'immediate knowledge' of beliefs, and our map analogy can find room for this: having put P on the map we simply act on that earlier decision, and use our map to steer by. No claim to a fully satisfactory analogy can be made however, for admittedly a mystery still remains: we have not explained just what this reference to the map, this using the map to steer by, comprises and, what is more, we must make sense of features being on the map which we have not placed there by deliberate decision.

CHAPTER III

THE ANALYSIS OF KNOWLEDGE

A long-cherished hope of philosophy was that questions of substance which lay beyond the reach of experience might be settled
by its practitioners. Such would include the supremely important
question of the existence of a God, conceived perhaps as creator
and prime mover of the universe, and the original source of
moral duty; of no less interest would be the existence of a distinguishable aspect of the individual which is a mind or soul, and
which might possibly have existence after the disintegration of
the body. Moreover the major questions of the finite or infinite
nature of the universe, both spatially and temporally, and the
existence of a cause for each and every phenomenon, though in
an obvious way of relevance to science are yet beyond being
settled by experimental investigation and were thought to fall
within the competence of the philosopher. Some philosophers
have approached such matters much more cautiously than
others, and have seen the need to pose a prior question before
entering on these matters of substance. Plato, Locke, Hume and
Kant[1] were members of this cautious school who recognised the
necessity of questioning the power of the human mind to come to
know the nature of things, the extent of the truths about the
world which might possibly lie within its grasp. A clear and
helpful answer to this prior question turns on the philosopher's
ability to give an adequate response to an even more fundamental
question: what is it for the mind to grasp truths about the world?
This, of course, is to ask for an account of knowledge.

But this might be to ask too much. Why should we assume that
anything much can be said about knowledge in general, that there
is anything which all cases of knowledge have in common?[2] The
obvious answer is that such an assumption need not be made
before an attempt to find a general characterisation of know-

ledge: clearly, it is a question to be settled only by that attempt. What is more, a general account of knowledge need not preclude a recognition of the diversity of phenomena which fall under the term, though admittedly it is a feature more of twentieth-century philosophy to stress the finer points of difference rather than the overall unifying features. It would, nevertheless, be too arrogant of us to assume that only now are philosophers able to see the important points of difference.

Kinds of Knowledge

Let us begin however by noticing some distinctions. It has become common to mark a distinction between 'knowing that' and 'knowing how', that is between knowing that some proposition is true, and knowing how to perform some action.[3] The simplest of examples would be something like knowing that today is Monday, or that $2 + 2 = 4$, and knowing how to whistle, or how to tie a shoelace. Other examples of 'knowing how' might be knowing how to recognise horses, which is a skill included in (and some would say commensurate with) the possession of the concept *horse*, and knowing how to use the word 'horse' itelligibly. Indeed the possession of a language is in itself a 'knowledge how' – knowing how to speak English for example – and moreover is a complex body of more particular items of such knowledge, such as knowing how to conjugate the verb 'to be'. To this common distinction between 'knowing how' and 'knowing that' we can add a further category of 'knowing a thing', understanding 'thing' to include people, places, and objects of various kinds and logical categories (Buckingham Palace, the Mona Lisa, the novel *Silas Marner*, the way to Rome, John Smith). A similar but distinguishable category of knowledge might be called 'knowing a truth', where this involves such matters as knowing the answer to some problem, knowing where someone is to be found, knowing who committed the crime, and knowing why he did it.

How many categories do we need to distinquish? That is obviously a matter for debate, but these distinctions are some of the more obvious ones. Within the context of some general philosophical position a particular distinction will seem of pressing importance, such as Russell's distinction between 'knowledge by acquaintance' and 'knowledge by description' of things.[4] For

Russell had a general theory about the nature of language which suggested that language acquires its meaning from our direct acquaintance with sense data, and where this involves no further knowledge of facts about these sense data or other things – hence Russell's special category of knowledge by acquaintance. It has, indeed, seemed highly implausible to many philosophers that there can be such a thing as acquaintance with some particular which involves no knowledge about it whatsoever.

The standard analysis of knowledge which we shall discuss at length in this chapter is at best an account of 'knowing that', yet it might be argued in its defence that the other forms of knowledge are all reducible to this one form. This seems plausible for what we have called 'knowing a truth', for knowing e.g. who committed the crime is knowing that X did it. Cases of 'knowing how' seem frequently reducible with little strain: knowing how to recognise horses is knowing that horses have such-and-such an appearance and exhibit such-and-such behaviour; knowing how to conjugate the verb 'to be' is knowing that the first person singular present tense is 'I am', the second person is 'You are', and so on. Not all cases of 'knowing how' are like this though, for knowing how to whistle might not involve any ability to say how it is done, and hence to say that you have to do X or Y: yet it still can be plausibly argued that knowledge that it is X or Y that has to be done must be present, even if the ability to put it into words is not. (One could as easily have argued that not being able to say how it is done shows that you do not know how to do it, but that would clearly be a mistake.) The most problematic category for this defence is 'knowing a thing'. What must be true for you to know Buckingham Palace? In one sense, at least, just having heard of it would seem to suffice; in another, having been there and seen it is necessary; in a further sense, where knowledge is a matter of degree, knowing a set of facts about its layout and history is necessary. 'Knowing that' is clearly required in some of these senses of knowing Buckingham Palace, yet not so clear is whether this is all that it comes to even then. Knowing John Smith also involves some knowledge of facts about him, but again in at least some sense of the term it involves having made his acquaintance.

The standard analysis is at least in need of further shoring up in terms of these different categories of knowledge. Within the category for which that analysis is best suited there are further distinctions to be made. One has already occupied our attention in Chapter I, that between basic and non-basic knowledge, and the closely allied one between immediate and inferential knowledge. (The difference between the two distinctions lies essentially in the stress on the foundational position of 'basic knowledge'.) To these categories must be added one which has less frequently been noted, but into which falls the greater part of what we know – knowledge on authority. What we have learnt from others, in as much as those others have been well placed to speak with authority on the matter, is of this kind: such would be knowledge imparted by institutions of learning, (some) newspapers, eye-witnesses, and so forth. It would be difficult to prove that this category is reducible to the basic or non-basic category. Sometimes, nevertheless, someone may regard another as *such* an authority that his pronouncements play something like the role of basic propositions as conceived by traditional epistemology – against propositions of this kind all others must be judged.

A further distinction is the historically important one between *a priori* knowledge and *a posteriori* knowledge, and the standard analysis must certainly be adequate for both kinds. We shall not delay here on this, for our final chapter is devoted to that very distinction. Other distinctions, from different points of view, mark off other categories and sub-categories for which the analysis must also suffice: perceptual knowledge, memory knowledge, scientific knowledge, knowledge (if such there be) by divination, and so forth; knowledge of the physical world, of the mental, the social, the future and the past.

The Platonic Definition of Knowledge

Though by no means universally adopted, there is one account of the nature of knowledge that deserves to be called the standard analysis. In one of the earliest works on Epistemology, Plato's *Theaetetus*, knowledge is said to be equivalent to 'true belief with an account' (*logos*)[5] where an account would show why what is believed must be so. Without an account knowledge cannot be present, though true belief may be: a jury can believe truly that the accused is guilty but cannot know that he is guilty without an account. (It is clear that Plato has a very demanding criterion for what would count as sufficient proof of such a proposition, and would not accept the possibility that the jury could indeed move from true belief to knowledge.) A modern version of this Platonic definition is that knowledge is justified true belief, or true belief on grounds which make the proposition certain. Ayer, for example, defines knowledge as true belief where the believer 'has the right to be sure'[6], and Chisholm as true belief where the believer 'has adequate evidence'.[7]

This analysis of knowledge has much initial plausibility. Beliefs can be true or false but clearly one cannot know something which is false. Again, there are some things which we believe and many which we do not, and we can hardly be said to know any of these latter. Finally, there are many things which are both believed and true, yet for belief to constitute knowledge we require that the belief is held for the right kind of reason and is not, for example, just a lucky guess or based on incorrect inferences. It will, however, be our major theme that this standard analysis of knowing is far from uncontroversial.

Two preliminary points must be noted about the form of the standard analysis. It is, first, in its standard presentation an analysis in terms of the truth conditions of the statement 'A knows that P' (and derivatively of associated statements in other tenses and moods). In full it claims that 'A knows that P' is true when, and only when, the more complex statement 'A believes that P, A has adequate grounds for his belief, and P is true' is also true. Such truth condition analyses have been much favoured in philosophy, particularly by empiricists who seek philosophical enlightenment from the reduction of complex concepts to their more elementary parts. It must be for us an open question whether such reductive analyses are generally possible of philosophically interesting concepts, but the problems to be explored in the present chapter will suggest that this is not true of knowledge in particular.

The second preliminary point is a terminological one. The standard analysis offers a set of necessary and sufficient conditions for the truth of 'A knows that P'. To say that X is a 'sufficient condition' for Y is to say that if X is the case then Y must be the case; to say that 'A knows that P' is sufficient condition for 'A believes that P' is to say that if the former is true then so must be the latter. Y's being a 'necessary condition' of X is the converse relation, such that 'A believes that P' is a necessary condition for the truth of 'A knows that P'. The standard analysis in effect identifies the conditions which are individually necessary and jointly sufficient for the truth of 'A knows that P'.

Is Knowledge Analysable?

Some philosophers have been critical of attempts like this to analyse knowledge, not simply because they object to their truth condition form, but because they think that no analysis is possible at all. Cook Wilson, for instance, thought knowing was a basic unanalysable state of mind and rather than including belief as one of its constitutents was totally incompatible with it.[8] Such a view can only be disproved by presenting a plausible analysis of knowing or by finding alternative explanations of those phenomena – such as the fact that we never say 'I know that P *and* I believe that P' – which are taken as establishing this unanalysability thesis. A different and ultimately more instructive unanalysability thesis has been defended by Austin who argues that the standard analysis is an example of what he calls the 'descriptive fallacy'.

The words 'I know that P' do not, according to Austin, serve to describe the speaker but serve instead to 'give others his word' that P, to 'give others his authority' for saying that P.[9] He compared the function of the phrase 'I know' with that of 'I promise', which also has a non-descriptive role. Saying 'I promise' is going beyond a mere expression of intention, to the point where the speaker is binding himself to others and staking his reputation in a special way; in saying 'I promise' he is not describing himself, even describing himself as so binding himself to others, but actually doing the binding. Saying 'I know' similarly involves taking a new plunge:

> But it is *not* saying 'I have performed a specially striking feat of cognition, superior, in the same scale as believing and being sure, even to being merely quite sure' ... Just as promising is not something superior, in the same scale as hoping and intending, even to merely fully intending.[10]

The words 'I know that P' are therefore words whose function is to give others the speaker's word that P rather than to describe the speaker.

This thesis is open to some obvious objections. In the first place Austin has attempted to describe the role of the first person singular present tense use of the verb 'know', and as such can hardly be said to have given a complete account of the verb. Saying such things as 'I knew that P', 'If I knew that P, then A', 'He knows that P' and so on, we need not be (and presumably usually are not) giving others our word that P. It looks, indeed, as if in such cases the primary function of the words is to describe the subject in some way, that is to characterise the subject as qualifying as a knower (whatever that comes to). Austin's account applies at most to his chosen case, and the only plausible form in which it could be defended as an adequate philosophical account of knowledge generally would involve the claim that all other cases are in some way derivative from the first person singular present tense use.[11] Clearly, however, 'I knew that P', does not say that I *said* 'I know that P', so the relation must be more subtle than that. As it stands, that Austinian account is not an account of knowledge ascriptions in general and makes no suggestion as to how it can be developed to become so.

A second objection reflects Austin's own later contributions to the philosophy of language following his adoption of this unanalysability thesis. In this thesis is the implicit assumption that a phrase cannot be both descriptive and performative – as he came to call such phrases as 'I promise' – at the same time. The phrase 'I know' is not descriptive, the thesis claims, but performative. Now this is clearly a mistake: I may insult you by calling you 'an insensitive buffoon', and my words are thereby serving at one and the same time to describe and to insult. What is more, it is only because of the descriptive meaning of such words that they can indeed serve as a mechanism of insult, just as they might serve as a warning to someone else to steer clear of you. It is plausible to suggest that the words 'I know that P' do in some circumstances have the performative role which Austin ascribes to them, and yet that this is a consequence of the descriptive meaning of these words. And, of course, in other circumstances the words may have another role but that would also be a consequence of their descriptive meaning. Austin came to recognise the distinction between performative and descriptive as characterising different aspects of an utterance rather than different kinds of utterances, and indeed to develop a general theory of the different aspects of utterances.[12]

A somewhat more esoteric problem, closely connected with the above, has been pointed out by P. T. Geach.[13] If the simple argument of *modus ponens* form

1 If I know that P, then Q
2 I know that P
Therefore
3 Q

is to be valid, the words 'I know that P' have to be construed in such a way in the premisses (1) and (2) as to ensure there is no fallacy of equivocation. If they are operating differently in (1) and (2) the argument cannot be valid. Perhaps the problem could be best put by saying that if the words are given a descriptive meaning in premiss (1) they must be given the same meaning in premiss (2), even if they have an extra force of giving one's authority for the truth of P.

A further shortcoming of Austin's theory is that it says nothing about *why*, i.e. on what grounds or basis, one is giving one's authority for the truth of P with the words 'I know that P'. It would appear that, at the very least, an implication of these words is that one is in a position to know that P, that one has perhaps the right kind of evidence on which to make the strong assertion that P is true. We might compare Austin's thesis with a similar one proposed by B. S. Benjamin[14] about the words 'I remember that P'. Benjamin claims that those words, rather than describing the speaker, are in fact performing the function of giving the speaker's authority for the truth of P. 'To preface one's remarks with the phrase "I remember . . ." (or a cognate),' he writes, 'is to indicate to one's audience that you certify the truth and accuracy of the information you are about to give . . . The nature of the status-label affixed to P in a statement of the form "I remember P" might, in part, be paraphrased "P is true (or his performance is an instance of P) and you have *my* word for it".'[15] Yet some difference must exist between 'I remember that P' and 'I know that P' or we would not have both locutions, and it is plausible to say that they differ in the implications they have about the *basis* of the claim that P is true. How else could we explain the difference?

These negative comments on Austin's thesis must not lead us to ignore what is of value in it. For one thing it encourages us to attend to the peculiarities of first person claims to know, and indeed claims to believe, which may well be absent from second and third person claims and will surely be ignored if we look simply for an adequate analysis of 'A knows that P'. Secondly, Austin has reminded us that such first person claims involve a commitment to others – we give others grounds for thinking that P, we give our authority – and as such lay us open to certain kinds of criticism if we have misled our hearers. Thirdly it is plain, as Austin says, that 'I know' goes beyond 'I believe' in the kind of commitment made to our hearers, much as 'I promise' goes beyond 'I intend to'. Finally, and following on from these points, we may reflect that we can mislead our hearers as much by saying 'I believe that P' where we ought to have said 'I know that P', as by saying 'I know that P' without sufficient warrant. For it will be inferred from our saying 'I believe' that a commitment of a limited kind is all that the circumstances warrant, and though 'I believe' may well be *true* if knowledge is present it is clearly misleading. It is, then, not just what is said but also the saying of it which is important.

The Truth Conditions of Knowing

The standard Platonic analysis offers three conditions for the statement 'A knows that P': (a) that the statement 'P is true' (or, more simply, 'P') is true; (b) that 'A believes that P' is true; (c) that 'A has adequate grounds for P' (or, as a variant, that 'P is certain') is true. In bringing out the difficulties facing an acceptance of this standard analysis it will be convenient to take these conditions one at a time.

(a) Few philosophers have denied that truth is a necessary condition of knowledge, but that does not show the thesis to be uncontentious. Some philosophers indeed have denied it, for example on the grounds that we wish to talk of the knowledge of earlier times (when we say, for instance, that the Greeks 'knew' that the gods lived on Mount Olympus) or the scientific knowledge of an age earlier than ours where we would now reject those beliefs as false.[16] Such cases could be treated as secondary or 'inverted commas' uses of the term, for the claim that they did not *really* know such things seems acceptable. Let us assume for a moment therefore that 'A knows that P' does entail 'P is true', that truth is a necessary condition of knowing.

This must nevertheless be clearly separated from a second thesis, that truth is a necessary condition for actually asserting of someone (perhaps yourself) that 'A knows that P'. We have argued at length in Chapter I that a proposition P can be 'established' as certain on evidence which does not logically entail it, and someone might therefore correctly claim that 'P is certain' and therefore *claim* to know that P although P is unfortunately not true. The truth conditions of 'A knows that P' are therefore not the same as the conditions of its *assertibility*.

As the origin of the major difficulty for the standard analysis it is worth dwelling on this distinction. Moore pointed out[17] that the following sentences are in some sense incoherent or odd:

(a1) P, but I do not believe that P
(a2) I believe that P, but P is not true.

If someone said, for example, 'I went to the cinema last night, but I do not believe it'; we would be hard pressed to understand these words. On the other hand it is clear that such assertions are not self-contradictions, for it could well be the case that P is true and that I do not believe it; the fault lies in their combined assertion. Such cases, constituting what is called 'Moore's Paradox',[18] underline the fact that assertion is a complex phenomenon which can misfire in more than one way: the moral is that we cannot infer from the oddness or incoherence of a form of words that we are dealing with a self-contradiction, and that we have therefore discovered a truth condition. The oddness of (a2), for example, does not imply that P's being true is a truth condition of 'I believe that P'.

Returning to the assumption made above that knowledge does entail truth we can now ask how this can be proved. Clearly the following

(a3) I know that P, but P is not true

is an odd statement, but we cannot conclude that P's being true is a truth condition of 'I know that P'. We can explain the oddness of (a3) in terms of conditions of assertibility in a manner which is quite simple: you are not warranted in asserting that you know that P unless you believe that P is true. Some way of establishing that a truth condition of 'I know that P' (or generally of 'A knows that P') is that P is true would have to be found, other than relying simply on the oddness of the locution (a3), to defend the standard analysis.

(b) The second part of that analysis is that 'A believes that P' is a truth condition of 'A knows that P', and this has been questioned by a number of philosophers. We are now in a position to understand why the debate has been so unsatisfactory. Two preliminary points in favour of the thesis may be noted. First, we often discover, as we say, that someone only believed that P rather than knew that P when we find that P is false; this suggests that there is no difference in the man himself which is so discovered. Secondly we have the expression 'He doesn't *just* believe, he knows' which suggests the inclusion of belief in knowledge. Regrettably, neither of these points provide conclusive proof of the standard analysis.

An argument might be constructed from the oddness of the statement

(b1)　I know that P, but I do not believe that P

but again that is inconclusive. Why is this not a consequence of assertibility conditions? It is plain enough that believing P is an assertibility condition of 'I know that P', if part of what this latter asserts is P itself. (This, by the way, rules out the Cook Wilsonian view[19] that knowing and believing are two incompatible states of mind.) How could it be shown that (b1) is self-contradictory rather than just in contravention of the conditions of assertibility?

We might try turning to the third person case:

(b2)　He knows that P, but he does not believe that P.

If this were a clearly acceptable locution it would show that (b1) is only in contravention of assertibility conditions, just as

(b3)　He believes that P, but P is not true

indicates that (a2) is not self-contradictory; unfortunately, (b2) is not itself clearly beyond criticism. Of course,

(b4)　He knows that P, but he cannot (or, can hardly) believe it

is perfectly acceptable, but (b2) is not (b4).

We must conclude that an argument from the oddness of locutions will not provide clear proof of the standard analysis. An alternative procedure has in recent years been favoured by a number of writers who hope to provide a clear *disproof* of the standard analysis. This negative aim can, they have assumed, be achieved by the description of cases which we would accept as cases of knowledge yet agree that belief is absent from them. Unfortunately the suggested cases lack plausibility. One such is Griffiths' unconfident examinee[20] who achieves consistent success in an oral examination while offering his answers with the least degree of confidence. We would, perhaps, accept this as a case of knowledge, but it is hardly a clear case of absence of belief; the examinee does lack confidence in his answers, even doubts them, yet that does not *clearly* entail that he does not believe them. A second case is described by Hamlyn as one of knowledge with a refusal to believe:[21] a mother is informed by the proper authorities that her son has been killed in action, so she obviously knows that this is so, yet she refuses to believe it and keeps his room prepared for his return. We are not forced to accept this case as knowledge without belief, as Hamlyn himself notes, for we could say simply that she *seems* not to believe he is dead, or *seems* to believe that he is still alive. Alternatively, we might describe her case as one both of belief that he is dead and belief that he is not, for people do hold contradictory beliefs and the woman is being irrational in these circumstances.

Radford offers the case of the French Canadian who engages in a guessing game, trying to guess various dates in English history.[22] After a run of successes he finally recollects that he had, years before, an English nanny who taught him some such history, and this explains his success. Radford takes this to be a possible situation which we would describe (because of the successful run of answers) as knowledge, e.g. that Elizabeth I died in 1603; yet we would also agree that belief is absent, for he took himself to be guessing. Again, it is not indubitably so. How we should construe the suggestion that he 'guesses' this date is hardly clear, but in so far as we do accept it as a case of guessing we would refuse to call it knowledge. After all, he only subsequently recollects his earlier experiences. In his discussion of Radford's case, Armstrong has suggested[23] that it is a case of inconsistent beliefs, yet this description is somewhat less plausible here than in Hamlyn's case.

This alternative procedure for deciding whether belief is a necessary condition of knowledge is therefore inconclusive, for alternative descriptions of these cases are forthcoming and we do not have to take them at their face value. Matters are in fact worse than that suggests, for they do not even have an obvious face value at all. This, it might be suggested, is a consequence of the fact that our concepts are not as carefully defined as they might be, so they lack a precise boundary in their applicability. Wittgenstein insisted that the concepts of everyday language lack the kind of precise definition which the sciences favour[24] and hence it is not too difficult to find cases where we cannot be sure whether or not a concept has application. It is a plausible conjecture that the unusual cases offered above fit this description.

Two further comments must be made about the alternative procedure just described. One is that even were cases forthcoming which we would be prepared to allow as cases of knowledge without belief it would still be open to us to treat them as peripheral examples of knowledge, and hence not indicative of the behaviour of our concepts in their central applications. There is no reason to expect that all cases of knowledge fit precisely the same pattern and some may easily fail to be at all representative of the central usage or usages. But secondly it should be obvious that this alternative procedure is not after all independent of arguments from the oddness of locutions. To decide whether a case purporting to be a refutation of the standard analysis is indeed so, is to decide whether the locution descriptive of such a case has the oddness or incoherence relied upon in the first form of argument. It follows from this that our resistance to a description of these unusual cases as knowledge without belief cannot be offered as proof that the standard analysis is correct. At most it indicates that there is *some* connection between the concepts of knowledge and belief, but not necessarily that it is as close as the standard truth condition analysis has it.

(c) The third truth condition offered by the standard analysis is variously expressed as 'A has adequate grounds for P', 'P is certain', 'A has the right to be sure that P', and so on. We may take the basic idea to be that the believer should be warranted in his belief by his epistemic circumstances, in the case of non-basic beliefs by the propositional evidence in their favour and in the case of basic beliefs by the set of other beliefs which bear closely upon them. Such a thesis has indeed been assumed in the previous two chapters of this book.

In as much as 'A has adequate grounds for P' goes beyond this central idea it is clearly mistaken. The only beliefs for which it is reasonable to ask for grounds are non-basic beliefs, for it does not make sense to ask for grounds for 'I am in pain' or 'It looks to me as if there is a table'. The third necessary truth condition of knowing cannot be put in these terms. A formula which recognises basic beliefs must be found, such as 'A is in a position to know'[25], 'A has the right to be sure'[26], or simply 'P is certain'. Such a formula has the additional merit that it can be taken to encompass beliefs which have been acquired on authority, for clearly our formula should permit the analysis of knowing to include knowledge on authority.

The sentence 'P is certain' does not mean the same as 'A is certain that P', although we have seen the close connection between these objective and subjective senses of certainty: if P is certain, then anyone in the relevant epistemic circumstances should *be* certain that P. Does knowledge require certainty in the subjective sense? The sentence

(c1) I know that P, but I am not certain that P

does indeed appear odd and its message incoherent, yet the corresponding third person case

(c2) He knows that P, but he is not certain that P

does not perhaps have the same effect; and if this is right, subjective certainty is an assertibility condition and not a truth condition of knowledge. (Woozley[27] has described sentence (c1) as 'epistemologically absurd' rather than self-contradictory.) More importantly, for us, is objective certainty such a truth condition, as our previous chapters have assumed? The idea has much *prima facie* plausibility. Surely, we may say, if the evidence is such as to make P only somewhat probable, or even quite probable, that is not enough for anyone to claim knowledge that P. Let the proposition be 'There is life on Mars' or 'Ned will win the Derby'; if P is true and someone believes it, we would not allow that he knows it if the grounds for P are insufficiently conclusive. They have, we say, to *establish* that P, to *justify accepting* it. (If the race is fair, no such grounds could exist and nobody could know that Ned will win.) Such thoughts do indicate some connection between knowledge and objective certainty but do not uniquely determine that relation.

The argument from the oddness of locutions would point to the incoherence of

(c3) I know that P, but P is not certain.

We know, however, from the comparison with (c1) that an incoherence of this kind could well be a function simply of assertibility conditions, and obviously if I do not believe that P is certain I ought not to assert that P nor, in consequence, that I know that P. We might attempt to rest the thesis on the oddness of

(c4) He knows that P, but P is not certain

by parity of argument with subjective certainty, for if (c2) shows that subjective certainty is not a truth condition of knowledge, (c4) surely does show that objective certainty is. This is not so, however. The unacceptability of (c4) can easily be explained as a function of assertibility conditions instead: in asserting of someone else that he knows that P I must *ipso facto* be asserting the same of myself. (This does not hold, of course, for the assertions 'He knows what the truth of the matter is', 'He knows how to do X', 'He knows Mr N', and possibly for other forms of knowledge ascription also.) If this point is granted, the rest follows easily, for we have just noted above that a condition for the assertion of 'I know that P' is that P is certain.

There is a case sometimes offered[28] to refute the standard thesis, in the manner of the alternative approach discussed in section (b), which is the boy in D. H. Lawrence's story 'The Rocking Horse Winner'. After his consistent predictions of the winners of horse races simply as a result of riding on a rocking horse, we have little alternative but to admit that he knows which horse is going to win – and not only now, but also that he knew on the first occasion as well. If we allow that there are grounds now for believing that some horse which he has just selected on the rocking horse will win the race, because of his past success rate, we cannot however allow that on the first occasion there were such grounds. We had no grounds for believing his first prediction, and neither did he, so it was not certain that his horse would win. Now the general comments made earlier on such extreme cases are equally applicable to this one, and its inconclusiveness therefore is clear. There are, of course, some simple and plausible ways of rebutting its threat to the standard analysis, for example by denying that it is a case of knowledge at all. Alternatively, we could say that there were after all sufficient grounds for accepting his prediction, for though we did not know it at the time his very prediction in these circumstances was conclusive reason for believing him and did make his choice a certainty.

The three truth conditions offered as necessary and jointly sufficient for knowledge by the standard analysis are therefore all open to dispute. The main difficulty lies in the complexity of assertion itself so that assertions can be defective for more than one kind of reason. Any attempt to analyse knowledge must face this difficulty, not only one which tries to provide a reductive analysis in terms of truth conditions, although the difficulties are most acute for analyses of this form. Considerations of the same nature as those outlined above are relevant to the assessment of other candidates which philosophers have offered as necessary for knowing, for example that 'A knows that he knows that P'[29] or 'A understands P'. It would obviously be very odd for someone to say

(c5) I know that P, but I do not know that I do

yet an explanation from assertibility conditions is easily found, and there are considerations in favour of allowing knowledge to be possessed by those who are unaware of it. Someone might, for example, possess all the relevant evidence for P and yet not realise that it is sufficient to make P certain even though he bases his belief on it. (It must be an open question for us whether he could be said to know if he does not draw the conclusion that P even though his evidence is sufficient for it.) Less plausible is Danto's argument[30] that knowing that one knows requires a philosophical understanding of the nature of knowledge itself, which is lacking in most people without detriment to their knowledge of other things. That 'A understands P' is a truth condition of 'A knows that P' is more plausible, since wherever knowledge is dependent on grounds it seems necessary that the knower grasp the connection between the evidence and what it is evidence for. On the other hand, cannot a schoolboy read in a standard algebra textbook the words 'The real field is perfect with respect to absolute value' and so know that it is, without understanding a word of it? And religious believers are not too ashamed to admit that they do not understand many of the propositions which they 'know on authority' to be true, for example propositions about the infinite nature of God's qualities, and the doctrine of the Trinity.

Alternative Approaches

If the truth conditions of knowing are so difficult to isolate, what implications does this have for the theory of knowledge? Clearly if the analysis of knowing has to take the form favoured by logical empiricists, a reductive truth condition form, it looks as if the prospects for the theory of knowledge are bleak. It would seem reasonable to be prepared to accept an analysis of a different kind, which might in fact take the form simply of indicating the incoherences on which a truth condition analysis was to be founded. For, it might be argued, each one of these incoherences does indicate something about the concepts involved, even if it does not clearly discriminate between possible sources of them.

An approach to the theory of knowledge of this sort would be in the tradition of 'ordinary language' philosophy, following the lead of Wittgenstein by marking the limits of what we can say about knowledge, belief, evidence and so on, to produce what Ryle called 'a conceptual map'.[31] Though such an enterprise would leave aside the attempt to formalise its results and relate them to a general theory of language, it need not be totally without direction. For Wittgenstein, and consequently for many other philosophers, the ultimate purpose of the enterprise was to dissolve the traditional and persistent problems of philosophy, and the sort of conceptual points brought to light in terms of the oddness of locutions discussed in the previous section would serve to meet the philosophical sceptic. Wittgenstein's own work *On Certainty*[32] is addressed, via a consideration of various remarks of Moore and Russell, to this traditional sceptical position, and it is apparent that an epistemology of this nature can offer a rich and varied product.

So much so, in fact, that it is tempting to progress beyond an amassing of detail to formulate an ordered system of conceptual remarks.[33] In recent years there has emerged an alternative to this ordinary language approach which gives hope to logical empiricism in finding room for truth conditions as part of the analysis yet seeks to include much more. Such is the formal epistemic logic of Jaakko Hintikka, which can only be briefly described here.

In his paper 'Epistemic Logic and the Methods of Philosophical Analysis'[34] he explicitly contrasts his method with what he calls the 'paradigm-case approach' of philosophers such as Ryle and Austin who seek to describe ordinary language in terms of standard cases. Hintikka shares their view that 'the philosophically interesting concepts which we want to study are largely embedded in ordinary usage'; but believes formal methods are needed. One major problem faced by the paradigm-case approach is that our linguistic intuitions frequently reflect not simply logical relations, but a more complicated interplay of factors, which formal epistemic logic can treat in a systematic and informative way. An epistemic logic provides 'an *explanatory model* . . . [which] may be thought of as bringing out the "depth logic" which underlies the complex realities of our ordinary use of epistemic words ("knows", "believes" etc.) and in terms of which these complexities can be accounted for'.[35] Such a model cannot be derived simply from a surface description of language but must instead be invented.

Within the model an epistemic expression is assigned a 'basic meaning', and the development of the logic shows how this meaning is modified by a multiplicity of pragmatic and other factors to produce 'residual meanings' which can be identified in ordinary usage. Typical modifying factors are those, such as the need to make as explicit a statement as possible, which virtually all discourse can be expected to serve; pragmatic pressures such as that not to use circumlocutions without some specific purpose; and pressures due to the particular context of utterance of the sentence. In contrast to his formal approach Hintikka finds the paradigm-case approach wanting on a number of counts. One is that the basic meaning may not itself appear in ordinary language – witness Hintikka's own assignment of the basic meaning to 'A knows that P' which makes it equivalent to 'A knows that A knows that P' – and, as a consequence, no paradigm-case appears in ordinary language which illuminates other uses. Furthermore, the lack of obvious surface connections between various uses of an epistemic term leads ordinary language philosophers to postulate a multiplicity of irreducible senses of words, whereas epistemic logic can indicate close interconnections.

One interesting question for Hintikka's approach concerns the decision procedure for competing epistemic logics which assign different basic meanings and alternative routes to the same residual meanings. In so far as ordinary language offers no choice between them, it would seem that the choice must be made in terms of such 'explanatory virtues' as coherence and simplicity: after all, it is in terms of the degree to which the theories cohere with previously accepted ones and the extent to which they effect a simplification in the overall account of nature that a choice is made in science between competing theories which have the same established observational implications. In what sense, though, can coherence and simplicity be called *explanatory* virtues in the case of Hintikka's epistemic models? The case of these models is different from that of scientific theories, for there is no obvious parallel to the actually existing unobservable entities of physical science. (The case is in fact similar to that of Chomsky's generative grammars in linguistics.[36]) There are, on the other hand, real social and linguistic pressures such as those indicated by Hintikka, which any adequate logic would need to reflect, and herein lies the real explanatory value of such a model. These are the best candidates for the 'unobservable entities' of epistemic logic.

The Gettier Problem

For the rest of this chapter we shall be concerned with a problem originating from a short paper which Edmund Gettier published in 1963.[37] Gettier tries to show, using two examples, that the standard analysis of knowing as justified true belief is incorrect in as much as the three conditions involved in this analysis are not jointly sufficient. It is clear that Gettier understands the standard analysis as a definition of knowing which is intended to apply only to that sub-class of cases of 'knowing that' which have been called non-basic or inferential, and the literature which Gettier's paper has generated has likewise limited itself to the standard analysis taken in this sense. Gettier, then, is attempting to show that 'non-basic knowing that' is not equivalent to justified true belief. Most philosophers have reacted to his paper by trying to find some fourth condition which, when added to the three standard conditions of knowing, will provide a set of jointly sufficient conditions.[38]

Gettier's first example is as follows:
Smith and Jones have applied for the same job. Smith has evidence that

(A1) Jones will get the job

and also that

(B1) Jones has ten coins in his pocket.

He conjoins these two propositions, arriving at the complex proposition

(C1) Jones will get the job, and Jones has ten coins in his pocket.

Finally Smith infers from (C1) the less specific proposition

(D1) The man who will get the job has ten coins in his pocket.

Ex hypothesi Smith has a justified belief in (D1). The difficulty now arises that Smith actually gets the job himself, and what is more he has ten coins in his pocket as well. Proposition (D1) is, therefore, true – but this case of justified true belief is clearly inadmissible as a case of knowledge.

Gettier's second example is this:
Smith has sufficient evidence to believe the proposition

(A2) Jones owns a Ford.

He conjoins this proposition, selecting three place-names quite at random, with propositions saying that Brown is in place X, and accepts these three propositions as true:

(B2) Either Jones owns a Ford, or Brown is in Boston
(C2) Either Jones owns a Ford, or Brown is in Brest-Litovsk
(D2) Either Jones owns a Ford, or Brown is in Barcelona.

However, Jones does not after all own a Ford, but quite by chance Brown is in Barcelona. Smith has justified belief in (D2) which is a true proposition, but again this is clearly inadmissible as a case of knowledge.

Gettier explicitly recognises that his examples depend on two assumptions. 'First, in that sense of "justified" in which S's being justified in believing P is a necessary condition of S's knowing P, it is possible for a person to be justified in believing a proposition that is in fact false.'[39] This assumption, saying that we can have a justified belief in a false proposition, has by and large not been questioned by Gettier's critics, and we have argued for the same point in an earlier chapter. 'Secondly, for any proposition P, if S is justified in believing P, and P entails Q, and S deduces Q from P and accepts Q as a result of this deduction, then S is justified in believing Q.'[40] This seems a plausible enough assumption.

The difficulties which we have been exploring in this chapter imply that a precise definition of 'knowing that', which will be adequate for each and every case of non-basic knowledge, is unlikely to be found, and certainly will not be discovered by listing what we would or would not admit as cases of knowledge. On the other hand, it is a plausible conjecture that Gettier has discovered a serious flaw in the standard analysis construed as an attempt to cover even central cases of knowing, for the intuitions of philosophers have coincided in an agreement that Gettier's two cases are very clearly *not* examples of knowledge. Some feature is present in central cases which is not incorporated in the idea of justified true belief.

It might be thought that Gettier's problem is contrived and of secondary importance, for his examples undoubtedly have an appearance of artificiality. On the contrary, it is not too difficult to find cases which are much more natural and which therefore illustrate the generality of Gettier's problem. Suppose Smith has very good evidence that a colleague of his is on the university campus today: he may have talked to him yesterday evening, so knows that he was only a few hours ago in the best of physical and mental health, and he also knows that he has to deliver a lecture this morning which his professional conscience and dedication would not allow him to evade, except on the most extraordinary turn of events. Smith concludes, therefore, that

>   (A3) My colleague is on the campus today to deliver his lecture.

It follows from this, and Smith infers from it, that

>   (D3) My colleague is on the campus today.

Now let us further assume that some extraordinary event has happened, and Smith's colleague has given up all interest in delivering his lecture but still comes into his office for some totally different reason, perhaps looking for his wallet. Of (D3) we would now say that it is true, that Smith believes it to be true, and that he is justified in his belief. We would not, it is clear, say that Smith knows (D3) to be true.

What might be the feature omitted from the standard analysis? A comparison of the two Gettier cases and this third case should provide the answer. In each there is an inference to a proposition (lettered (D) in each case) which is *less specific* than the proposition from which it is inferred. In Gettier's first case the generalisation involved takes the form of inferring from a proposition about a specified person to one about some unspecified person; in his second case, the generalisation is to a disjunction; in our example, we generalised by leaving out the explanation of the man's presence in his office. Now clearly such generalisations lead to propositions which can be true even though the propositions from which they are inferred are false: for example, (D3) is true even though (A3), from which it is inferred, is false. And the reason why the conclusion is true in each case is quite independent of the facts claimed in the premises.

Looked at in this light a solution to the Gettier problem seems simple enough. For a justified belief to constitute knowledge it would appear that there should exist a connection between the truth of the proposition believed and the grounds on which it is believed. The reason why the proposition is true must not be independent on the facts asserted in the propositions constituting the grounds for the belief. Or to put it in different terminology, those justified true beliefs which constitute knowledge are those in which it is not just a *coincidence* that the believer is right, but where the belief has been arrived at on the basis of facts which are relevant to the truth of the belief. In each of our examples it seems from this point of view to be purely by chance that the believer is correct in his belief, for the propositions from which he derives his belief are false and therefore cannot explain the believer's success.

The solution of the Gettier problem involves the recognition that the standard Platonic analysis of knowing allows the three conditions to be satisfied quite independently of one another. It claims that A knows that P if and only if A believes that P, A has sufficient grounds for his belief, and P is true. That such conditions can be satisfied independently is obvious enough. We might notice that someone could fail to know because he bases his belief not on the sufficient grounds which he has at his disposal, but on something else such as a whim, a prejudice, or irrelevant evidence. The Gettier problem concerns the possibility, particularly, that the grounds for P which A uses to arrive at his belief are irrelevant to the truth of P itself. This flaw in the standard analysis can be eliminated, not by adding some fourth condition to the other three, but by insisting that these three previously recognised conditions should not be independently satisfied.

Such seems a straightforward and effective way to solve Gettier's problem. Certainly there are points in it which need greater clarification – we shall need to say a little more later about the precise nature of the connection between believing and truth – but it has the merit of pointing out an intuitively plausible condition of knowing. It is somewhat surprising, therefore, that it is not a response to the Gettier problem which has found much support in the considerable literature on the subject.

Defeasibility and Causality

We come now to the two approaches to Gettier's problem which have been most influential: one relies upon the idea that justifications for believing are defeasible; the other insists that a causal connection exists between the truth of the proposition believed and the believing of it in cases of knowledge. Both approaches seek, in effect, to add a fourth condition to the Platonic definition of knowledge as justified true belief.

On the defeasibility approach, knowledge is *undefeated*[41] justified true belief. The notion of defeasibility was first introduced in moral philosophy where it was applied to concepts such as duty, obligation, and responsibility. Such concepts were said to be defeasible in that their applicability could be *negated* or *overridden* by one or other of a set of circumstances. For example, a man can be said to have a duty to return borrowed goods, but this is negated or overridden by a variety of circumstances such as the knowledge that such action will lead to disastrous consequences – your duty to return a borrowed knife is overridden by the fact that its owner is in a suicidal state of mind.[42] The idea of defeasibility was transferred from this to epistemology where it has been used to make a valuable point about the nature of justification and knowledge. But it does not, as we shall show, hold the key to Gettier's problem.

The most natural way of applying the notion of defeasibility to justification in order to parallel its use in moral philosophy would be something like the following.[43] Someone S may be said to be justified, by a body of evidence e, in believing proposition P; however, there may be further information relevant to P, e', which is such as to override or negate the force of e, and if S comes to possess e' as well as e he will no longer be justified in believing P. We shall say, therefore, that S's original justification (e) for believing P is *defeated* by e'. We may note two points about this explanation. First, it concerns the situation of the believer, that is it concerns the evidence which he possesses and the beliefs which he bases on that evidence. To defeat e as a justification e' must be possessed by S as evidence. Secondly we have assumed, following much of the literature, that defeating evidence must be true, although a case could be made for widening the notion of defeasibility so that even false evidence might be said to defeat a justification. After all, if S believes falsely that not-P is true, this would appear to negate any justification he had for believing P.

We can illustrate this idea of defeasibility by adapting one of Gettier's cases. Suppose, as in Gettier's first example, Smith has evidence which justifies his believing

> (C1) Jones will get the job, and Jones has ten coins in his pocket

and he infers

> (D1) The man who will get the job has ten coins in his pocket.

We have argued that Smith is indeed justified in believing (D1). But suppose Smith learns that (C1) is false: his original justification may be said now to have been defeated by this new piece of evidence, so he is no longer justified in believing (D1).

Yet this illustration itself shows that defeasibility does not hold the key to Gettier's problem, for the simple reason that Smith does *not* know that (C1) is false in the original Gettier case. Defining knowledge as *undefeated* justified true belief fails to solve that problem, as each of Gettier's examples (as well as our own third example) would thereby qualify as knowledge. In none of these cases is the original justification defeated by the appearance of new evidence.

Moreover, it may seem that there can be cases of defeated justified true belief which are nevertheless cases of knowledge. Consider an adaptation of our example where Smith believes

(D3) My colleague is on the campus today.

Suppose Smith has been informed by his wife that an event such as would in fact keep his colleague away from the lecture room has happened, and that there were therefore no grounds for expecting him to appear. Smith believes this proposition – his belief here is a justified one – and his original justification for believing (D3) is therefore defeated. But, as can clearly happen with new pieces of evidence, the information provided by Smith's wife is misleading, for his colleague is blissfully unaware of the event happening which would stop him lecturing. (If Smith were to learn this further fact, we would say that the original defeated justification for believing (D3) was reinstated.) Now clearly in this example Smith's justified true belief is defeated, and clearly also Smith is now in no position to *claim* to know (D3); on the other hand, is it so clear that Smith does not know (D3)? We, who are in the position of knowing that his colleague is unaware of the event in question, can judge Smith's wife to be misleading him (albeit unintentionally), and may want to say that Smith does know (D3) after all.

If this seems too strong (and to accept it would require us to give up the Platonic idea that knowledge requires a *justified* belief, at least in any simple form), the possibility of misleading information shows at least that the defeasibility approach cannot be saved from the first objection by redefining knowledge as *indefeasible* justified true belief.[44] The Gettier cases could be handled by such a definition, for in each example the justification could be defeated were Smith to come to know the relevant proposition (i.e. (C1), (A2), or (A3) in the three examples) to be false. However, if misleading information can be said to defeat a justification, this revised definition of knowing would always lead us to refuse that title whenever misleading evidence was possible – whether it was possessed or not. If Smith knew that his colleague *was* unaware of the unfortunate event which had occurred, on this definition he would even then not be allowed to know (D3), even if his colleague does come on to the campus to lecture. And if Smith's wife has never informed him of the occurrence of the event and his colleague comes on to the campus to lecture, Smith would on this definition not know (D3) either.

One version of the defeasibility approach does appear to deal with Gettier's problem successfully.[45] Lehrer and Paxson have defined knowledge, in effect, as justified true belief which is *indefeasible by a proposition which the believer has a justification for believing false*:[46] the problem, for example, with Gettier's first case is that Jones will not get the job – (C1) is false – and Smith's reason for believing (D1) is his justified belief in (C1). The Lehrer and Paxson definition seems successful in marking off Gettier's cases from cases of knowledge, and in that sense must be allowed to have solved Gettier's problem. It does so, however, at a price. In the first place it is obvious that the notion of defeat really plays no essential role in their solution at all, for what is important is the *truth* of the proposition that Jones will not get the job, and not whether or not it is believed – a fatal defect in any move from an 'undefeated' to an 'indefeasible' definition which is shared by Swain's approach as well.[47] In the second place the definition provides no intuitively satisfactory explanation of the shortcomings of the Gettier cases as cases of knowledge, but offers only a complicated description which such cases fail to satisfy. Our own solution makes good this defect by indicating that the belief must be based on something relevant to its truth. If we recognise that a requirement for knowledge is that the grounds on which one bases one's beliefs are relevant to the truth of those beliefs, it is easy to see that one cannot have knowledge when those grounds are false. Our solution therefore explains whatever success is achieved by the defeasibility approach.

But can our solution be spelled out in more detail? It is tempting to construe the relationships invoked by that solution as causal ones, in the following manner. We have said that in non-basic knowledge the justification for the belief must be relevant to its truth, and a simple formula which might be taken[48] as making the same point is that the *reason why* the proposition is believed should be the *reason why* it is true. And then 'reason why' might be interpreted causally leaving us with the formula that the *cause* of the belief should be the *cause* of its truth, a simple version of the causal analysis of knowing.

The objections to this simple causal theory are easy enough to state. In the first place, a distinction must be made between the reason why someone holds a belief and the cause of that belief. The first occurrence of 'reason why' in the above formula, describing as it does the kind of inferential step involved in cases

of knowing – and even in the Gettier problem cases – is a jus-
tificatory or epistemic notion. It refers to the reason (or reasons)
which the believer takes as evidence or grounds for his belief,
which he takes as sufficient to warrant his belief; and into this
notion enters a logical dimension which is absent from the causal
notion. Of course, there will always be causal factors responsible
for the believer's believing some proposition P, and presumably
in the kind of cases which we are considering one of these causal
factors will be his believing true that proposition which expresses
his 'reason for' believing P. His reason for believing P will
nevertheless be grounds for the truth of P itself – 'having adequate grounds for P' can certainly not be construed as there being
causal factors sufficient for believing P. What is more, our
believer may have these grounds only in the sense that these are
the reasons he would give if questioned about his belief, rather
than there being a conscious inferential process on his part in
which they have figured.

The second 'reason why' in the above formula is also construed
wrongly if taken to be causal. Our Gettier problem cases illustrate
this well, for the 'reason why' the believed propositions lettered
(D) in each case are true – the origin of the proposition's truth in
each case – is so far from being causal it might better be termed
'logical'. In Gettier's first case the reason why

(D1)   The man who will get the job has ten coins in his pocket

is true is because

(E1)   Smith has ten coins and will get the job

is true, and here we are dealing with a logical entailment between
(E1) and (D1). Similarly in Gettier's second case, it is true that

(D2)   Jones owns a Ford or Brown is in Barcelona

because it is true that

(E2)   Brown is in Barcelona

where once more (E2) entails (D2). It would be wrong, nevertheless, to think that our demand that reasons for beliefs be relevant
to their truth will always be satisfied by such a close connection as
entailment, since that would be to assume that all grounds for
believing logically entail the beliefs they support.

One of the first of the causal theories offered as a solution to Gettier's problem is that of A. I. Goldman.[49] This theory is more sophisticated than the one given above, but seemingly no more successful. Goldman holds[50] that S knows that P if and only if 'the fact P is causally connected in an "appropriate" way with S's believing P', and gives some examples of what such 'appropriate ways' might be. The theory is intended to cover non-inferential as well as inferential knowledge, and Goldman instances perception and memory as two non-inferential knowledge-producing causal processes. He also offers two patterns for causal chains which would be appropriate to produce inferential knowledge. One of them is illustrated by the case of knowing that smoke was coming out of a chimney on the previous evening: S remembers perceiving a fire in his fireplace, and infers that the fire caused smoke to rise out of the chimney. The fact that there was a fire in the fireplace, says Goldman, was the cause both of S's believing that smoke was coming out of the chimney and of the fact that smoke was coming out. The other pattern is perhaps even simpler, and is illustrated[51] by S's inferring, from the presence of solidified lava on a mountainside, that there was at one time an active volcano there. If S is to know that the mountain erupted in the past, then the eruption must be the beginning of a causal chain producing (via the lava's being recognised) the belief that it took place.

Goldman thinks other patterns are possible, but takes one important element in such patterns to be that the causal connection between the known fact and the grounds for it is 'correctly reconstructed by inferences' in the rest of the causal chain.[52] This idea has much to commend it from the point of view of our theory, for it comes close to our own stipulation concerning the actual relevance of the reasons for believing to the truth of the belief – at least, were our stipulation to be limited to beliefs about the causal connection among events, for only there are *causal* chains part of the story. From the point of view of the causal theory, it is not a happy move on Goldman's part, for it requires him to extend the notion of 'causal chain' beyond its ordinary sense. For Goldman, such chains must then include inferential steps (as for example where an inference is made from the lava to the eruption of the mountain)[53] and we have seen that basing one's belief on evidential propositions is not the same as being caused to believe by the evidential facts.[54] Goldman also needs to see connections such as that between (E1) and (D1), and (E2) and (D2), as steps in a causal chain,[55] and again we have seen that the connections here are logical instead of causal.

The greatest problem for our own attempt to salvage the Platonic analysis – always remembering the reservations consequent on the earlier part of the chapter – is undoubtedly in spelling out the idea of the justification being 'relevant' to the truth of that for which it is a justification. This will sometimes, as we have seen, involve a logical relation, sometimes a causal one as in Goldman's two examples; but presumably many other kinds of relation will occur, as varied as there are kinds of relation between grounds and the propositions for which they are grounds. Perhaps the kind of connection which would provide this essential aspect of the concept of knowledge, and satisfy Goldman's requirement that the inference involved in the believer's justification for his belief should reconstruct the facts of the matter, could best be captured in the following formula: to constitute knowledge the belief that P must be based upon facts which actually figure in the *explanation* of the truth of P itself. To say this, of course, is only to take another small step towards a fully adequate Platonic analysis, but in so far as causal explanations are just one kind among many it does underline our reservations over a straightforward causal analysis of knowing.

CHAPTER IV

PERCEPTION

The Common Sense View of Perception

It will be useful to start our discussion of sense perception by considering what people of ordinary common sense think about the information that our senses give us. There can, of course, be no clear and definite specification of what constitutes the beliefs of 'common sense'. The phrase is a vague one. The content of such beliefs will vary to some degree from age to age, and from one civilisation to another. We may take them to be the commonly assumed and unargued assumptions that we all take for granted in everyday discussion and reflection. That the sun will rise tomorrow is such an assumption; or that other people are not mere robots but have minds very like one's own. Such assumptions may very well be put in doubt in philosophical discussion. But in everyday discourse, we all take them for granted.

It is a characteristic of such beliefs that they are felt to require some specially cogent arguments to put them in doubt; and that in the absence of such arguments they are assumed to be reliable. This is not to say that they cannot be rationally discredited, but only that they are taken to be true in the absence of strong evidence to the contrary. For this reason, a consideration of common sense beliefs gives a useful starting point for many philosophical discussions. We first of all clarify our own opinions on the topic that we are considering, and then subject these opinions to sceptical criticism. The outcome will be that our common sense, or 'pre-analytic' concepts, will either survive the scrutiny and emerge promoted from the level of common sense assumption to that of justified belief or they will be suitably modified by the process of enquiry.

Sense perception gives us information about physical objects.

But what is a physical object? Clearly, it is a chunk of matter. But not any chunk of matter is ordinarily reckoned to be a physical object in the common sense of the phrase. What we usually include under the title are what Austin called 'moderate-sized specimens of dry goods'[1] – rocks, apples, dogs, people, furniture, houses and the like. These are all bits of matter which are neither too large nor too small to be sensed and which can be conveniently categorised as being of a certain kind. Clearly, there is no very good reason, other than convenience for illustrating an argument, that has led philosophers to use these examples. There are all sorts of other pieces of matter that do not fall into this general class of identifiable, medium-sized objects which are familiar to us. The atmosphere, a molecule of sodium chloride, the Pacific Ocean, the plague bacillus, and the dark companion of Sirius are just as much pieces of matter as the pennies, tables and tomatoes that philosophers are apt to take as their standard instances when they discuss perception. Moreover, we learn what we can know about these less familiar objects through perception if only in most cases indirectly and by inference. However, this does not matter. We may legitimately start with the common sense assumption that perception gives us what knowledge we have of pennies, tables and tomatoes and see where the argument takes us. If common sense can be justified in these familiar cases, it would be to that extent corroborated. And if it fails us even here, we need not consider more outlandish examples.

What, then, does common sense assume about these medium-sized familiar objects? (1) They are taken to be independent of our perceiving them in that they continue to exist when they are not being perceived. In this they differ from the tables and tomatoes that we meet in dreams or from after-images or hallucinations. (2) They are taken to be 'public' to use Russell's term. That is, they can be perceived by any number of observers – again, unlike dreams or after-images. These two properties are certainly necessary to the concept of a physical object; but they are not sufficient. True propositions like '3 + 4 = 7' or 'oxygen is heavier than hydrogen' are independent and public in this sense. They do not cease to be true when they are not being thought of, and they can be simultaneously entertained or believed by any number of people. So we need some further properties to characterise the common sense notion of a physical object. (3) A physical object is said to be 'neutral' between several senses of the same person. I can see, touch, smell and taste the same apple. All the very different sensible qualities that it manifests, colour, shape, smell, taste, texture and the rest are supposed to belong, in some sense of that vague word, to the same thing. (The exact nature of this relation of 'belonging' is a question of some difficulty. But we are dealing here just with the assumptions of common sense.) This third condition, neutrality between senses, puts some restrictions on the things that we can recognise as candidates for our limited category of 'physical objects'. Clouds, stars, holograms, magnetic fields and rainbows all seem to be excluded for this reason from the restricted group of standard physical objects that we are considering. The basic kind of neutrality that is relevant here is neutrality between sight and touch. Few objects give us information through all our senses.

(4) Perhaps the most fundamental defining property of a physical object is that it has both location and extension in space and time. The exact implications of this condition cannot be spelt out without raising difficult problems about the nature of time and space. But at the level of common sense we do not have to concern ourselves with these complex problems. The spatio-temporal location of a material object is perhaps the only property that will uniquely identify it. To give the *exact* spatial position of this particular apple, its exact latitude, longitude and height above sea level, for example, together with the time of observation will mark it off from all other apples. (And here we are appealing to the fact, to be commented on later, that no two material objects can occupy the same place at the same time.) Further, we ordinarily claim that a physical object must have a certain finite extension and duration. Such a thing cannot be infinitely small, nor can it have a merely fleeting and transitory existence, like a flash of lightning. But exactly how large or how enduring a thing must be to qualify as a material object is not a matter on which common sense has to adjudicate.

(5) Physical objects must possess the property of being *solid* in two quite distinct senses of that term. (i) They must be three-dimensional in the sense of occupying a volume of space and so have a continuous two-dimensional boundary separating the outside from the inside. As H. H. Price expressed it: 'a three-dimensional whole, with back, top, bottom as well as front, and

having an inside as well as an outside: something which does not exist from any special place'.[2] (ii) A second sense of *solidity* is *impenetrability*. This impressed Locke as the most important defining property of matter. 'This, of all others, seems the idea most intimately connected with and essential to body, so as nowhere else to be found or imagined, but only in matter. . . . The mind . . . finds it inseparably inherent in body, wherever and however modified.'[3] If we confine ourselves, as we have done here, to common sense notions of physical objects, we can agree with Locke in regarding solidity, in this second sense, as an essential property of such objects. There are, of course, many exceptions to be found if we move a little away from the material objects of common sense. Two pieces of ice are mutually impenetrable; but not so the respective volumes of water or steam that they become on being suitably heated. And to meet these cases, we have to leave common sense for physics.

So far then we have seen that material objects, in the everyday meaning of the phrase, have the following properties: independence of observers, publicity, neutrality between different senses, spatio-temporal location and extension and solidity in the two senses of three-dimensional compactness and mutual impenetrability. But is this a complete account, even in rough outline, of the everyday notion that we are trying to determine? Surely there must be at least one more property, namely, that of being sensuously manifested? Material objects affect our senses; that, indeed, is how we come to know of their existence and their properties. They are sensuously manifested in virtue of having sensible properties – colour, shape, taste, smell, texture and the rest. Moreover, they must be manifested to more than one sense. A simple patch of colour can no more be a material object than a shadow or a mirror image can. So a material object must possess a complex of sensible qualities and these are manifested to us by means of our sense organs. And it is this last property of material objects that raises philosophical difficulties, as we shall see.

The Argument from Illusion

This phrase is not the name of a single identifiable argument, but rather is a way of referring to a number of logical considerations that help us to answer the question: what does perception tell us about material objects?[4] We have seen that an essential part of the common sense notion of a physical object is that it has various sensible properties, colour, shape, texture and the rest. The list will differ with different objects. Now since these sensible properties are given to us via our senses, it is natural to suppose, and we ordinarily do suppose, that things are as we perceive them. The apple is literally red, smooth and sweet; the coin is literally circular; the rose is literally fragrant. And the word 'literally' here is intended to imply that these objects have the sensible properties assigned to them in their own right. They are part of the nature of the objects, and share the independence and publicity which common sense attributes to material things. The apple does not cease to be red, smooth and sweet when no one is looking at it, touching it or tasting it. However, there are strong reasons for believing that this cannot be so.

Locke, and after him Berkeley, used a persuasive example.[5] Put one of your hands into ice cold water and the other into very hot water and keep them there for a minute or so. Then put both hands into lukewarm water. The lukewarm water will seem distinctly warm to the hand that has been cooled, and distinctly cool to that hand that has been warmed. Since the water cannot be simultaneously warm and cool, it cannot have just those sensible properties that it seems to us to have. In other words, the *felt* temperature of the water cannot literally be a property of the water. Such variations in sensible properties like taste and smell are familiar to everyone. A sweet orange will taste sour to one who has just been eating chocolate; and so on. A particularly striking instance of the general principle that felt sensory properties cannot straightforwardly be properties of the things that they seem to belong to can be obtained as follows: Shine a red light in your left eye and a green light in your right eye for a minute. Then look with your left eye and your right eye alternately at a piece of bright yellow cloth. The cloth will seem a washed out pale yellow to your left eye and a rich orange to your right eye.

Examples of this kind can be multiplied. The general form of the argument underlying them is as follows:

(1) It is impossible for the same thing to have incompatible properties at the same time.
(2) Properties P and Q are incompatible.

(3) One and the same thing, X, is sensed as P by one sense organ and as Q by another.

(4) A sensed property is really an intrinsic property of the thing perceived.

It is clear that if we accept (1), (2) and (3) which seem incontrovertible, we cannot consistently accept (4). So we are driven to the conclusion that some sensed properties are not really intrinsic properties of the material object that we perceive. Arguments of this sort can be applied to colour, taste, smell, sound, and texture.

But what do such arguments really show? They show at least that many of the sensed properties that common sense counts as properties of material objects depend not simply on the nature of the objects concerned but also on a number of other factors. They depend also on the state of the sense organ, on the condition of the percipient's nervous system and, in the case of colour, the nature of the medium through which the light passes, and the nature of the light itself. They cannot, therefore, be straightforwardly properties *of the object*.

Consider next the familiar cases of the shapes of objects distorted by perspective and the angle of sight. We all know that table tops, which we believe to be rectangular, appear in a variety of more or less irregular quadrilateral forms when seen from most angles; that railway lines are parallel but do not look to be so from most points of view; that coins are usually circular but from most angles are seen as ellipses. Such variations are, in a sense, 'explained' by the laws of perspective. But an appeal to the laws of perspective does not help to refute the argument from illusion. These laws explain the appearances only in the sense that they enable us to correlate the various appearances of objects with the distances and angles from which they are viewed. What they do not explain is how we are to reconcile the changing shapes and sizes of objects as they are seen with what we know to be true about such objects, namely, that they are not in fact changing but are constant in shape and size.

There are important differences, as we shall see, between properties like colour and felt temperature on the one hand, and shape and size on the other. And we must not make too much or too little of the distortions of perspective in stating the argument from illusion. Human beings do not, in any case, see things in strict perspective owing to what psychologists call the 'constancy phenomena'. It has been shown experimentally that there is a tendency for us to see objects as having shapes and sizes some way between what strict perspective would require and what we 'know' them to be. However, the fact remains that the varying shapes and sizes of objects seen at varying distances and angles cannot all accurately represent the objects as they actually are. No doubt it is to some extent necessary, if we are to see the world at all, that things should occupy different proportions of our visual fields at different distances. It is impossible to imagine a world in which perspectival variations in size did not occur.

The philosophical difficulty does not arise from the fact that the distortions of perspective are 'subjective' in the sense that they do not correspond to differences in the independent world of material objects. The apparent shapes and sizes of objects seen at a distance depend on the angle which the edges of the objects project on the eye. But, as Professor Price has pointed out, such edges project an angle from *any* point in space, whether or not it is occupied by an observer. 'It is just an objective fact of Nature that the angle which an object subtends at a point P varies with the distance between the object and P.'[6] But does this 'fact of Nature' weaken the impact of this phase of the argument from illusion? It seems that it does not, for the following reason.

Perspectival appearances of objects, though they conform to laws of nature, namely, the laws of perspective, still do misrepresent the actual shapes of objects. And the actual sense content that we get in these situations is not just, for example, a circle appearing as an ellipse but is actually an ellipse. It is important to stress this point because critics of the argument from illusion have argued in the following way:

> That the coin appears elliptical to me is no reason whatever for concluding that there is anything (a sense datum) that *is* elliptical. There is just *nothing* in the situation described that *is* elliptical; there is nothing elliptical to be sensed. There is something – the coin – however, which, though it is round, *appears* to be elliptical . . . There is no elliptical existent, only a round existent, the coin, which appears elliptical from this angle.[7]

This objection can be dealt with like this. Gaze for a minute or so at a bright circular object, such as a circular mirror, placed at an angle with your line of vision so that it presents an elliptical appearance to your eye. Then turn and look at a white surface. You will see an elliptical after-image projected on the white surface. Now it is clear that an elliptical after-image cannot be caused by anything but an elliptical stimulus. There must therefore have been an elliptical something in your visual field causing an elliptical impression on the retina. So it must be false to say 'there is nothing elliptical to be sensed'.

A second type of argument that is often advanced under the general heading of 'the argument from illusion' is concerned with the physical and physiological mechanisms that are necessary for sensation. Consider the question: What is a sense organ? We can get a rough idea of the answer to this question by asking what functions all our sense organs have in common. Each of them (eye, ear, skin receptors, taste buds and so on) are biological devices for giving us information about the external world (and also, to some extent, about the internal world of our bodily states). And the work of physicists and physiologists has shown in some detail how they carry out this job. Each of them is a mechanism sensitive to some specific form of energy. The eye, for example, is sensitive to electro-magnetic radiation within a rather narrow waveband, from 760 mμ at the red end of the spectrum to 380 mμ at the violet end.* This type of radiation, which we call 'light', enters the eye and excites the retinal cells at the back causing complex chemical changes there. These chemical changes cause electrical changes in the optic nerve fibres to which the cells of the retina are attached. These changes in turn are transmitted in the form of electric currents along the optic nerve to the visual centre at the back of the brain. When all this has happened, we become conscious of light, the exact felt quality of which will depend on the nature of the original radiation and on the state of the eye itself. This is a complex story and the exact details of it have not yet been completely unravelled by the scientists. But the general point, which is of great importance for the philosophical problems of perception, is that it applies in its general outlines to all the information that comes to us from our senses. This information is all transmitted to the central nervous system in the form of

---

* A millimicron (mμ) is one ten millionth of a centimetre or 10^{-9} metres.

electrical currents along the afferent nerves. And these electrical currents are of the same form from whichever sense organ they originate. The special group of sensations which they elicit depends on the part of the brain to which the nerve carries its electrical message.

We shall be considering later some consequences of the fact that our sense organs work in this particular way and that they are sensitive to certain types of energy only and to rather restricted ranges of these types. For the moment, let us ask the question: what do these facts show about the reliability of the information that our senses give us about the world of material objects? They do not, in themselves, show that the information is not entirely veridical, so far as it goes. The fact that my eye is sensitive to electro-magnetic radiation only in the range 760 to 380 mμ is not evidence that the greenness of grass is not a genuine and independently existing property of the grass. For that conclusion we have to look more closely at the physics and physiology of sensation.

First, we need to make an obvious but important distinction. Words relating to human sense experience such as heat, light, sound and the rest have a double meaning. In the *physical* sense, they relate to various forms of energy; in the *psychological* sense, they refer to specific and unique types of sensory experience. The colour *green* for the physicist is primarily electro-magnetic radiation of about 530 mμ in wave length; but for the ordinary man it is the characteristic sensation that we get from looking at fresh grass. Let us distinguish these, for convenience, as 'green-P' (for 'green-physical') and 'green-M' (for 'green-mental'). Now there are very good reasons for supposing that green-M is not literally and independently of any observer a property of grass or, indeed, of any other physical object. The reasons are as follows.

Consider what happens when we see something green. White light, normally from the sun, falls on the grass. Part of it is absorbed by the grass and part is reflected. The parts of the light that are absorbed and reflected respectively will depend on the molecular structure of the grass itself. The part reflected is that with a wave length in the general neighbourhood of 530 mμ. This enters our eyes, in the way described above, and after setting off the appropriate electrical currents in the optic nerve, results in a sensation of green, that is, in green-M. Now what is the bearing of these facts on the question: Is green-M a property of the grass independently of any observer?

The first point to note is that there is very good evidence indeed that grass is green-M only because the surface of grass reflects light which is green-P, that is, light of the appropriate wave length. The laws of physics on this point are as well founded as any knowledge that we have. And there is absolutely no evidence that the surface of grass is green-M, in its own right so to speak, and independent of any observer. That hypothesis is (a) entirely unnecessary, because greenness-M is adequately accounted for by physics and physiology, and (b) impossible either to verify or to falsify, for it makes no sense to ask how things appear when they are not being observed. The way in which the question is put effectively pre-empts the possibility of it ever being answered.

And this is not just a point about greenness or about colour in general. The argument applies, *mutatis mutandis*, for sound, smell, taste, and touch. So we have no reason to believe and very good reason not to believe that the looks and feels of material objects are properties intrinsic to the objects and possessed by them independently of observers. Moreover, the ways in which physical objects appear to observers depend, among other conditions, on the nature of the observers' sense organs. Our eyes see things like tomatoes, blood or rubies as red-M. The eyes of a dog or a bee do not. There is good evidence that dogs like most mammals are completely colour-blind and see things only in shades of black, white and grey. Bees' eyes are sensitive to a different range of radiation than are our own. Their visual capacity runs from about 670 mμ to almost 300 mμ, well into the ultra-violet part of the spectrum. So bees, though they cannot see red light can, unlike ourselves, see ultra-violet, as can many insects. Thus the supposition that grass is really and intrinsically green-M, even if it were not an empty hypothesis, rests on the assumption that the human eye has a privileged insight into the nature of things, denied to other animals. And in the light of what is known about human and animal senses, this seems a perfectly absurd suggestion.

Sense Data

The outcome of the arguments that we have been considering is that there are serious difficulties in maintaining that some of the observed properties of physical objects are really properties *of those objects*. It seems rather to be the case that colours, warmth, sounds, smells, tastes and so on, in the everyday senses of these terms, are the effects of a complex set of causes. And the most essential of these causes is the presence of an observer with sense organs and nervous system in good working order. At this point we need to introduce a term that will apply to the contents of these felt sensory experiences – patches of colour, smells, sounds and the rest. In the eighteenth century, the word in common philosophical use was 'ideas'. But in contemporary language, this word is too vague and ambiguous. Since the work of Russell and Moore on the problems of perception, the favoured term has been 'sense datum' or, sometimes 'sensum'.[8] We may define the term 'sense datum' as 'part of a sense field'. So that a visual sense datum, for example, is a part of a visual field, a tactual datum is part of a tactual field, an auditory sense datum part of an auditory field, and so on. No one who is not totally blind can deny that he has a visual field and that it is extended and diversified so as to have distinguishable parts.

By explaining the term in this way, we can avoid a number of useless questions about the nature of sense data which have confused discussion in the past. For example, how many sense data are there at a given moment? How long do they last? Do they have properties that they do not appear to have? And so on. The answer to all such questions is that sense data have just those properties that parts of our sensory fields are found to have, and no more. The question of the nature of sense data becomes an empirical one if we define the term in this way. We can now proceed to the question: What is the relation between sense data and the world of material objects? To this question there have been, in the history of philosophy, three main types of answer.

(1) Realist theories claim that sense perception is a direct relation between the observer and the material object which exists idependently of him. To the question raised in the previous paragraph, the realist will reply that sense data are literally parts of the surfaces of objects in the case of sight and touch. (2) Representative theories claim that perception is a three-term relation between the observer, his sense data and the material objects which he perceives. (3) Phenomenalist theories claim that material objects are simply ordered collections or 'families' of

sense data and that the relation of perceiving is a two-term relation between the observer and his sense data. Material objects, for
the phenomenalist, have either no independent existence or are
no more than, in Mill's phrase, 'permanent possibilities of sensation'.[9]

Described in this summary way, realism, representationalism
and phenomenalism are no more than programmes for theories
of perception. There are a number of theories falling under each
of these general descriptions. The progress from (1) to (3) is a
progress from a 'common sense' point of view to a position very
far removed from common sense, so far indeed, that it is hard to
find reputable philosophers who have consistently tried to maintain it.

The arguments that we have considered so far have tended to
persuade us to move from the common sense starting point to a
rather indeterminate version of a representative theory. We have
seen good reason to suppose that sense data, the contents of our
sense fields, are not literally parts of the external world; rather
they are facets of consciousness brought about by a complex of
causes of which the physical objects are only a part. But before we
try to sharpen this sketch of a theory into something more substantial, we should look at some of the objections to representative
theories that have persuaded some philosophers to move on to
phenomenalism, and others to stick to direct realism, in spite of its
difficulties.

The first objection is this. It will be said that our conclusion that
what we are immediately aware of in perception are sense fields
rather than material objects depends on the evidence of physics
and physiology; and that these are natural sciences which start by
assuming the truth of common sense observations about the
external world. And unless such observational propositions, from
which the sciences start, are themselves true, no scientific conclusions that are derived from them can reliably be taken as true. So a
refutation of common sense by science is self-refuting in that it
denies the truth of the premises from which the refutation starts.

This objection has force only if it can be shown that the rep-
resentational theory of perception assumes the truth of anything
that its conclusion denies. But this is not so. The theory does not
start from the premiss that the experienced sensuous properties
of physical objects do really belong to them. It does not deny that

there are material objects or that we can know a great deal about them. Indeed, it is the enormous success of natural science over the past hundred years in telling us about the micro-structure of matter and the details of its causal interactions that makes the theory in its modern form so much more persuasive than it was in the form advanced by Locke at the end of the seventeenth century. Modern physics and chemistry have shown that we can have a great deal of reliable and detailed knowledge about hypothesised material particles which are unobservable. That such knowledge is true and reliable is shown by the efficiency and dependability of its applications, radio, radar and television, for example, and the various developments of nuclear technology. The conclusion that we have drawn here from the theory is simply that *some* of the properties of material objects, namely, their so-called secondary properties of colour, sound, taste, smell, felt temperature, and texture, are the product of energy emissions working on our sense organs. The felt qualities themselves do not belong to the objects as they are in themselves and apart from their interactions with those who observe them.

A second well-known objection to representative theories arises in the following way. My sense fields are private to myself; and your sense fields are private to you. Even though we may both experience qualitatively identical sense data, that they are identical is an inference, and a precarious one. The fact that they are private prevents a direct comparative check. Now if all my experiences are inescapably private in this way, how can I ever be justifiably certain of the nature of the world of material objects or, indeed, even of its existence? What legitimate inference can there be from my private world of sense experiences to the public world of physical things in which we all believe?

This is an argument that was used by Thomas Reid in the eighteenth century in his critique of the theories of Locke, Descartes and their successors. It has subsequently been used by opponents of a representative theory of perception. And even at the present day, it is accorded much more credit than its merits warrant. The first step in the way out from what has been called 'the egocentric predicament'[10] was pointed out by Berkeley, himself no friend of representative theories. When we distinguish features of our experience that are believed to be due to causes external to ourselves, we do so by noting that these features are independent of our will and are forced upon us, whether we welcome them or not.

> But whatever power I may have over my own thoughts, I find the ideas actually perceived by sense have not a like dependence on my will. When in broad daylight I open my eyes, it is not in my power to choose whether I shall see or no, or to determine what particular objects shall present themselves to my view; and so likewise as to the hearing and the other senses, the ideas imprinted on them are not creatures of my will.[11]

Berkeley himself believed, of course, that these causes external to ourselves were mental and not physical. But at least he correctly observed that the contra-volitional nature of the contents of our sense fields was good evidence of their independent causation. The second phase of the escape from the eogcentric predicament consists in raising the question: What is the nature of these independent causes? And to this question, the development of physical science has given a complete and convincing answer.

Primary and Secondary Qualities

To appreciate this point, it will be useful to consider a distinction between two kinds of properties of physical objects made famous by Locke. (Locke borrowed the distinction from predecessors and contemporaries, in particular, Descartes, Boyle and Newton, but it was the doctrine of his *Essay Concerning Human Understanding* that made it influential in philosophy.) 'Whatsoever the mind perceives in itself or is the immediate object of perception, thought or understanding, that I call *idea*; and the power to produce any idea in our mind, I call *quality* of the subject wherein that power is.'[12] There are three kinds of qualities: primary, secondary, and powers of bodies to affect other bodies. The primary qualities of bodies are those which are 'utterly inseparable from the body in what state soever it be'.[13] He gives as a list of these qualities, solidity, extension, shape, motion or rest, and number. And he explains (i) that no mechanical sub-division or deformation of a body can deprive it of these properties, and (ii) that the ideas that we have of these primary qualities really resemble them. Secondary qualities 'in truth are nothing in the objects themselves but powers to produce the various sensations in us by their primary qualities'. And he adds that the ideas of secondary qualities are produced in us 'by the operation of insensible properties on our senses'.[14] Colour, sound, taste, smell and felt temperature are *ideas* of secondary qualities. The principal difference between primary and secondary qualities is that the latter, unlike the former, do not in any way resemble the ideas that they cause in us.

It is clear that Locke's theory, as he stated it, is difficult to defend. Physical science was in a primitive state in his time and, indeed, consisted in little more than Newtonian mechanics. It is also clear, however, that if we interpret his doctrine with a little charity he can be seen to be anticipating the distinction between those sensible qualities that are *directly* measurable (extension, mass, velocity and the like) and those that are *not* directly measurable (colour, temperature, sound and so on). When we measure something, we express its dimensions in the form of an arithmetical ratio between an arbitrary standard unit (metre, pound, second or whatever it may be) and the measured object expressed in terms of the standard unit. 'John is six feet tall' means that the ratio of John's height to the standard foot is 6:1. Measurement so understood is a perfectly objective procedure which can be checked by as many independent observers as we please.

We can carry out this procedure of measurement with primary qualities (though not with all those in Locke's list); we cannot do this with ideas of secondary qualities. To measure colour, sound or temperature, we have to translate the property into a form that can be directly measured, usually into a pointer reading of some kind. There are other less important differences between primary and secondary; for example, that primary qualities can often be detected by more than one sense (length, motion, for example) whereas the ideas of secondary qualities are specific to one sense (colour to sight, sound to hearing, temperature to skin senses). But it is the measurability of primary qualities that is fundamental.

The development of physical science since Locke's time has made it quite clear that it is the fact that the primary qualities of matter can be measured, expressed in numerical terms and treated mathematically that has made science possible. Mathematics is, as Galileo said, the language in which the book of nature is written. But it is so only because nature's primary qualities are directly measurable. The secondary qualities, as they are sensed, can be shown to be dependent on the micro-structure and micro-behaviour of matter; and it is these which can be measured directly in terms of size, mass, velocity and so on. That the material world apart from its interactions with sense organs is simply a world of primary qualities was expressed by A. N. Whitehead in a classic passage:

> Thus the bodies are perceived as with qualities that in reality do not belong to them, qualities which are in fact purely the offspring of the mind. Thus nature gets credit which should in truth be reserved for ourselves: the rose for its scent: the nightingale for his song: and the sun for his radiance. The poets are entirely mistaken. They should address their lyrics to themselves and should turn them into odes of self-congratulation on the excellency of the human mind. Nature is a dull affair, soundless, scentless, colourless; merely the hurrying of material, endlessly, meaninglessly.[15]

The ironic tone of Whitehead's rhetoric should not lead us to believe that what he says is false. On the contrary, it is the extraordinary fertility of the study of the primary qualities of matter that has led to man's understanding of the workings of nature and to the unparallelled control of natural forces that is the main feature of contemporary civilisation. Scientific knowledge is not infallible; but it is the most reliable kind of knowledge available to us. And the fact that we do have this knowledge at our command shows that we are not locked in the private world of the egocentric predicament. Two features of the world of sense data show where the escape lies from this so-called predicament; that they occur independently of our volition suggests that they have external causes; and the success of physical science based on the study of the measurable properties of sense fields confirms this hypothesis in abundant detail.

The theory of perception that we have been outlining so far is a causal or representative one. These two terms are not synonymous. A representative theory of perception is a more detailed and specific theory than a causal theory need be. To establish that our sense data have external causes is to say less than that they represent the external world to us. For to say that A is a representation of B is to imply that there is some kind of systematic relationship between features of A and corresponding features of B. Maps, models, portraits, musical scores, codes, cassette tapes, texts of any kind – all of these are representations in different ways of their respective subject matters. And to claim that a particular theory of perception is a representative theory, we have to show, at least in principle, how sense data correspond to their causes. That they do have causes may be taken as proved by the argument that we have previously considered. It will be remembered that this was an argument in two stages: (i) we accept, as a hypothesis, that sense data are externally caused in as much as they are imposed on us against our will; (ii) that this hypothesis is abundantly confirmed by the development of science which starts from certain features of our sense data (the fact that their primary qualities can often be measured) and builds up an enormous complex interlocking system of highly reliable knowledge from this basis. It is necessary to emphasise the importance of this line of argument because critics of causal and representative accounts of perception have often claimed (i) that causes can only legitimately be proved when both effect and cause are equally events which we can experience; and (ii) that A cannot be shown to represent B unless we can be acquainted with both A and B in order to check the mode of representation. Berkeley argues for (ii).[16] And even as empirically minded a philosopher as Ayer has argued for (i).[17]

But we may reply to both these objections that they are pre-scientific. Available knowledge in Berkeley's day did not offer any plausible counter-instances to his principle. But contemporary physics and physiology give us innumerable instances of reliable representative accounts of the phenomena of colour or of sound, for example. And though we cannot check by direct comparison that sense data of secondary qualities are represented in nature by the primary qualities described by physical theory, the success of the total interlocking system of scientific theory shows that this must be so: similarly with objection (i). Once we can plausibly outline the micro-behaviour of matter we are appealing – and appealing successfully – to reliably inferrable, though unobservable causal events. In other words, the justification of a representative theory of perception lies in the history of science. And this is something on public record that need not be elaborated in detail here.

The Phenomenalist Alternative

Let us call the causal-representative theory that we have been arguing for 'scientific realism'. This is a less clumsy title and emphasises the scientific basis of the theory's justification. Our argument has so far tried to show that common sense realism leads to unacceptable difficulties. But many philosophers who would agree that common sense realism is incoherent have believed nevertheless that scientific realism offers no better outcome. And it is true that the *pre-scientific* forms of the arguments about the egocentric predicament and the impossibility of confirming statements about causes or about forms of representation were not easy to answer. These philosophers have been driven to accept some variety of phenomenalism, a theory which maintains that a physical object is no more than a set of actual and possible sense data, that is, those sense data which would normally be said to be *of* a particular material object.

Thus whereas common sense realism tries to explain perception in terms of minds and physical objects and scientific realism does so in terms of minds, sense data and physical objects, phenomenalism uses only minds and sense data. The objects are abandoned as unknowable and therefore unexplanatory. It is a theory which is adopted only because of the supposed irremediable defects of its rivals and runs counter both to common sense and natural science. It has been propounded in two forms, a factual form and a linguistic form.[18] We shall look briefly at both of them.

The factual version of the theory claims that material objects are no more than ordered sets of 'families' of sense data. And though this claim has a certain elegant economy, it contradicts three basic beliefs about material objects shared by both forms of realism and by ordinary common sense: (i) that such objects are independent of the observer; (ii) that they are public in being accessible to any number of observers; (iii) that they have causal properties in that they are able to affect other material objects (including, of course, sense organs). And it is clear that sense data, whether singly or in ordered groups, are neither independent, nor public, nor capable of affecting other groups of sense data.

Moreover, the theory makes the world discontinuous and fragmentary in a nightmarish way. Every time I blink, or fall asleep, or move to another place, a whole group of material objects, under the phenomenalist interpretation, are annihilated or put into a state of suspension. And the continuous processes of physical nature sketched by the scientific picture of the world are made intermittent in a way that would destroy their essential properties. To meet this type of objection, phenomenalists have supplemented actual sense data with possible sense data. But possible sense data are not existing features of the world. They are nothing but contents of sense experiences that *would* occur if an observer *were* to behave in a certain way. And even less than actual sense data are they public, independent or endowed with causal powers.

These difficulties have been recognised by phenomenalists who have tried to circumvent them by adopting a linguistic variant of their thesis: that all *statements* about material objects can be analysed or translated into *statements* about actual and possible sense data. Exponents of this version of phenomenalism have tried to show that any physical object statement can be translated, without loss of meaning, into a *logically equivalent* statement about sense data. Thus if P is a physical object statement (e.g. 'This is a dog'), and Q is the corresponding sense datum statement ('Here are such-and-such sense data') P must be true or false whenever Q is true or false, and vice versa. But this programme has proved impossible to carry into practice for even the simplest physical object statements. (Note that the phrase 'such-and-such' in the example above would have to be *completely* unpacked in sense data terms.) In particular, it is impossible to find a uniquely descriptive set of sense datum statements that will identify a particular physical object without covertly re-introducing into the analysis the notion of a physical object. We may not, for example, talk of 'dog-like' sense data or refer to observers, who are, of course, themselves physical objects. Indeed, this last point is an important one. To any given observer, other people are just as much material objects as stones or tables. So they too have to be accounted for as sets of actual and possible sense data. Thus solipsism is always lurking in the background of phenomenalism.

In any case, the linguistic version of the thesis must be parasitic on the factual version. For it is a basic function of language to describe the world. And if the linguistic version of phenomenalism purports to be an account of the correct working of language, it must also be, indirectly, an account of the way the world works. In other words, the linguistic version cannot be true if the factual version is not. So it is not possible to evade the weaknesses of the factual version by taking refuge in the linguistic version. And it is very easy to see the unacceptable consequences of the factual version. To take two examples among many: (1) We have very good reason to believe that our planet was formed rather less than five thousand million years ago. Geologists can offer good evidence for the earth's antiquity and describe its development during periods when there were no animal or human observers.

(2) As I look at the paper in front of me, there are all sorts of complex chemical and electrical processes going on in my sense organs and nervous system which are necessary conditions for my having my present visual field. These processes cannot possibly be regarded as even possible sense data, for they are over as I write these words. Berkeley met objections of this sort by appealing to God as the omnipresent observer; but this device is not open to the phenomenalist. Now we have much better reasons for believing in geology or in neuro-physiology than we have for accepting phenomenalism. So phenomenalism must be rejected as false.

The Realist Alternative

The principal weakness of a realist theory has been exposed by the argument which led to our present position, the so-called argument from illusion. A realist theory can be supported only at the cost of denying seemingly incorrigible propositions such as (1) to (3) on pages 93–4, and maintaining, equally unplausibly, that when I see something which appears as X (e.g. elliptical, convergent or grey) when it really is Y (e.g. circular, parallel or green) I am not really seeing anything X at all. In recent years, the main weapon of realists against representative theories has been a criticism of the concept of the sense datum. If that can be shown to be incoherent, it is not easy to state a representative account of perception.

A particularly detailed and extended attack was made by Austin in his book *Sense and Sensibilia*.[19] Many of his points were trivial and many were directed against accounts of sense data which had been imprudently phrased. It will not be necessary to examine his objections here as they were very conclusively refuted by Ayer[20] in a close examination of Austin's arguments. It is particularly noticeable that Austin made no reference at all to the physical and physiological evidence for sense data. And it is this evidence, as we have seen, that constitutes the strongest support for making the distinction between sense data and physical objects. In particular, nothing that he said has any bearing on the rather modest version of the theory offered in this book, namely, that a sense datum is a part of a sense field.

A more fashionable critique of the concept of sense datum relies on a well-known argument of Wittgenstein's about the impossibility of a private language. Hamlyn uses this approach.[21] The argument is as follows. (1) Language depends on rules. (2) The concept of a rule is empty unless there is a way of checking that the rule has been correctly applied. (3) Any such check must be a *public* check. It follows from these three premises that there can never be a private language in the sense of a language which cannot be learned by anyone other than its single user.[22] Hamlyn considers that this argument was a criticism of the concept of sense data in so far as it was an attack on the possibility of the private naming of sensations.

> Given this general argument, the private naming of sensations would be feasible only within an already established public language, since that language provides a means of giving sense to the words that we use; we would come to the sensations with an already established concept of sensation, which would bring with it criteria of identity, i.e. some way of giving sense to the idea of speaking of the 'same sensation again'.

There are at least two weaknesses in this. (a) Wittgenstein's argument against the possibility of the private naming of sensations is an extraordinarily feeble one. There is absolutely no good reason to accept that the required check must be a public one. The check may very well be, and often is, my own memory of experiencing a particular sensation. My 'criterion of identity' for recognising the sensation as the same again would simply be the memory that it is the same. And if it be said that this criterion is inadequate, the reason can only be that my memory is held to be unreliable. But if it is unreliable in this particular, why should it be more reliable in any other? In other words, premiss (3) of Wittgenstein's argument, if it is to be taken seriously, is simply a covert expression of scepticism about the reliability of personal memories. But such scepticism will do far more than throw doubt on the possibility of a private language. It will, among other things, throw the same doubt on the reliability of any public testimony that I may wish to use to establish the language's public status. The very uncritical enthusiasm with which this strange argument has been acclaimed seems to rest on a misunderstanding of another of Wittgenstein's gnomic utterances: 'An "inner process" stands in need of outward criteria.'[23] This is true only in the trivial sense that A needs behavioural evidence for the existence and nature of B's inner processes. It cannot, without absurdity, be read as meaning that B needs outward criteria for the existence and nature of his own.

(b) But even if we waive these objections, it is doubtful whether the use to which Hamlyn puts this doctrine is defensible. 'Furthermore,' he says, 'whereas to have the feeling is to be aware of it, it is not *eo ipso* to be aware of it as a such-and-such, as a feeling of a certain kind. For the latter to be the case, we need the concept of a feeling of this kind, and this, as we have seen, is not something that can be derived directly from the feeling itself. Thus nothing is "given" in having that feeling.'[24] This is intended to be a refutation of the view that we are originally 'given' sense data and build up our perceptual world from them. But why is it supposed to be impossible that the concept 'feeling X' is derived from experiencing X, in one's early infancy, let us say? Presumably Hamlyn does not believe that concepts precede sensations in our life history. How then are we to acquire the concept? With the reservation that the acquisition of concepts is a matter for experimental psychology and one which has so far not been fully investigated, let us consider the following suggestion. In the case of sensations (pain, blue, sweet and so on) we can take the first step towards the concept *by comparison* not of this sensation with a previous one (for we are momentarily accepting the Wittgensteinian argument) but of one part of this sensation with *another homogeneous part*. For all sensations are extended in time and some in space as well; and so they offer their parts for comparison in one specious present. So there is no difficulty in seeing, in principle, how the progress is made from feeling X to feeling X as such-and-such, that is, *as X*.

Sensing and Perceiving

We have seen that causal or representative theories of perception require as a basis some assumptions about the nature and functions of sense data. We now need to say a little more about sense data and about the distinction between sensing and perceiving. To have defined sense data as parts of a sensory field does not tell us much of their function in perception. We need to assume that they are (1) really distinct from material objects, (2) that they are private to the individual of whose sense field they form a part, and (3) that they are immediately or directly present to his consciousness.

That they are really distinct from material objects follows, as we have seen, from the impossibility of an object having incompatible properties at the same time. This by itself shows that no more than *one* of the incompatible properties can be a genuine property of the object. But the known details of the physical and physiological mechanisms of sensation show that all sensed properties are private to the observer. And this in establishing (2) shows that there can be no reason to suppose that any of the sensed properties can literally be an independently existing property of the object.

Point (3), that sense data are immediately or directly present to consciousness, calls for explanation. Of course, it makes perfectly good sense to talk of being directly aware of the material things in the world about us if we are looking at them in a good light with normal eyesight. So if we are to insist that the visual field is more directly or immediately presented to us than the visual world, we must be using language in an unusual and perhaps misleading way. But it is surely clear on reflection that this claim amounts to, however maladroitly it may often have been expressed. The visual field is more primitive than the visual world. It is its basic unconceptualised raw material. New born infants and patients blind from birth recovering from surgery to restore their sight are doubtless the only human creatures with unconceptualised visual fields. We no longer remember what it was like to have one. Professor Bruner has remarked how 'it is curiously difficult to recapture preconceptual innocence'.[25] Certainly we cannot hope to divest ourselves of the complex conceptual network woven into our sensory field that gives our experience meaning and intelligibility. We can perhaps occasionally approach that state of 'pre-conceptual innocence' in artfully contrived situations in the psychological laboratory or in delirium or, momentarily, in awakening from sleep or coming round from an anaesthetic in unfamiliar surroundings. But for us, such situations are now disturbing and unpleasant. However, as infants, we all had such raw unconceptualised sensory fields. They were given to us prior to the world of material things; and they were the material necessary for our gradually learned concepts to mould into the now familiar sensory world.

Let us talk for simplicity in terms of the visual field. (Analogous arguments can be put forward for other sensory modalities.) Our visual fields as now given to us are so conceptually saturated, so moulded by learning the structure of the visual world, that it is almost impossible for us to prescind from the conceptual load that gives meaning to what is presented to us. Certainly any expression in language of a visual experience, however primitive and ill-defined, is already conceptually tainted. (Even, for example: 'I see yellow'.) For language is pre-eminently a device for the storage of ideas. But with special training and care it is sometimes possible to see the world, for short periods, as a patchwork of light, colour and shade instead of a world of material objects and their environment. Many painters have this skill.

This distinction of perceptual attitudes towards the visual field and the visual world is important. If we attend to it, we can see what is wrong with Ryle's well-known argument against sense data. Ryle argued that 'this whole theory rests on a logical howler, the howler namely, of assimilating the concept of sensation to the concept of observation'.[26] Perhaps some philosophers have committed this 'howler'. Certainly some of them have talked of 'perceiving' sense data. And if our perceptual attitude to things observed were the same as that towards sense data, we would indeed be involved in an infinite regress. But if we distinguish the conceptualised visual world from the unconceptualised world of raw sense data, we can see that the visual stance appropriate to one is quite different from that appropriate to the other. We sense sense data; we perceive objects. And when we perceive something or purport to perceive it, we clothe a portion of our visual field with concepts.

So visual sense data, that is, the contents of our visual fields, are historically or developmentally prior to our having a visual world. It has been shown from studies of patients blind from birth who have their sight restored surgically that the transition from a visual field to a visual world has to be developed slowly over a long period of time. Towards the end of the seventeenth century, William Molyneux, a friend of Locke, wrote to ask him whether a blind man, on recovering his sight, would be able to distinguish a cube from a sphere from their visual appearances alone. (He would, of course, have learned earlier to distinguish them by touch.) Molyneux conjectured, and Locke agreed with him, that the previously blind man would not be able to distinguish the two shapes by sight alone.

This was no more than an intelligent guess, but subsequent work by psychologists has supported it. In fact, most psychologists have been concerned with the question: What, if anything, does such a patient see? rather than with Molyneux's question: Can such a patient name what he sees? But the results of their investigations are of great importance for the theory of perception. An examination of more than seventy cases of patients blind from birth who had their sight restored by surgery was made by the German psychologist, Dr Marius von Senden.[27] The reports of the subsequent visual experiences of these patients are difficult to interpret for a number of reasons. But, in general, it is clear from the reports that a great deal of learning is required to interpret the new range of sensations conferred by these surgical cures. A recent investigator in the field, Professor R. L. Gregory, summarises the outcome:

> They could see but little at first, being unable to name or distinguish between even simple objects or shapes. Sometimes there was a long period of training before they came to have useful vision, which indeed in many cases was never attained. Some gave up the attempt and reverted to a life of blindness, often after a severe period of emotional disturbance. On the other hand, some did see quite well almost immediately, particularly those who were intelligent and active and who had received a good education while blind. The overall difficulty which these people have in naming even the simplest objects by sight, and the slowness in the development of perception, so impressed the Canadian

psychologist D. O. Hebb that he gave a lot of weight to this evidence, suggesting that indeed it shows how important perceptual learning is in the human infant.[28]

It would be dangerous to draw any very specific conclusions from the evidence available. But this much at least is clear: sensory abilities are innate; perception is to a large extent learned. Locke and Molyneux were right in the answer they gave to Molyneux's question. Our raw experience of the world, conveyed through our sense organs at birth, has to be interpreted; and we learn only slowly how to do this. Sensation gives us merely raw sense impressions – sense data; perception gives us the familiar world of physical objects. But this familiarity is won only slowly and at such an early stage of our lives that we have all forgotten what it was like. Von Senden's blind patients, newly restored to sight, experience some of the learning difficulties that we all went through in our infancy in making the progress from the immediately presented world of sense data to the gradually learned world of material objects. This is the sense in which sense data are more directly and immediately apprehended than are material objects.

There is one further point to be borne in mind considering what information the senses give us about the world. Our sense organs are very limited in two different ways: (i) They are limited in their sensitivity to the forms of energy to which they do respond; (ii) and they are limited in the different types of energy to which they are sensitive.

Examples of the first sort are common enough. The human eye responds to only a very tiny range of the spectrum of electromagnetic radiation in the wave band from 760 to 390 mμ. X-rays and radio waves, for example, differ from light only in wave length, that is, in the way that red light differs from blue. Yet our eyes are not sensitive to them. Our noses and ears, as is well known, are vastly less sensitive to their respective stimuli than are the organs of many other animals – dogs, fish, bats, moths and many others. So it is clear that our senses can detect only a small range of the forms of energy to which they are specially adapted. And to turn to the second limitation, it is plain that there are forms of energy for which we have no sensory detectors at all. Magnetic fields, for example, and most forms of electrical energy, have to be translated by suitable instruments – magnetometers, galvanometers and the like – before we can detect them. Even forms of energy which are highly dangerous to life like gamma radiation, must be detected by the clicking of a Geiger counter or the like before we are aware of them.

It may be asked what these examples are intended to show. After all, if we had sense organs which could detect all types and degrees of energy output we would be overwhelmed by the magnitude and diversity of our sensory input. There are good biological reasons why our sense organs are not of this variety and range. Evolutionary processes have worked to adapt the types and capacity of our senses to the sort of lives that human beings live, as they have for all other animals. This is true. But it does not affect the point which these examples bring out, namely, that the picture of the world that is given to us through the senses is a very selective, limited and restricted one. We build it up from only a tiny sample of the information at large in the world. This must be borne in mind when the question is raised: Does sense perception give us knowledge? It does; but the knowledge is necessarily very limited. A recent book on sense perception by the American psychologist Lloyd Kaufman has the title: *Perception: The World Transformed*.[29] The title points to an important truth. But we should remember that it is only a very tiny selection of the world that is transformed.

CHAPTER V

MEMORY

The Ways of Remembering

Remembering is a way of knowing. So we may reasonably be asked to consider the problems raised by memory when we are talking about the theory of knowledge. But what are these problems? We may want to know, for example, how memories are stored so that they can later re-appear in consciousness. We may ask by what mechanism they can be voluntarily recalled to mind, as when we are trying to remember a name. But these questions about physical mechanisms are not problems for the philosopher. They lie in the province of the physiologist of the nervous system. It has been suggested, for example, that the physical memory trace lies in some modification of the synapses of certain brain cells or in the formation of special proteins or RNA in the brain or in some combination of these factors. But whether such theories turn out to be right or wrong, they are scientific theories established by experiment, and are not part of philosophy. Again, psychologists over the last hundred years have devised many theories to explain human and animal learning, that is to say, the ways in which memories of various kinds are acquired and lost. But such theories, like those of the physiologists, are scientific and not philosophical. None of these questions, real and important as they are, have to be considered by philosophers, though naturally, anything that philosophers may say about memory must at least be consistent with well established scientific theories. What then are the questions about memory that *do* concern philosophers?

If we examine recent philosophical writings about memory we find discussions of the following questions: Is memory a source of knowledge? Are we directly in touch with our past experiences when we remember, or are we inferring truths about the past from our experience of the present? How do we distinguish genuine memories from putative or mistaken ones? How do we acquire our *concept* of the past? And, most basically, what is remembering?

Such questions, like all questions in philosophy, are connected very closely so that the answers that we give to one of them will determine, to some extent, the answers that can be given to the rest. This makes it a matter of some importance to start with the most basic and important question, if there is one. And to do that it will be useful to survey the different sorts of memory to see which of them presents us with philosophical problems. Perhaps the most obvious distinction between types of memory is based on the well known distinction between types of knowledge on which Ryle laid so much stress, the distinction between knowing *how* to do something or other and knowing *that* such-and-such is the case. I may remember, correspondingly, how to swim, how to ride a bicycle, how to play the piano and also remember, though no doubt in a different sense of the word, that I watched the Cup Final at Wembley in 1969, or that I stood at the top of the amphitheatre in Verona on 2 April 1977. We have chosen these two very different types of remembering simply to emphasise the obvious difference between what is called habit memory and what we may call perceptual memory. An American psychologist has suggested the useful phrase 'episodic memory' for this very specific kind of perceptual memory.[1]

If we survey the different types of beliefs which we might call memory-beliefs, two things stand out: first, that there are a large number of different kinds and, secondly, that there are no very clear differences between the kinds. It is rather that they can be arranged in a kind of spectrum where one type merges into the next without any very sharp distinction between them. Let us look first at the instances of episodic memory mentioned above. These are very special types of memory-belief in that I not only remember *that* I had these particular experiences but also remember *having* them. That is to say, I can put these experiences into a specific time and place in my past history and can recall various perceptual details – the colours of the jerseys of the two competing teams, for example. I can also remember details that are not supported by images of any kind. For example, I can remember the names of some of the players. And these are memories of a propositional kind, rather than a perceptual. It is true, of course, that if I have an episodic memory M, then I also have a corresponding propositional memory – *that* I had the experience preserved in M. But I can have many propositional memories of which I do not have a corresponding episodic memory. And here we must distinguish again between two distinct, though related, types of memory – personal and impersonal. I can remember, for example, *that* I took various school examinations, although I have no recollection of taking them. Such memories are propositional and personal, but they are not episodic. They relate to events in my own past, even though the events themselves are not now remembered in the way in which I remember the 1969 Cup Final or standing at the top of the amphitheatre in Verona.

And, of course, I have very large numbers of memories which do not relate to events in my own past, even though it is directly due to some event (or events) in my own past that I now have the memory. For example, I may remember Pythagoras' theorem and perhaps even the proof of it. Clearly, I must have learned these things on some occasions in my past, even though it is unlikely that I can now recall the occasion in the way that I can recall the 1969 Cup Final. Indeed, all our knowledge, with two principal exceptions, is memory knowledge of this sort. All our knowledge of our own native language, for example, is of this type as well as all the concepts that we possess which enable us to make sense of the world about us. The two principal exceptions are, first, the content of our immediate present awareness and, secondly, any knowledge which we obtain *by inference* from this content or from what we remember. And this, too, is remembered even though its content was not given to us in our personal experience. (We shall be discussing problems raised by our immediate present awareness later.)

Thus we may move along the memory spectrum from episodic memories of myself doing or experiencing something to propositional memories of a personal kind – memories *that* I did or experienced such-and-such. The next step in depersonalising our memories is to remember that so-and-so is the case – that the square root of two is irrational or that Napoleon won the Battle of Austerlitz, where the memory content does not relate to my past experience. Consider some examples.

I remember *that* I travelled by air from London to New York sometime in June 1959, even though I have no episodic recollections of the journey. Perhaps this is no more than an inference from the undoubted episodic memory I do have of breakfasting in New York on a June morning after arriving from England. However that may be, I certainly remember *that* I flew to New York on that occasion, though I retain no perceptual details of the journey.

Now let us look at an example of impersonal propositional memory – say, Pythagoras' theorem. If I say to myself 'the square on the hypotenuse of a right angled plane triangle is equal to the sum of the squares on the other two sides', is this just habit memory or is it a genuine propositional memory? Clearly, we cannot answer this question without further information. If I can give a proof of the theorem or explain what the terms 'hypotenuse' and 'right angle' mean, it would be conceded that I am remembering a proposition. If not, then by reciting the phrase may amount to no more than habit memory, like reciting a chain of nonsense syllables, or a phrase in a language that I do not understand. And this fact raises a difficulty.

Some philosophers have tried to make a sharp distinction between habit memory and what is sometimes called 'cognitive memory', memory of propositions or of propositions as expressing facts. This distinction was the basis of Bergson's account of memory[2] and was strongly defended by Russell and by C. D. Broad. Russell speaks of our beliefs that certain images 'refer to past occurrences' and emphasises that this is genuine memory knowledge. 'I shall speak of it as "true" memory to distinguish it from mere habit acquired through past experience.'[3] According to Broad,[4] we must make a sharp distinction between various acquired motor-habits, whether muscular or verbal (such as swimming, playing a musical instrument, speaking a language, and so on) and genuine memory which is 'a peculiar kind of cognition in which we seem to be in contact with a part of our own past history and with events which we then experienced.'[5] Only cognitive memory, so described, is real memory.

It is not difficult to see why such philosophers have wanted to make this distinction. Cognitive or 'true' memory can be genuine or misleading and the propositions which it embodies may be true or false. But in the case of pure habit memory, swimming, cycling or even speaking our native language, there seems little or nothing of truth or falsity involved. Empirical evidence may bring me to realise that even a vivid episodic memory may be false. But what would it mean to say that a habit memory was false? A case of habit memory such as swimming or serving at tennis may be more or less perfectly established and more or less fitted for its purpose. But truth or falsity hardly apply to it.

On the other hand, if we look at the very varied forms that our memories take, it is not easy to draw any hard and fast lines between them. One type seems to shade off into another. We have memories *of* events in our past, clear episodic memories often accompanied by very distinct imagery, we have such memories where the imagery is vague, scanty or even absent altogether, we have memories *that* a certain event happened without any memories of the happening itself. All these are clearly cognitive, to use Broad's term, and may be true or false. But the truth or falsity, like the accompanying imagery, seems to be a matter of degree. Some memories are more detailed and vividly representative than others, though some details are right and others wrong. The next class of cognitive memories are those relating to facts or events which do not form part of our own past, though we must have learned them at some time in our past. Most of our knowledge of history, geography, and science is of this sort. I remember *that* the Battle of Waterloo took place in June 1815 even though I cannot remember it actually taking place. But such cases of impersonal memory are clearly of secondary rank. Although they must necessarily have been acquired during our past, they are not memories of our own past even though we may sometimes remember the occasion on which we first acquired the knowledge. What is hard to appreciate about impersonal memories is the way in which they are basic to our whole way of thinking and looking at the world.

This question was briefly mentioned earlier; but as it is a matter of great importance, it is worth looking at in more detail. All of the conceptual apparatus which we have to use in order to understand and make sense of the world around us is derived from our memories. Our chief source of stable concepts is, of course, our native language. But beyond that, there is a wide range of habits and social conventions which we learned in early life and which have now become so much a part of our established ways of reacting to our fellow human beings, to animals and to the rest of nature that we are unconscious that these patterns of behaviour are a part of our memories. To bring home to ourselves just how important such memories are, consider the case of a man from an environment entirely alien to ours, an Arctic Eskimo, for example, or a native of central New Guinea, who is suddenly transported to contemporary London. Everything which makes his life natural and easy for him in his native surroundings will have vanished and will have been replaced by an alien ambience. His native language, his familiar concepts, his social habits will now be like keys whose locks have been altered. They no longer work in the new environment. And the new conceptual apparatus which will enable him to live more or less comfortably in his new surroundings will have to be established by new memories. It is hard to realise the very basic function of such memories simply because they are so basic. And they are not obviously propositional memories at all. They are habits of adjustment which have to be acquired by every animal, human or not, which is born into the world. We can appreciate to some degree how much more important they are than the propositional memories that much philosophical argument has been concerned with, if we look at what commonly happens when someone is afflicted with a sudden amnesia. Such a person may have no personal memories at all and so may be quite unable to tell doctors or police anything of his family, his background or his origins. He literally does not know who he is as all his personal memories have been obliterated. But he still speaks his native language and retains the concepts that enable him to make sense of his environment.

But even if such basic habit memories are important in these ways, it may still be doubted whether they are of any philosophical importance. Although they store knowledge acquired in the past, they do not represent the past directly to us as personal and episodic memories do. And it is the problems raised by the representation of the past that have traditionally been considered to be the philosophical problems of memory. We shall be in a better position to consider the relations between these two varieties of memory when we have looked at the claim of personal memories to represent the past.

The Representative Theory of Memory

When I recall an event which I experienced in the past, it seems to me that my present state of mind is (i) informing me of a past event, (ii) is good evidence that the event took place, and (iii) is good evidence that the event was experienced by me. So that my present state of mind offers both information and a guarantee. The information is of a past event. And the guarantee is that the event really took place and was experienced by the person who recalls it. Any of these features of an apparent memory may, of course, be doubted, as we shall see. But the characteristic feature of this unreflective 'common sense' account of memory is that a present experience is a reliable record of a past experience. And, indeed, this common sense account has been the basis of what is called the representative theory of memory which, in various forms, has been adopted by many philosophers from Aristotle to Russell. But stated in this skeleton form, it is only a programme for a theory. And as soon as we try to fill out the programme with some explanatory detail we meet serious difficulties.

What indeed are the characteristics of a present experience that lead us to suppose it to be a memory? We are accustomed to talk of 'memory images' and some philosophers have thought, or at least have talked as if they thought that imagery was essential to memory. 'Memory, even the memory of concepts,' says Aristotle, 'cannot exist apart from imagery.'[6] Such images are supposed to represent the original experience in the sense that (i) they are more or less perfect replicas of the experience and (ii) that they bring to mind the experience that they stand for. Later philosophers, and in particular, Hume and Russell, have tried to elaborate this account by giving answers to a difficulty first raised by Aristotle.[7] If we remember through images impressed upon us by the original experience, are we just remembering the image or the event which caused the image? If we are remembering the image which is present to us, we could not be remembering, as we obviously are, events which are not present to us. And if we are remembering the event, how do we remember something which is absent from us through the experience of what is present to us? Aristotle's own rather unsatisfactory solution of his difficulty is that the image functions in a double capacity, as a picture in its own right and as a representation of something else, namely, the event remembered. But this is merely a restatement of the representative account of memory. It still leaves open the question of how we can distinguish images which genuinely represent our own past to us from all our other images which do not. In short, how is memory to be distinguished from imagination?

Philosophers who have adopted a representative theory of memory have commonly tried to answer this question by specifying a mark or sign present in our immediate experience which will serve as a more or less reliable 'memory indicator'.[8] David Hume tried to find the required criterion in characteristics of the memory image which he believed would distinguish it from the images of imagination. He suggested two such marks. The first is that memory images have a characteristic 'vivacity' or liveliness which those of the imagination do not possess. The second is that while imagination 'is not restrained to the same order and form with the original impressions; while the memory is in a manner ty'd down in that respect, without any power of variation'.[9] But Hume himself immediately concedes that the second mark is useless as a memory indicator. Clearly, I cannot compare the content of a present experience with that of a past experience which I may believe that the present experience represents. So we are left with the criterion of 'vivacity'. But this too fails for a number of reasons. In the first place, it is not true that even totally reliable memory experiences are always, or even usually, more clear, lively and distinct than undisputed deliverances of our imaginations such as dreams, reveries, hypnagogic images, hallucinations and the rest. As we all know from experience, these can be very vivid indeed. Secondly, liveliness and vivacity are matters of degree and can be placed on a continuum from very faint to very distinct and detailed. There is no clear cut-off point on that continuum which must exist if Hume's distinction is to be sustained. Even if he were right to the extent that products of the imagination are usually and on the average less clear and lively than memory images, it would still not be possible, on his criterion, to differentiate between a rather faint memory image and a rather clear product of the imagination. And, thirdly, we can raise the important question: What exactly is it that Hume supposes to bear this mark of vivacity? We can look at this question after we have considered Russell's attempt to improve upon Hume's account of memory.

Russell concedes[10] that the 'mere occurrence' of images, 'by itself, would not suggest any connection with anything that had happened before.' And if we are to suppose that they are sometimes bearers of memories, we have to be able to point to some characteristic of memory images which distinguishes them from other images. Russell claims to detect two such properties. The first is a feeling of familiarity which accompanies our memory images; and the second is a collection of marks which enable us to refer a particular memory to its place in the past. Russell calls this 'the feeling of "pastness" ' which is usually accompanied by a remembered 'context' which enables us to place the memory, with more or less accuracy, to its appropriate position in our past experience.[11]

This account is certainly an improvement on Hume's in that it is a fair description of the way in which we do experience the past. It is true that some images seem familiar to us and that, by and large, such images are memories or parts of memories. And it is true also that we are helped in placing a particular memory to its location in our past by the aura of associated memories that fills out the picture, so to speak. The richer and more distinct the detail of a given memory, the more easily and confidently we are enabled to assign it to its place in our past history. However, if Russell meant to claim that these are infallible memory-indicators, he was surely wrong. In the first place, as he admits, these criteria are very much matters of degree. A given memory experience may feel more or less familiar and may have a vivid or faint sense of pastness and a more or less rich context of associated memories. It is well known that some imaginary experiences may stamp themselves on our consciousness with some or all of these properties. And it is precisely in consequence of this that we can be genuinely uncertain as to whether a given putative memory is a real memory or not. So Russell's memory indicators are subject to the same criticism as Hume's in that they do not reliably distinguish between memory and imagination. We must concede, however, that Russell's indicators are more dependable than Hume's. If Hume's term 'vivacity' refers to the force and clarity of images — and he does not trouble to specify his meaning more closely — these are properties that images may possess for all sorts of reasons unrelated to memory. Vivid dreams or drug-induced hallucinations will normally possess a 'vivacity' far in excess of anything that memory may offer. But feelings of familiarity and a sense of pastness are normally concomitants of memory and accompany the products of imagination only in rather aberrant cases.

Yet to admit this is certainly not to justify Russell's version of the representative theory of memory. The theory in any form has still to meet a serious objection first formulated by Thomas Reid in his *Essays on the Intellectual Powers of Man*. [12] Hume had assumed in his account of memory that we 'find by experience, that when any impression has been present with the mind, it again makes its appearance there as an idea.'[13] And this is, of course, a fundamental premiss of his philosophy – that all ideas come from experience. But how does Hume know this, if not by memory? Russell too claims that 'images are regarded by us as more or less accurate copies of past occurrences because they come to us with two sorts of feelings', namely, those of familiarity and of pastness.[14] But how does he know this, if not by memory?

Reid's point is that 'all experience presupposes memory; and there can be no such thing as experience, without trust – to our own memory, or that of others: So that it appears from Mr Hume's account of this matter, that he found himself to have that kind of memory which he acknowledges and defines, by exercising that kind which he rejects.'[15] The same objection can be made against Russell's theory. When Russell says that images purporting to represent past occurrences 'come to us with two sorts of feelings', he is relying on memory for this information. But is memory, in this sense of the word, the same as the memory that Russell is trying to explain? Reid's objection can be put in a way that directly challenges any attempt, such as those of Hume and Russell, to find reliable memory-indicators in our experience: how do we know that such-and-such a memory-indicator (a feeling of familiarity or whatever it may be) really is one without relying on the very notion of memory that we are trying to elucidate? To this question, there are several possible answers. We may agree that to argue for Russell's theory, for example, we are relying on memory, in a general sense of the word – a biological habit, let us say – for the information which justifies *particular* memories as being veridical.

However, this general sense of 'memory', memory as a biological residue of experience, is not the sense at issue in the attempts of Hume and Russell to find reliable memory-indicators in our everyday recollections. Such purely habitual adjustments to the world do not ordinarily carry any such indicators. Their very familiarity goes unremarked. It is true that when Hume says 'we find by experience' that our present ideas are derived from our previous impressions, he is indeed invoking memory, but memory in this generalised and unspecific sense and not the episodic type of memory that he is trying to explain. So Hume and Russell cannot fairly be accused of arguing in a circle by invoking the explicandum in their explicans. What they are purporting to account for are particular episodic memories of specific identifiable events in our past experience. They are not talking of the general biological tendency of all animals to guide their present actions by a generalised knowledge of the way the world works. This knowledge is no doubt based on individual memories of an episodic kind. But the specific details of these memories have long since been forgotten. What we retain of them is an accumulated residue that makes up our knowledge of our language, our concepts, the regularities and customs of our environment and the rest of our social and intellectual habits. So Reid's criticism is beside the point.

What would it mean, in any case, to say that we are trying to explain memory, in this biological sense of the word, the tendency of all animals to retain enough of the general pattern of their past experiences to guide their present and future actions? Nowadays we would surely give an evolutionary explanation. The better developed these retentive powers are in a particular species, the more likely is that species to live successfully in its environment and to pass on this life-preserving trait to its progeny. Any individuals of the species which had minimal or poor capacity for memory would quickly succumb to the local predators and other dangers and would not survive to pass on this forgetful habit of mind to their offspring. It is on this general pattern that most animal capacities are successfully explained by biologists. The problem is not a philosophical one at all.

Reid, living in pre-Darwinian times, did not have such models of explanation available. Indeed, he took a strictly agnostic view of the matter: 'Memory is an original faculty given to us by the

Author of our being, of which we can give no account but that we are so made.'[16] Reid is fond of rebuking scepticism in other philosophers; but to be sceptical about the possibility of explanations is just another form of scepticism, and one to which he was much addicted. Any operations of mind on body or vice versa have causes 'inscrutable to the human understanding'.[17]

So far then, we might accept the representative theory of memory in the form that Russell gives it. It does assign reliable, if not infallible, memory-indicators to our states of consciousness. But if we look more closely at the character of these supposed indicators, Russell's account looks less plausible. In his summary of the theory of memory set out in Lecture IX of *The Analysis of Mind*, Russell concludes: 'Memory demands (a) an image, (b) a belief in past existence.' But is it true that images are essential for memory? And if they are not, how are we to describe the conscious states that we recognise as memories, if they are not composed of, or accompanied by, images?

The Role of Imagery

It is a fact of experience that most human beings have images of various kinds and that many of these images are associated with remembering. But is it true, as Russell assumes, that images are a *necessary* feature of memory so that, were someone incapable of forming images, he would also be incapable of remembering? The answer to this question is certainly: No. The evidence for this negative lies in the studies by psychologists on the nature and function of imagery.[18] Any of the various sensory modalities — sight, hearing, taste, smell, organic sensations and the rest — are capable of yielding images. These images may occur in varying degrees of vividness and intensity and they may occur with varying functions. A vivid visual image may be a bearer of memory but so may a very faint auditory image. And very intense images may occur with no associated memories at all. Hallucinations, whether drug-induced or the result of disease, can be of quite frightening intensity and indistinguishable from experiences of the perceptual world. A very familiar type of image is the so-called hypnogogic image which occurs in the period when we are just on the point of falling asleep but have not quite done so. These occur as very vivid pictures, noises or other sensations and are, as it were, semi-waking dreams. They are, in fact, very similar to the imagery of dreaming.

But these different sources and types of imagery and the different degrees of vividness with which images may be endowed are not the only differences of importance in assessing the role of imagery in memory. Even more important is the way in which the degree and type of imagery varies from one person to another. We are all naturally disposed to think that the types, frequency and intensity of images which each of us experiences in his own mental life is substantially the same as that of other people. But this is certainly not so; and the fact that it is not is a matter of some consequence for the role of imagery in human memory. The earliest systematic investigation of the role of imagery in human thinking was made by Sir Francis Galton about a hundred years ago and published in his *Inquiries into Human Faculty and its Development* in 1883. Galton's inquiries were concerned mainly with visual imagery although the questionnaire with which he initiated his investigations concerned imagery in all the sensory modalities. Galton was surprised to find that many educated people, particularly among the men of science with whom he started his inquiries, claimed to have no experience of mental imagery. 'They had no more notion of its true nature than a colour-blind man, who has not discerned his defect, has of the nature of colour.'[19] Many others, however, particularly women and children, 'declared that they habitually saw mental imagery, and that it was perfectly distinct to them and full of colour.' The outcome of his inquiries was that the occurrence of mental imagery is not universal among humans, that its occurrence varies very widely in vividness, persistence and the degree to which it can be voluntarily controlled and that, most important of all, it seems to have no sort of correlation with memory or with any other intellectual powers. Galton's investigations were by the standards of modern experimental psychology, crude and naïve. But his general findings have not been seriously discredited by later and more sophisticated methods of inquiry.

These facts are of some importance for the philosophical problems of memory. If imagery is not essential for memory, and it is clear that psychological findings show that it is not, what ingredients of our conscious life do carry the information that memory gives us? Clearly, to put the question in this way may look as if we are presupposing that some form of the representative theory of memory is correct. But this is not necessarily so. When I am having an episodic memory, there is something in my present state of consciousness that I can identify as being (or perhaps as bearing) the memory. Now if it is not an image, or a set of images, what is it? States of consciousness which carry veridical information may be of varying kinds. Whether I am perceiving, reasoning or remembering, there is some characteristic feature of my current state of awareness which carries the information. If, in the case of remembering, it is not imagery, what is it? The answer presumably must be that there is no one feature of our awareness that is uniquely identifiable as being a memory-carrier. Our vocabulary for describing our consciousness is limited and imperfect. Any ways we devise of offering such a description will usually be found to beg the question in favour of some particular philosophical theory about mind and its workings. And yet it cannot be doubted that for the majority of human beings who do enjoy imagery, images do often, and perhaps usually, convey memories. So we are tempted to ask: what does this job for those equally reliable memories where no imagery is present?

The fact that this question is not obviously answerable in any straightforward way should make us suspect both it and the role assigned to imagery in memory. There may be a sense in which images are memory carriers; but if memory can work equally well without them their role is clearly an inessential one. And by attending too closely to imagery and its functions, we may be overlooking more important ways of approaching the questions at issue. It may be that the decisive objection to any representative theory of memory is just that the nature of the alleged 'representatives' cannot be clearly specified. Images are neither necessary nor sufficient for remembering. And there is no other identifiable content of our conscious life which can serve in their place. May it not be that, when we remember specific events, we are not using any symbolic substitute for the remembered events but rather we are directly aware of the events themselves?

The Realist Theory of Memory

That this is so is the contention of philosophers who espouse what may be called a realist account of memory.[20] If an ordinary man of unreflective common sense were to be asked: 'Exactly what are you now remembering when you recall, let us say, arriving in Italy for your last summer holiday?' he would probably reply that he was recalling exactly that, namely, the event of his arrival. In other words, when we remember past events, what we are aware of is just those past events, and nothing further. Whether our rememberings are accompanied by images which highlight or clarify the memory is an accidental matter which does not affect the basic fact that we believe that in remembering we are in some kind of direct touch with the past. This theory, or rather, this point of view, (for it can hardly be called a 'theory' at this undeveloped stage) has obvious similarities with the so-called 'naïve realist' theory of perception. It shares with that theory the advantages of evading the difficulties presented by any kind of representative account of knowing. But it is not without serious difficulties of its own.

The first is concerned with the nature of time. We ordinarily suppose that past events are over and done with and though they may leave their traces in the present, they do not now exist. How then can I be in direct touch with events of my past experience if these events no longer exist? Moreover, how is it that the events that I can be 'in touch with' are all events of *my own* past experience and not those which occurred in the experience of others? It is not sufficient to reply that this is exactly what remembering *means*, to be in touch with events of *my own* past and not the events of anyone else's past. No doubt this is so. But a theory which claims that I can be in direct and unmediated touch with past events has to explain what it is that differentiates events of my own past experience from those of others so that my direct contact with past events is confined to the first class alone. The answer to such a question is obvious enough. Only events of my own past experience have left the brain traces which physiology has shown to be a necessary condition of memory. So that this supposed direct contact with the past turns out, after all, to be mediated necessarily by present traces in the nervous system of the person who remembers. Thus the supposed direct character of remembering, on the realist account, has to be qualified. (This point will be taken up again when we discuss the origins of our concept of the past.)

A second difficulty is this: if in remembering I am in some sense *directly* in touch with the past events that I am recalling, how does it come about that my memories are so often indeterminate, or accompanied by incorrect details or indeed mistaken on crucial issues? The analogy with directly realist theories of perception, which is sometimes invoked here, breaks down at this point. If my senses put me in direct touch with the physical world, I can correct any apparent gaps or flaws in my perceptions by critically re-scrutinising the same scene, from a different angle perhaps, or in a different light. But there is no possibility of amending my faulty memories in this way, *as there would be* were I in direct touch with the past. It is hard to believe that talk of being in direct touch with the past through memory is anything more than a hopeful metaphor which cannot be developed into a theory.

Memory, Perception, and Scepticism

Memory, like perception, is a way of knowing. Unlike perception it does not also constitute a source of knowledge, for we do not discover things about the world by remembering them. Nevertheless, like perception our 'faculty' of memory marks off a particular form of knowledge, for we talk of perceptual and of memory knowledge. To talk of memory is to talk (at least centrally) of retained knowledge – knowledge which we 'have learned and not forgotten', to use Ryle's phrase to describe propositional knowledge[21] – and to talk also of our recollected experiences, our episodic memories. We have memory knowledge, for example, that crows are black, that Jimmy Carter lost the last American presidential election, and that $2 + 2 = 4$ as well as memory knowledge that we parked the car on the left side of the road. Now, as we saw in Chapter I, the sceptic typically raises his worries about one area of knowledge at a time, and we must therefore expect to find scepticism about memory knowledge and perceptual knowledge developed independently. That is not to say, however, that such sceptical positions will have nothing in common, for if what we said in Chapter I is correct there should be at least a Cartesian form and a Humean form of sceptical argument

in each area of knowledge. We shall concentrate mainly on scepticism about memory in this section and the next, though the
points raised will, by and large, have an obvious relevance to
perceptual knowledge as well.

In questioning the reliability of memory or of perception the
sceptic is questioning those criteria on which we rely to make the
judgement that a proposition P, which expresses what we *seem* to
remember or to perceive, does in fact really express something
which we *do* remember or perceive. In other words – and limiting
our attention now to memory – the sceptic finds fault with those
'criteria of certainty' which are used in the field of memory
knowledge and which enable us to say, when they are satisfied,
that what we 'ostensibly remember' or 'seem to remember' is
indeed remembered. The sceptic believes that such criteria of
certainty are defective and hence provide no warrant for that
move.

A Cartesian sceptic would find the criteria defective in that they
are not logically conclusive, that is that although they are satisfied
they do not guarantee that what we ostensibly remember actually
constitutes memory knowledge. How do we check upon our
ostensible memory knowledge? That depends, of course, on the
kind of belief involved, for clearly seeming to remember that the
car was parked on the left side of the road and seeming to
remember that 123 times 12 came out at 1476 would present to
some degree a different kind of problem. However, we can suggest that in general we shall go by the way in which such ostensible
memories cohere with other such memory experiences, and with
what other people now say and what any other relevant records
show. Even the best evidence, so the Cartesian sceptic will insist
nevertheless, fails to prove that our ostensible memory constitutes memory knowledge. The satisfaction of the standard
criteria for certainty does not entail the reality of the ostensible
memory.

A possibility described by Russell[22] brings out this point in a
vivid fashion. The possibility envisaged was that the world sprang
into existence only a few minutes ago, and this is something which
cannot be logically excluded on the basis of the totality of current
evidence. The status of Russell's hypothesis, that the world came
into existence just five minutes ago, is that of Descartes' evil
demon hypothesis: it serves to point to the logical inconclusive-

ness of our criteria of certainty. Russell writes:

> There is no logical impossibility in the hypothesis that the world sprang into being five minutes ago, exactly as it then was, with a population that 'remembered' a wholly unreal past. There is no logically necessary connection between events at different times; therefore, nothing that is happening now or will ever happen in the future can disprove the hypothesis that the world began five minutes ago.

A Humean sceptic would rest his case on something more than this logical inconclusiveness of our criteria. For him, it is important that those criteria lack a justification. Hume's argument concerning 'moral reasoning' was that it cannot be provided with a non-circular justification, one which does not rely on the validity of the very form of argument concerned. Humean scepticism about memory would point out similarly that no non-circular justification of our memory criteria can be given: any attempt to show that those criteria are trustworthy will of necessity rely at some point on memory itself and hence on those very criteria.

A general argument along these lines might be this. Any attempt to show these criteria to be reliable would have to make reference to the past, for it would involve establishing that our memory beliefs about the past do indeed conform to it. But all knowledge of the past relies at some point on memory: for instance, if we refer to the testimony of others, perhaps eye-witnesses, we are of necessity relying on their memories, and in any case we have to rely on our memory knowledge of what words mean and our memory knowledge of people's general veracity; if we refer to records, photographs, or other physical traces we are necessarily relying on our memory knowledge of how the world goes in relevant respects, as well as on such things as our memory knowledge that *we* wrote in the diary or took the photograph rather than some practical joker. This is not to say, of course, that all knowledge of the past is memory knowledge – clearly we can come to know about the past by looking at our diaries or photographs to gain information which we have forgotten or even by looking at someone else's diary or photographs to gain information which we have never before had – but it does show that our knowledge of the past is intimately connected with such memory knowledge, and hence that no non-circular proof of the merits of our memory criteria is possible.[23]

The grounds of this Humean form of scepticism have been disputed by some philosophers, who argue that ostensible memories can be checked without reference to the past and hence without dependence on memory itself. R. F. Harrod, for example, thought[24] that individual ostensible memories might be tested by making predictions on their basis, and if these are found to be correct then a start has been made on proving the general reliability of memory. If we ostensibly remember that lightning flashes have always instantly vanished, we can predict that such will be true of the next lightning flash: if this turns out to be so, it confirms that ostensible memory. Clearly there are problems here, not the least of which is that the sceptic will insist on the logical gap between the experience 'confirming' the ostensible memory and the actuality of the memory itself. Why, he would ask, does the vanishing of this lightning flash show that others have done so in the past? Why does it show, what is more, that we *remember* them doing so? And how can we make predictions from ostensible memories without introducing more information about the ways of the world? To make these moves we must rely on a great deal more than is given so far, and clearly we shall be involved in the kind of reliance on memory described above. Much the same is surely true of Holland's example[25] of an ostensible memory being checked against a present experience: if I ostensibly remember putting some money into a box, this can easily be checked by opening the box and investigating its contents. If the box had been destroyed, says Holland, I would have had to rely on other people's memories and other remembered facts, but in this case the box and the money are there to be seen. Once more, however, the sceptic can insist that much more is involved in coming to the conclusion that I remember putting the money there, than the presence of the money now.

J. T. Saunders has pointed out[26] that Holland fails to distinguish between an explicit and an implicit appeal to memory in the process of justifying any particular memory belief. Holland is right in as much as no explicit appeal to memory is involved in his example, yet it is clear enough that an implicit appeal is involved for a full statement of the argument from the presence of the ostensible memory to its reality as a memory of the past would depend on memories of one kind or another. Indeed, Saunders wants to insist that the very reliance on any empirical generalisations in such an argument would involve a commitment to memory beliefs, in so far as 'to have inductive evidence for an empirical generalisation one must have reason to believe in the occurrence of a sizeable number of its instances . . . And there would appear to be no way to assure ourselves of this if we distrust our ostensible memories'.[27]

Cartesian and Humean versions of scepticism about memory are, therefore, simple enough to establish. There are various ways in which such sceptical positions might be met, which follow the pattern discussed in Chapter I in terms of scepticism generally. For example, Holland's paper mentioned above includes a subtle defence of our memory criteria from the point of view of ordinary language philosophy; and a paper by J. O. Nelson,[28] which distinguishes between 'memory-statements' and 'past-tense grounds statements' which both express our beliefs about the past – the latter, however, being such that we are not prepared to admit the possibility of error in them – is reminiscent of Malcolm's discussion of what he claimed to be the two senses of 'know'. The merits of such approaches having been explored in Chapter I we can simply restate here our general solution to scepticism of a Cartesian or Humean form.

The first move is to point out the devastating consequences of accepting Cartesian scepticism and adopting only criteria of certainty which are logically conclusive (given, that is, that no criteria are available which are guaranteed by God's goodness). So much of what we now call knowledge will be lost to us, for by far the greatest part of our knowledge is memory knowledge acquired in the past and since retained. We would lose also that memory knowledge which constitutes our episodic memories, our knowledge of our past experiences, intentions, expectations and so on.[29] Finally, in so far as our knowledge of the past in general is closely tied up with memory knowledge, that would have to go as well. It follows that we must adopt some criteria which are logically inconclusive, and the next step is to insist that the ones which we have now have not simply sprung from nowhere, but represent a refined and evolved set of criteria which have shown their merits. This move obviously falls foul of the Humean sceptic's criticism of the circularity involved in arguing from past successes, so finally we have to insist that these criteria do at least have the merit of not failing in their own terms. We do claim to remember (using standard criteria) that the standard criteria have been relatively successful – as far as we could tell using our general knowledge criteria including these standard memory criteria themselves. If things seemed to us to have been otherwise, that would have been reason to adopt a different way of deciding what constituted memory knowledge. As it is, there is clearly no need to do so.

Are Perception and Memory Necessarily Reliable?

Our general solution of Cartesian and Humean scepticism would be redundant if it could be shown that the basic assumption of both forms of scepticism – that the connection between the satisfaction of our standard memory criteria and the reality of the memories themselves is a contingent one – was an assumption that could be rejected. We have argued ourselves in Chapter I, in general terms, that our knowledge criteria are not such that their satisfaction logically entails knowledge, but there is no need for that thesis to come into question here. Our solution of the sceptical problem would be redundant if it could be shown that it was not a contingent matter that the satisfaction of the relevant memory criteria is *in general* associated with the reality of the memories themselves.

In other words, if it could be shown that our memory criteria are *necessarily* reliable in leading to truth *for the most part*, no such considerations as we have adduced are needed to answer the sceptic. Of course, the sceptic might even then try to point out that the *general* reliability of our criteria does not allow us to say with absolute certainty, of any *individual* ostensible memory which met those criteria, that it was indeed a memory, but a simple answer to this lies readily at hand. If the general reliability of memory criteria is a necessary truth, we are warranted in using those criteria, and the criteria themselves precisely permit us to say with absolute certainty that individual ostensible memories are indeed memories.

We shall look, therefore, at an attempt by S. Shoemaker to defend such a thesis in relation to both memory beliefs and perceptual beliefs. Shoemaker's thesis[30] is not offered in precisely our terms, for he does not talk of the criteria of memory and perceptual knowledge, but in as much as his interest is in 'the sincere and confidently asserted perceptual and memory statements' his discussion is of close relevance to our theme. If anything, the class of statements which his thesis covers would be somewhat wider than the class of ostensible memory and perceptual beliefs which have been found to satisfy the relevant criteria for knowledge, so a proof of the general truth of his class might be expected to carry over to our own.

In his own words, Shoemaker wants to argue 'that it is a necessary (logical or conceptual) truth, not a contingent one, that when perceptual and memory statements are sincerely and confidently asserted, i.e. express confident beliefs, they are generally true';[31] and he makes clear that the expression 'perceptual and memory statements' is not restricted in his application of it to statements that actually *say* that the speaker perceives or remembers something, but includes statements that are 'directly based on observation or memory, i.e. are putative reports of what the speaker perceives or remembers'.

His first argument to show that such statements are, necessarily, generally true is the following:

> A primary criterion for determining whether a person understands the meaning of such terms as 'see' and 'remember' is whether under optimum conditions the confident claims that he makes by the use of these words are generally true. If most of a person's apparent perceptual and memory claims turned out to be false, this would show, not that the person had exceptionally poor eyesight or an exceptionally bad memory, but that he did not understand, had not correctly grasped, the meanings of the words he was uttering, or was not using them with their established meanings, i.e., was not using them to express the perceptual and memory claims they appear to express.[32]

To provide support for this argument, Shoemaker asks us to consider a newly discovered tribe whose language we are trying to translate. Suppose someone proposes translating a certain class of statements as perceptual statements and another class as memory statements. Suppose further that these statements are most commonly uttered, confidently and assertively, in circumstances in which their proposed translations would be false:

For example, the expression translated by the English sentence 'I see a tree' is commonly uttered, confidently and assertively, when the speaker's eyes are not open or not directed towards a tree, and the expression translated by the English sentence 'I ate meat last night' is frequently uttered by vegetarians but seldom by anyone who did eat meat on the previous evening.[33]

Now in such circumstances, argues Shoemaker, what we would do is reject the proposed translations, rather than believe these people to be involved in such widespread mistakes:

Anything that might seem to show that the confident and sincere perceptual and memory statements that people make are generally false would in fact show that we are mistaken in regarding certain utterances as expressing certain perceptual and memory claims.[34]

Shoemaker's claim about the criterion for whether someone understands the term 'see' or 'remember' does not seem correct. It would appear to imply that someone who, for whatever reason, comes to make what are generally false memory or perceptual claims is no longer in possession of the relevant concepts. Someone, for example, who through senile decay comes to make wildly inaccurate claims about his experiences or, suffering from a disorder affecting his senses, makes wholly inaccurate claims about his environment would be said to have lost an understanding of 'remember' or 'see'. This does not appear at all plausible, just as it does not seem plausible to say that a deterioration in one's memory or sight involves a gradual loss of this understanding. Perhaps in reply, Shoemaker could argue that in such cases we are not dealing with 'optimum conditions', for which the above criterion for the possession of these concepts is appropriate; and perhaps in these circumstances the person would be unlikely to make confident and sincere claims about what he remembers and what he perceives. The possibility must be allowed, nevertheless, for such cases to arise; and for this defence of the criterion to be successful the notion of 'optimum conditions' must be understood to mean something other than 'conditions in which a person's claims are generally correct' on pain of reducing Shoemaker's thesis to a tautology.

If we applied Shoemaker's criterion to the terms 'expect' or 'foresee', however, its implausibility should be even more apparent. We make 'sincere and confident' claims about the future, which express our expectations in the way in which memory claims express our beliefs about (*inter alia*) the past, and these take the form sometimes of 'I expect (or foresee) that P' and sometimes simply report what we expect (or foresee). Now Shoemaker's criterion demands that someone who understands what 'expect' or 'foresee' means, that is someone who has the concept of expectation or foresight, must make claims about the future which are generally true. However, it would clearly be possible for someone to be mistaken in all such claims, if some catastrophic event were to bring the world (or even his world) to an end, and yet we would not take such an event to indicate that he had no concept of expectation or foresight.

The force of Shoemaker's example of the tribe has been disputed by Don Locke, who contrasts the case of a purported translation of certain statements as statements about spirits and demons. Shoemaker's example would seem to imply that we could not accept this translation as correct, and at the same time believe all such statements about spirits and demons to be false.[35] We do, on the contrary, allow superstitious tribes to have their false beliefs. Because of some major mistake over that fact, it is possible for such beliefs to be one and all mistaken. If this holds in the case of the superstitious tribes, why could it not hold also in the case of our own memory judgements if (as Russell thought was at least possible) the world had only come into existence five minutes ago, or Descartes' evil demon was misleading us in our perceptions of the world?

Shoemaker has a second argument of a different kind.[36] This begins with the claim that one cannot question one's *own* confident perceptual and memory beliefs:

> It is precisely one's confident beliefs, and especially one's confident perceptual and memory beliefs, that one expresses by saying 'I know . . .'; it is not a psychological fact, but rather a logical fact, that one cannot help regarding one's confident perceptual and memory beliefs as constituting knowledge.[37]

One has to concede that one's *own* confident perceptual and memory beliefs are generally true. Moreover, one must concede that every other person would have an equal right to claim that *his* confident perceptual and memory beliefs are generally true, for the same argument holds for each person. Finally, if it is necessarily true (it makes no sense to deny) of each and every person that his confident perceptual and memory beliefs are generally true, it is necessarily true of confident perceptual and memory beliefs in general that they are generally true.

The logical flaw in this argument is the move from the 'logical fact' about what makes sense in one's own case to the need to recognise the truth of someone else's claim concerning his own confident beliefs. Of course, one recognises that the other person cannot question his own confident beliefs, but this is not the same as accepting them as true, or even generally true. What one cannot do, according to Shoemaker, in one's own case, one can clearly do in someone else's. But the 'logical fact' used as a premiss does not seem to be true either. Assuming one can question the general truth of other people's confident memory and perceptual claims, and recognising the important point that one's own perceptual and memory beliefs rest heavily on those of other people, it seems one can intelligibly raise doubts about one's own confident beliefs.

Of course, in so far as these beliefs remain confident the doubts will be of a 'theoretical' kind; if one came to doubt others in a practical way, one would have to lose confidence in one's own beliefs and hold them much more tentatively. But a theoretical doubt lies easily at hand: one can recognise, without this having any implication at all for one's own beliefs, that the criteria in accordance with which perceptual and memory judgements are judged to constitute perceptual and memory knowledge are not such as to guarantee logically that this is so. And without begging the question at issue, Shoemaker cannot argue that there is at least a guarantee that these criteria ensure truth for the most part. The necessity of the general reliability of memory and perception has therefore not been established, no more by this second argument of Shoemaker's than by the first, and a reply to scepticism along the lines we have ourselves developed is far from redundant.

The Concept of the Past

Memory knowledge is a particular kind of knowledge of the past. It is, in one of its forms, a knowledge of some events which occurred in the life history of the person who remembers. Some events, perhaps a majority of them, from my past history are known to me only from the testimony of others – that I was born on a certain day and in a certain place, for example. But any events that I do remember must (logically) be events from my past history. But how do we come by the concept of the past? We must have such a concept in order to make sense of the concept of memory. I cannot meaningfully say that I recall a certain event if I do not already possess a concept of the past. Yet it is not obvious how we acquire such a concept.

According to the empiricist tradition, we acquire concepts in the ordinary way by experiencing instances of the thing or quality in question. I acquire the concept *red* by meeting instances of red things. If I were blind from birth, I could never come by the standard concept *red* (though no doubt I could get some imperfect substitute in terms of other sensory images). But the concept *past* seems to present an obvious difficulty for such a tradition. I never directly experience anything that is past, any more than I directly experience anything that is still in the future. Once an event is past, it is beyond the range of direct experience. Nor does it seem to make sense to say that I acquire the concept of the past from memory because memory knowledge is knowledge of past events. As we have seen, unless I already had some notion, however vague, of what it means to be past, I could not even understand what it is to remember. We seem to be faced here with a dilemma: either the concept of the past is an exception to the standard type of concepts which we derive from experience or there must be something unobvious in our experience which generates the concept.

Some philosophers have grasped the first horn of his dilemma by claiming that temporal concepts (past, present and future) are given to us as a precondition of sense experience rather than acquired from such experience, giving up therefore the empiricist approach. Immanuel Kant held a theory of this sort though he did not use the term 'concept' in this context.[38] Such theories are usually associated with elaborate metaphysical systems, as in

Kant's case, and they cannot be usefully discussed outside the context of the theories in question. However, they do raise all the difficulties of theories of so-called 'innate ideas' to which rationalist philosophers were driven by the apparent difficulty of accounting for the existence of indubitable concepts whose origins in experience were hard to explain. If we can find a plausible foundation in experience for these concepts, it will not be necessary to retreat to the 'asylum of ignorance' offered by the hypothesis that such ideas are presupposed by experience rather than discovered in it.

Some philosophers have claimed that pastness is, in Samuel Alexander's words 'a datum of experience, directly apprehended'.[39] But unless it is possible to offer some evidence for this proposition other than that we do 'directly apprehend' our memories, the statement is not illuminating. It amounts to no more than to say that our memories appear to us to be information from the past. But this is a definition of memory rather than an explication of it. It is true that there is a sense in which past events may be said to exist still even though they are past. If they did not, it would be hard to distinguish between true and false statements about the past. For example: 'Julius Caesar was assassinated', 'Julius Caesar died in his bed'. That the first is true and the second false has to be attributed, in some degree, to the reality of the past. But the point at issue here is not the reality of the past, but our present access to it. How do we acquire our concept of pastness without experiencing past events *as past*?

Broad, recognising the force of this question, makes a distinction between empirical concepts like *red* or *sweet* and what he calls 'categorial' concepts such as *pastness* and *cause*. Instances of this second type of concept occur in experience without being completely suggested by experience. The contents of our memories, according to Broad, are neither past nor seem to be so. But they do have a special characteristic which Broad, like Russell, calls 'familiarity'. And it is a psychological fact about human beings that when they encounter this characteristic 'we inevitably apply the concept of pastness'. 'Familiarity is an empirical characteristic and pastness is a categorial characteristic; but the former "means" the latter to such beings as we are.'[40] But this seems a desperate way of evading the conclusion that pastness is an empirical property. For what could 'familiar' mean except something like 'recognised because of past acquaintance'? In other words, it is hardly possible to assign a meaning to the word 'familiar' which does not involve the notion of pastness.

A more plausible explanation of the origin of the concept of the past attributes it to a directly empirical source – our experience of the passing of time. A passage from William James' *Principles of Psychology* makes the point well. 'The practically cognised present is no knife-edge but a saddle-back with a certain breadth of its own on which we sit perched and from where we look in two directions in time.'[41] This 'saddle-back' of experience, to which a contemporary of James had given the name 'the specious present', presented a challenge to early experimental psychologists who tried, without much success, to measure its duration. (The experimental difficulties were formidable, and it seems that their experiments may have measured sensory acuity rather than the duration of the specious present.) However, there can be no real doubt that the units of our experience of time are not instantaneous moments but short bits of awareness which fade gradually into the past. Indeed, if this were not so, pains and pleasures would not be pains and pleasures at all. No one would mind an instantaneous pain, however acute. Pains are distressful only because they have some *felt duration* in our present consciousness, and not because they are remembered as having been unpleasant. Were they instantaneous, they would not be so remembered. So too with other sensory modalities; we actually see movement and hear musical phrases within the specious present. And it is a feature of the specious present that it is experienced as dying away into the past, and that within its short duration, we experience events as occurring before and after. In this way we are able to acquire an empirically-based concept of the past and, indeed, of the future as well.

Conclusion

In discussing Reid's criticism of Hume, we made a distinction between two types of memory, episodic memory of incidents in the rememberer's own past and the biological residue of experience embodied in our familiar concepts, native language and habits of adjustment to the physical and social world. And although we may start, as we did, by contrasting specific episodic memories with habit memories embodying skills rather than information, it is not difficult to realise that all memories, of whatever type, originate in personal experiences of an episodic kind. Our memories, whether of personal experiences, propositions, concepts, habits of every type, can be arranged in a kind of spectrum starting with individual experiences and ending with an accumulated compost of experiences stripped of their individuating properties and their wealth of perceptual detail. This residue of all we have learned is, indeed, hardly recognised as memory at all. But reflection makes clear that it is indeed just the sediment of what we have learned at some time and exists only in virtue of being remembered.

The glossary of a well-known textbook of psychology defines 'memory' thus: 'technically, retention of any learning; used popularly to refer only to what the human subject can recall or report'.[42] And it is to what the individual can recall or report that philosophers interested in memory have devoted nearly all their attention. That I can recall perceptual details of the 1969 Cup Final is a standard case of memory for philosophers; that I remember that 361 is the square of 19 is not held to be so philosophically interesting. And that I can speak English, or swim, or serve at tennis seems not to be a problem for philosophy. Yet all are instances of memory. They differ chiefly in retaining or in lacking the specific perceptual detail that accompanied their original imprinting. Why one end of the memory spectrum has engaged the attention of most of the philosophers who have written on the theory of knowledge is itself an interesting question. It would, in any case, make for a more uniform treatment of the philosophical problems of memory if they were dealt with as special cases of the problem of belief. And this, indeed, they are.

CHAPTER VI

A PRIORI KNOWLEDGE

Knowing Without Experience

The term *a priori* is applied in philosophical discussions to know-ledge, to propositions, and to concepts. It, and its contrary *a posteriori*, have had a long history – their literal meaning is 'from what is prior' and 'from what is posterior' respectively – and they had a common usage in Scholastic philosophy. Their contem-porary meaning was given by explicit definition by Kant in the Introduction to *The Critique of Pure Reason*, along with those of certain closely associated terms which we shall dicuss later, although the ideas involved were current under one name or another in the writings of the Rationalists and Empiricists of the seventeenth and eighteenth centuries.

A proposition is said to be *a priori* if its truth can be established by means independent of empirical investigation or observation. We can know, in this way, the truth of the proposition 'All bachelors are unmarried', since all we need to know is the mean-ings of the terms involved. We cannot know *a priori*, for example, that 'All copper conducts electricity', or that 'This table is brown' – or even that we have some mental state such as fear or pain, for it is usual to exclude self-observation from *a priori* knowledge. A subtle point should be noticed, however. Many philosophers would admit that *a priori* propositions, or at least some of them, might be established empirically, as, for example, someone who was unaware of the normal connotation of the word 'bachelor' might (presuming some method of identifying bachelors which leaves the question open) discover that bachelors are one and all unmarried. We have called propositions *a priori*, however, if they can be established independently of experience and this does not rule out such empirical verifications.[1] When the term is applied directly to knowledge it does not have this subtle complication: to call someone's knowledge *a priori* is to say that he knows what he knows independently of experience.

Agreement on the use of philosophical terms, nevertheless, hardly guarantees agreement on the question of their scope of application, and the basic controversy between rationalists and empiricists is over the extent of *a priori* knowledge. Rationalists believe it possible to attain a substantial body of knowledge about the world independently of experience, empiricists, that no such knowledge of the world can be so achieved. The impressive but conflicting metaphysical systems of Descartes, Spinoza and Leibniz, erected by 'reason unaided by the senses' have therefore no real counterparts in the works of empiricists like Locke and Hume. Locke did, admittedly, break the empiricist rule by holding that we can attain some *a priori* knowledge of the world in that we can have what he called a 'demonstrative knowledge' of God's existence and, on the basis of that, a demonstrative knowledge of morals. He did, indeed, think we had *a priori* knowledge of even wider scope, but it is fair to say that the rest of his *a priori* propositions, being concerned with the various relations between our ideas such as identity, difference and inclusion, have generally been thought by empiricists to be unproblematic in having no real import about the structure of the world as such. These philosophers have recognised *a priori* knowledge of the truths of mathematics (including geometry as well as arithmetic) and the truths of logic (e.g. 'Whatever is, is' and 'If P is true then not-P is false'). They have recognised also what might be called 'the truths of language' (such as our example above that 'All bachelors are unmarried') which reflect the way in which we use words.

Some Distinctions

It is convenient to begin our account of the major theories of *a priori* knowledge of propositions with Kant's discussion, in the Introduction to his *Critique of Pure Reason*, of the notions of *a priori* and 'analytic'.

There are, Kant claims, two marks of the *a priori*. The first is that of *necessity*: from experience we can learn that a thing is so-and-so, but not that it *must* be as it is. 'If we have a proposition which in being thought is thought as *necessary*, it is an *a priori* judgement.'[2] An example (one of Kant's own) might be that we can learn from experience that events have causes, but not that every event *must* have a cause. Secondly, and much more questionably, Kant claims that *a priori* judgements are characterised by a special kind of *universality*, a 'strict universality' which is not found in the judgement 'All bodies are heavy' but is found in the *a priori* judgement 'Every event must have a cause'. He does believe these two characteristics to be independent, in that we might more easily establish one than the other in any given case: we must take it, therefore, that 'strict universality' cannot be equated with necessity, and regret the absence of further explanation.

Kant then goes on to draw his second distinction between 'analytic' and 'synthetic' judgements.[3] We shall, for the moment, merely register his thesis. When a judgement is made affirming of a subject A some predicate B – when we judge, for example, 'All bodies are extended' – the predicate, Kant claims, is sometimes 'contained in this concept A', and otherwise 'lies outside it'. In the first case we are adding nothing to the concept of the subject A 'but merely breaking it up into those constituent concepts that have all along been thought in it', and such a judgement is 'analytic' or 'explicative'. In the second case, the judgement is indeed adding something new to the concept of A, and is called 'synthetic' or 'ampliative'. Kant's example of an analytic judgement is 'All bodies are extended', of a synthetic judgement 'All bodies are heavy'. Apart from this method of introducing the present distinction, Kant does in fact hint at a second method: an analytic proposition is such that its truth can be discerned from the concepts involved 'by the principle of contradiction'.[4]

The distinction between analytic and synthetic judgements is not, except for this last comment, made by means of epistemological notions. It is, in other words, not the same kind of distinction as that between *a priori* and empirical. It concerns, instead, the *form* of the proposition or judgement, and might be said to be a logical rather than an epistemological one. It is not at all obvious that the two distinctions are coextensive – nor does Kant claim them to be.

It is interesting to see how Kant's predecessors marked off what they took to be important divisions in our knowledge. We shall look at the contributions of Locke, Leibniz and Hume.

Locke recognised two distinctions, which paralleled Kant's.

We have, he thought, 'sensitive knowledge' of the existence of substances in the physical world and of the coexistence of the perceptible properties of those substances; and, on the other side, 'intuitive knowledge' and 'demonstrative knowledge' of various 'relations of ideas'.[5] Examples of these latter *a priori* cases of knowledge would be that red is not green, or that 3 is more than 2, for the intuitive cases, and such demonstrative propositions as that the sum of the three angles of a triangle are equal to two right angles. But Locke also thought we had intuitive knowledge of existence (namely of our *own* existence) and demonstrative knowledge of existence as well (namely of God's); and, what is more, a demonstrative knowledge of moral truths. Indeed Locke was quite clear that his *a priori* versus sensitive distinction failed to coincide with a second, one which looks very like Kant's analytic-synthetic distinction.[6] Some propositions are 'trifling' or 'merely verbal', he claimed, as opposed to being 'informative'. These trifling cases include (i) all purely identical propositions, such as (the most general case) 'What is, is', and 'Whatever is red, is red'; and (ii) all propositions 'wherein a part of the complex idea which any term stands for is predicated of that term', such as 'Gold is a metal'. Not all intuitive or demonstrative knowledge is of this trifling kind, as is witnessed by the examples of God's existence and moral rules.

Leibniz and Hume, on the other hand, can be seen to run together distinctions which Kant and Locke were at pains to keep apart. Leibniz recognised a metaphysical distinction, in the first place, between the contingent truths which hold of this world but not of all possible worlds, and necessary truths which are true in all possible worlds.[7] Now truths of *both* classes are all such that the concept of the predicate is contained in the concept of the subject (though he did not use the term, they are all 'analytic' in Kant's sense); so it is possible, by analysing the subject concept, to come to see that any truth expresses an identity.[8] However, the great difference between these two classes is that, with contingent truths, this analysis is an infinite process, which can only be completed by God, and then only in terms of the principle of perfection which states that this world is the best of all possible worlds. The human mind can know contingent truths only by experience, so contingent truths of fact are *a posteriori*. Necessary truths, on the other hand, can be shown by a finite number of steps to be such that the predicate concept is contained in the subject concept. Necessary truths, therefore, are knowable *a priori*: indeed, they are knowable by *reasoning*.

Hume even more clearly insisted on the overlap between a logical division of propositions and the epistemological one between *a priori* and empirical. For Hume divided all propositions into those expressing 'matters of fact or real existence' and those expressing 'relations of ideas'[9], where the former are knowable only through the use of the senses and the latter are knowable *a priori*. Hume's distinction between propositions is very similar to that of Leibniz, between truths of fact and truths of reasoning, and hence is comparable to Kant's analytic-synthetic division. Relations of ideas hold in virtue of the nature of the ideas themselves: for example, ' 'Tis from the idea of a triangle, that we discover the relation of equality, which its three angles bear to two right angles; and this relation is invariable, as long as our idea remains the same.'[10] Unlike Locke, Hume takes such relations to be deniable only on pain of contradiction. What is more, the very distinction of matters of fact and relations of ideas is made in terms of the epistemological division, and, being what is standardly called 'Hume's fork', constitutes an important forerunner of the logical positivists' Verification Principle. In Kant's terminology, that Principle states that all propositions are either *a priori* and analytic, or empirical and synthetic.

Theories of the *A Priori*

What should we demand of a theory of the *a priori*? Two questions, in particular, should be settled by any adequate theory of this kind of knowledge: first, the theory should explain the nature of necessity which (as Kant insisted) is the mark of *a priori* propositions; and, secondly, it should explain how we can recognise necessity, that is, how we can know that some sentence expresses a necessary truth. It is not too difficult to establish that the major theories in this field fail on one or both of these counts, and it is not unreasonable to suspect that the explanation may lie in the diversity of those propositions which fall into the class of the *a priori*. We have suggested ourselves that this class includes truths of language (such as 'All bachelors are unmarried'), truths of mathematics, and truths of logic. Perhaps a different account should be provided for these different sub-classes of the *a priori*.

The innateness theory

Many philosophers have been attracted to what in some ways is the simplest theory of *a priori* knowledge, the innateness theory. Locke, its most famous critic, reported that it was (in the seventeenth century) 'an established opinion amongst many men that there are in the understanding certain innate principles, some primary notions, . . . characters, as it were, stamped upon the mind of man, which the soul receives in its very first being and brings into the world with it.'[11] Locke took it upon himself to establish that, on the contrary, the mind is a *tabula rasa* at birth and comes upon the knowledge of whatever sort it has only during its existence in this world.

Locke was directing his arguments, in particular, against the innateness theory in two of its manifestations: it was commonly believed that demonstrative argument depended on the presence in the mind of certain abstract innate principles such as 'Whatever is, is' and 'It is impossible for the same thing to be and not to be'; and it was frequently asserted that man's knowledge of moral principles was an example of such knowledge stamped on the mind 'in its very first being'. The innateness theory was, however, widely adopted by philosophers of the rationalist persuasion, as an attractive explanation of our supposed knowledge *a priori* of substantial truths about the world. Descartes and Leibniz, for example, held that certain ideas were innately possessed, and truths utilising such ideas were available to the 'natural light of reason' as written into the mind itself. Plato argued, similarly, that our knowledge of the Forms predates the soul's existence in this world and that our knowledge of truths concerning the Forms, in so far as we appear to come to it in this world, is no more than our recollecting in a conscious manner something we have possessed all along.[12]

Apart from offering an alternative explanation of *a priori* knowledge, Locke provides arguments against innateness which are incontrovertible. The theory is supported by the consideration that the propositions treated of are given universal consent among mankind, and Locke's reply is twofold. In the first place he points out that universal consent would fall short of proving innateness, for other explanations might be forthcoming. In the second place he can provide sufficient cases of people who fail to give these propositions their assent; for children and idiots 'have not the least apprehension or thought' of principles such as 'Whatever is, is', and there are and have been many people who have failed to give assent to the moral principles which we recognise. A revision of the argument to the claim that these principles gain universal consent when people acquire the use of reason, is as easily met: 'a great part of illiterate people and savages pass many years, even of their rational age, without ever thinking on this, and the like general propositions'. A second revision, to the claim that these principles are assented to as soon as proposed and understood, hardly provides proof of innateness unless propositions such as 'All bachelors are unmarried' (which contains undeniably non-innate ideas) are also innate. A final revision, to the claim that the principles are *implicitly* known, really means the collapse of the theory altogether, for what can that mean except that the mind is *capable* of affirming them when proposed and understood, and how can that prove any proposition innate?

We can add to Locke's arguments the following considerations. The innateness theory was seldom introduced to account for all *a priori* knowledge, only for a sub-class of the propositions which are known *a priori*, and so would at best provide only a partial answer to the overall problem. It does not even do that, however, for it hardly explains *how* we know the innate propositions in the first place, offering only the explanation that we know them now because we knew them before. And, of course, it offers no account whatsoever of the nature of necessity itself. On all these counts we should look for another theory.

The traditional theory

The approach first followed by Aristotle in his discussion of our knowledge of essences has been adopted by many, even through to the twentieth century. Aristotle thought that we had the ability to know, by an act of intuitive apprehension, the relation between two or more properties.[13] For example, we could apprehend the connection between being human and being rational, so that we have intuitive apprehension of the essence of humanity. With a change of terminology but arguably in the same tradition,

Descartes wrote of our ability to recognise the relations between ideas by 'the natural light of reason': we could know thereby, for example, that seven is greater than five, as well as such complex propositions as the law of non-contradiction and that 'the cause is as real as the effect'. Locke favoured this account as a reasonable alternative to the innateness theory. Knowledge is nothing other than 'the perception of the connexion and agreement, or disagreement and repugnancy, of any of our ideas,' he wrote. 'When we possess ourselves with the utmost security of the demonstration that the three angles of a triangle are equal to two right angles, what do we more but perceive that equality to two right ones does necessarily agree to and is inseparable from the three angles of a triangle?'[14] And Russell, writing in 1912, explained our *a priori* knowledge as the preception of relations between universals: the proposition 'Two and two are four' states, he wrote, 'a relation between the universal two and the universal four'.[15]

This approach to *a priori* knowledge, venerable and simple though it is, quite obviously fails on both the criteria we introduced above. It cannot be said to have provided any account of the nature of necessity itself, offering only talk of the relations between propositions, ideas, or universals; nor can it be said to have provided an account of our knowledge of such relations, for it does no more than describe this knowledge in metaphorical terms. What explanatory value can 'the light of reason' have, or talk of perceiving relations between ideas or universals?

The Leibnizian account

We saw earlier how Leibniz distinguished truths of reason from truths of fact, in that they are reducible by a finite number of steps to explicit identity statements; and we saw how Kant suggested, as one account of analyticity, that analytic judgements are of this nature. This approach to *a priori* knowledge was adopted in the nineteenth century by Frege, who was particularly intent on establishing his 'logicist thesis' that arithmetical truths are reducible, by the use of definitions and logical transformations, to the laws of logic.[16] More recently, such an account was adopted by Waismann, and by other logical positivists, as an account of the class of analytic statements which they took to be co-extensive with that of *a priori* statements. According to Waismann, analytic statements are reducible to logical truisms when synonymous expressions are replaced for terms in the original statement: for example, the analytic statement 'All bachelors are unmarried' becomes an instance of the logical truth 'All things which are A and B, are A' when 'bachelors' is replaced by 'unmarried men'.

In terms of our two criteria, however, this approach must also be found wanting. Leibniz indeed thought of necessary truths as those propositions which are true in all possible worlds, and though this has by some been thought illuminating, the term 'possible world' can hardly be explained independently of the term 'necessary truth' – the philosophical problem is, of course, to explain modality generally, whether it be necessity or possibility. It is clear, that in so far as an account of the necessity of reducible truths is given in terms of the notion of a logical truth, no general account of necessity has been provided by Leibniz's approach. Nor, obviously, has a general account of our knowledge of necessity been given, for the question remains how we can recognise the necessary truth of the laws of logic and of the logical rules of transformation which allow us to proceed with the reduction of reducible truths.

We should not conclude, however, that this approach has no value in explaining any of our *a priori* knowledge, for it is plausible to suggest that it provides a partial account at least of the truths of language and of mathematics. Frege's logicist programme, which was pursued further by Russell and Whitehead in their monumental *Principia Mathematica*, cannot be said to have been wholly and obviously successful, but the programme has at least shown how much (both logical and arithmetical) can be reduced to intuitively plausible premises of a simple kind. Undeniably, too, the truths of language depend on the meaning we give to our words, and frequently identity of meaning or synonymy is for us an acceptable explanation of our *a priori* knowledge.

The conventionalist account

Logical positivists standardly combined the Leibnizian account with a conventionalist theory of necessity, as for example in the case of truths of language. 'All bachelors are unmarried' depends for its truth on the linguistic convention whereby 'bachelor' means the same as 'unmarried man'. But the conventionalist approach was supposed by these philosophers to explain the necessity of all *a priori* truths, even those of logic. 'In saying that the certainty of *a priori* propositions depends on the fact that they are tautologies,' wrote Ayer, 'I use the word "tautology" in such a way that a proposition can be said to be a tautology if it is analytic; and I hold that a proposition is analytic if it is true solely in virtue of the meaning of its constituent symbols.'[18] Truth of logic, just as much as truths of language and mathematics, they supposed to be tautologies in that sense: 'If one knows what is the function of the words "either", "or", and "not", then one can see that any proposition of the form "Either p is true or p is not true" is valid, independently of experience. Accordingly, all such propositions are analytic.'[19]

Ayer, in particular, was careful to state this theory in a way that avoided some obvious objections. It seemed that the theory, in effect, equated *a priori* propositions with empirical propositions about the way in which symbols are used, and it is clearly not the case that 'All bachelors are unmarried' means the same as 'The word "bachelor" is used in such a way that it is equivalent to the phrase "unmarried man"'. Ayer insisted that his version of the theory claimed only that the validity of *a priori* propositions depended on certain facts about verbal usage, not that such propositions were equivalent to empirical propositions about usage.[20] He was careful to deny, what is more, that they were themselves linguistic *rules*: 'for apart from the fact that they can properly be said to be true, which linguistic rules cannot, they are distinguished also by being necessary, whereas linguistic rules are arbitrary'. He added, however, that 'if they are necessary it is only because the relevant linguistic rules are presupposed'.[21]

Conventionalism was in fact adopted by Wittgenstein in his *Tractatus Logico-Philosophicus*, in explanation of the necessity of logical truths, and that text was a major influence on the positivists. According to the *Tractatus*, logical truths are one and all 'tautologies', meaning in this case that they are true under all consistent assignments of truth value to the propositions which appear as their constituents. For example, the proposition 'If P or Q and not-P, then Q' is true no matter which propositions are substituted for P and Q, as long as one proposition is substituted for P throughout, and another for Q throughout. Moreover, Wittgenstein argued that tautologies were true because of the definitions which we have given to the 'logical constants' such as 'or', 'and', and 'if . . . then'; he showed how definitions in terms of 'truth tables' of these constants leads to the tautologous nature of all truths which are expressible in logic of the lowest order. This *Tractatus* theory had two undeniable advantages. First, it offered a clear account of what Leibniz called truth 'in all possible words': logical truths are true under all possible assignments of truth values. Secondly, in providing a decision procedure whereby we can easily show the tautologous nature of a logical truth, it provided an account of how we could know some propositions *a priori*. Its success was, however, limited; for though Wittgenstein thought he had solved completely the nature of logical (and indeed of all) necessity, it is clear that only logical truths of the simplest order are truth-functionally tautologous, and even the necessity of such a truth as 'If all A's are B's, then no A's are not B's' cannot be captured by Wittgenstein's theory.

In his later writings, such as the *Philosophical Investigations*, Wittgenstein continued to hold some version of the conventionalist theory. Necessity he saw as a function of the use of words, a use which was only to be understood in terms of the context of our interaction with the world and with other people. When we have understood the 'language games' in which our words have a role, we can see how those uses can be abused so that nonsense occurs. We might see, for example, how 'This surface is red and green all over' cannot possibly convey any fact; and we would therefore see why 'Nothing is red and green all over at the same time' *must* be true. *see Kant's notion hr*

The ultimate inadequacy of the conventionalist theory can, perhaps, be most plausibly argued in terms of this very example from Wittgenstein. It is surely correct to notice that the way in which we use the words 'red' and 'green' plays an important role in the sentence 'Nothing is red and green all over at the same time' expressing a necessary truth. There seems, however, to be rather more involved in its truth than the use of words, something which has to be brought out in terms of the properties which those words are used to designate. The word 'red' designates one particular colour, 'green' another, and it is a fact about the nature of colour that green and red are mutually exclusive. Similarly it might be objected to Ayer's account that he has at best reminded us that the usage of words is *in part* responsible for the fact that *a priori* propositions express necessary truths: the validity of such propositions depends on the arbitrary conventions of language, but only in so far as these conventions dictate what truths are expressed by what words. Given the meaning of 'bachelor' and 'unmarried', it is true that 'All bachelors are unmarried' expresses a necessary truth, but the truth is not itself a consequence of meaning. The truth is a function of the nature of the properties concerned.

Such would be argued against conventionalism by a traditionalist, and perhaps the argument could be made stronger if some clear idea could be given of how relations between properties (such as bachelorhood and unmarriedness) might differ from and be logically prior to relations between words. It does appear, at least, that facts about experience underlie the way in which we do use words, and that is an avenue worth investigating. Concerning truths of language we must conclude that the conventionalist theory has not been shown to be wrong.

But it is pretty clearly at fault in its account of logical truths. It is an implication of both Ayer's and Wittgenstein's accounts (at least in the *Tractatus*) that the logical truths which are now recognised are a function of the conventions of language, and that we could well have adopted different definitions of such words as 'not', 'or' and 'and'. Take the most important example, the law of non-contradiction which holds that 'not both P and not-P can be true'. Is this necessity true just because of our linguistic conventions? The conventionalist would hold that we could adapt our usage of words in such a way that what it expresses would be false, and 'P' and 'not-P' could both be true together. That is clearly so, but it can be argued that the principle which the law of non-contradiction states would have, in one form or another, to be recognised and conformed to. A change of linguistic conventions would allow our present words to express something other than they now express, but whatever they expressed would only be possible at all because we accepted that restriction on our sentences. As Aristotle argued, the law of non-contradiction is a condition of thought and language, something which could only be denied at the expense of ending all thought and talk.[22] The sentence 'S' can only make a claim on the world because it rules out something as well; a belief that the world is so-and-so presupposes that the world is not some other way. A contradiction, however expressed, using whatever linguistic conventions, fails to make any claim whatsoever about the world.

Does this show that the law of non-contradiction is necessarily true? It shows that we must abide by the logical principle – that we do not, in a sense, have a *choice in the matter*. A conventionalist theory is therefore inadequate as an account of logical truth, at least for this particular truth. Whether other laws of logic could find the same defence against conventionalism is not so clear: it has been argued by Strawson that we do not, in fact, abide by the law of excluded middle ('Either P is true or not-P is true') in ordinary usage, but we cannot investigate this here.[23] What does seem clear though is that *a priori* truths are not all of one kind, and different accounts should be expected to prove adequate in different fields. Truths of language are probably adequately handled by a conventionalist account, though that breaks down as we have seen for truths of logic. Which account is most adequate for mathematical truths is still unresolved.

Scepticism and the *A Priori*

As we might have expected from our earlier discussion of scepticism generally, various kinds of sceptical stances have been taken in respect of *a priori* knowledge of propositions. Few philosophers have wanted to take a position of total scepticism here, except those who, for reasons to do with the general fallibility of the human mind, have wished to deny that any knowledge at all is possible. Mill, who was possibly unique in the scope of his empiricism, did treat arithmetical truths as generalisations from experience;[24] but it would be difficult to find even an empiricist who denied the possibility of any *a priori* knowledge at all. A general consideration can be offered, in any case, which establishes the total implausibility of such scepticism. We do possess concepts, or 'ideas' in the terminology of earlier philosophers, and their possession is inconceivable without the ability to recognise relationships between them. We could not, for instance, have the concept of red if we could not know that red and green exclude one another; we could not have the concept which we do have of bachelor, without knowing that bachelors are necessarily unmarried.

Assuming that we do have *a priori* knowledge, can we say

anything about its general structure? We should expect, from our earlier discussions, something like the division between basic and non-basic empirical propositions. Historically such a division has been assumed, for example by Hume in his distinction between intuitive and demonstrative knowledge. In arithmetic, for instance, we can recognise a difference in our knowledge of such 'primary truths' as '$1 + 1 = 2$' and '$1 \times 2 = 2 \times 1$', and such higher level truths as 'There are prime numbers greater than the fifteenth prime'. In logic, too, though the application must vary from system to system, the distinction between axiom and theorem has central importance; and no doubt some truths of language are more immediately decidable than the rest. Our previous section, nevertheless, should make us hesitate to expect too simple an application of the notion of basic *a priori* knowledge, and certainly not expect any simple account of everything falling under that head.

One interesting question which we cannot pursue, would be the extent to which our knowledge of basic *a priori* propositions involves certainty beyond all possible doubt: our discussion of the principle of non-contradiction provides a case for its inclusion in that category. If our basic propositions are known in that sense, and the steps by which we arrive at a non-basic one accord with truths known also in that way, then we might be said to know beyond all possible doubt that non-basic proposition also. In this connection Hume offered an interesting argument against *a priori* knowledge of a demonstrative kind, for though 'in all demonstrative sciences the rules are certain and infallible . . . when we apply them, our fallible and uncertain faculties are very apt to depart from them, and fall into error'.[25] A scepticism such as Hume's would be met, if at all, by the recognition that we have criteria in accordance with which we are frequently certain beyond all *reasonable* doubt that error has been eliminated.

The most influential kind of scepticism, however, is that definitive of the empiricist confrontation with rationalism. The empiricist countenances *a priori* knowledge of a limited kind, typically embracing truths of language, mathematics and logic; but, in Kantian terms, the empiricist refuses to countenance *a priori* knowledge of *synthetic* propositions. The rationalist, of course, makes use of just such *a priori* knowledge in building his metaphysical system. How might such a grand disagreement be adjudicated?

For a start, the rationalist has been shown by Locke to have no retreat into innate knowledge, either of ideas or of truths, and has not provided a clear alternative account of his *a priori* knowledge. But, by the same token, the empiricist cannot claim an adequate account has been provided from which his thesis can be demonstrably established. The best move open to him would seem to be to rest his case on the absence of any agreed knowledge criteria which allow us to go beyond such *a priori* truths as he sees fit to treat as analytic. The rationalist, for his part, can point to the claimed inadequacies of the very notion of analyticity itself[26] and indeed can question whether those truths which his opponent does embrace can be treated as analytic anyway. One proposition which was much discussed this century, as providing such a worry for the empiricist, was 'Nothing is both red and green all over at the same time': 'red' and 'green' are certainly not *defined* to be the negations of each other, so that proposition cannot be easily reduced to an instance of the law of non-contradiction. The empiricist's case could be amended by a readjustment in his understanding of analyticity, without perhaps departing much from the original Kantian idea. Not so easy for him is the law of non-contradiction itself, as we have already noted. Nor could he be content that he had limited the apparent exceptions to his thesis to such basic logical laws, for synthetic *a priori* propositions which are not logical laws seem easy to produce as counter-examples. What, for instance, of the propositions 'Something has happened' and 'Today is the first day of the rest of my life'?

A philosopher who saw his work as resolving the conflict between empiricism and rationalism was Kant, who in effect took a sceptical stance quite as radical as that of the empiricists. Like these philosophers, Kant insists that there can be no body of synthetic *a priori* propositions comprising a metaphysical account of reality. The concepts, such as cause and substance, which metaphysicians made so central in their theories are being misused when applied beyond the bounds of any possible sense experience. An attempt to so apply them can produce only contradiction, confusion and illusion.

But Kant's *Critique of Pure Reason* does allow a limited amount of synthetic *a priori* knowledge. They are, thinks Kant, certain propositions which make use of the metaphysician's favourite concepts but which assert no more than the conditions, or presuppositions, of objective experience. Two such propositions in effect proclaim the inevitable applicability in every objective experience of the concepts of cause and substance: 'All events have a cause' and 'In every change a substance persists'. In all experience of an objective world, these concepts of necessity find application. We can know *a priori*, therefore, the truth of such synthetic propositions. Yet Kant's theory is really an extreme sceptical stance, for he is certain that such propositions are not descriptive of reality 'as it is in itself'; we have synthetic *a priori* knowledge only of the conditions of experience, and such experience is only of the *appearance* of the world to us as sentient and thinking creatures. We can, in effect, have no *a priori* knowledge of *reality*.

Kant's thought is complex and obscurely stated, and we cannot do it justice here. Besides the twelve 'categories', or *a priori* concepts which have necessary application in experience, Kant thinks that space and time are dimensions in which we can invariably place our experienced world, but which cannot be applied to reality as such. His arguments are frequently general, as for example when he tries to derive the twelve categories from what he thinks are the twelve forms of judgement, though he does offer more specific arguments for chosen concepts. It is plain, however, from his writings that he is attempting to accommodate what he takes to be established and unshakeable science – Euclidean geometry, as descriptive of our spatial experience; and the deterministic picture of Newton's universe, as witnessed in the causal principle above. Regrettably, this represents one of the great weaknesses of Kant's work, since, in so far as such science has in fact been found wanting and superseded by later science, Kant's arguments can only be judged mistaken and misguided. In that respect his account of *a priori* knowledge must be rejected.

Nor can Kant be said to have provided any adequate account of the necessities which he takes the synthetic *a priori* propositions to express. Not only do these, on his theory, fail to describe reality as such, but apparently fail in the last analysis to express necessities at all. In what he was proud to call his 'Copernican Revolution', Kant was establishing the possibility of synthetic *a priori* knowledge only in so far as our experience reflected the concepts (and space and time, the 'forms of intuition') which *we* imposed on it *ourselves*. The so-called 'necessities', of cause and substance and so forth, simply reflected the constitution of the mind itself, and there is no reason Kant can provide as to why that constitution should be (or indeed remain) as it is. These necessities, then, rather than being true in all possible worlds, or even true in all possible experiences of worlds, are only true in all possible experiences of worlds by creatures with the same constitution as ours. Such necessities, if that is what they might still be called, are a far cry from the Leibnizian notion which has traditionally been taken as a mark of the *a priori*.

Critics of Analyticity

For empiricists, as we have seen, the class of *a priori* propositions is coextensive with that of analytic propositions, and any general assault on the notion of analyticity must therefore reflect on that of the *a priori* also. One such assault might be to suggest that the notion has not been clearly defined or explicated, and the implication would be that more work remains to be done. A more damaging criticism would argue that the supposed analytic-synthetic distinction, and consequently the *a priori*-empirical distinction, are purely illusory and all propositions are on a par with respect to their logical and epistemological status. A more plausible thesis, and one which has been forcibly argued by Quine, is that though distinctions do exist they are more distinctions of degree than of kind.

Kant's explicit definition of analyticity will clearly not suffice as a general account of the intended class. For one thing, talk of one concept being contained within another, or being already thought in thinking another concept, invites rather than meets the demand for clarification. Such metaphorical talk needs supplementation at the very least. For another thing, the definition given could at best apply to propositions of subject-predicate form, for only there could analyticity be a function of the subject and predicate concepts. What is more, Kant's definition related analyticity to the mental act of judgement, and what is really needed is a characterisation of the conditions under which a sentence can be said to express an analytic proposition.

Can Kant's definition be revised to something like Ayer's favoured version – namely, that a sentence expresses an analytic proposition when the truth of the proposition is a consequence of the meaning of the terms in the sentence? In other words, can analyticity be understood as truth in virtue of meaning? Many philosophers think not.[27]

Quine's criticisms of analyticity as developed in his paper 'Two Dogmas of Empiricism', are detailed and somewhat complex, but can be summarised as follows. The notion of analyticity is quite naturally associated by its proponents with that of synonymy, or sameness of meaning: Ayer's idea, applied to analytic propositions which are not themselves explicit logical truths (such as 'All bachelors are unmarried'), implies that such propositions are reducible to explicit logical truths by replacing synonyms for synonyms. The problem, therefore, Quine sees as that of giving an adequate account of synonymy.

Quine discusses attempts to provide such accounts, arguing forcibly that the only plausible versions lead immediately back to the very notion of analyticity itself which synonymy is supposed to explain. Such accounts would not, therefore, provide the desired illumination. He concludes that the commitment of empiricists to an analytic-synthetic division is purely dogmatic; and, he suggests, closely associated with a second dogma to the effect that the truth of statements in science is decided on an individual basis, with such statements 'facing the tribunal of experience' one at a time.

Quine's own positive proposals are that the analytic-synthetic distinction, as traditionally drawn, is an attempt to treat what is a difference of degree as a difference in kind. There is a gradation amongst our beliefs to do with the degree of willingness on our part to give them up in the light of experience forcing some change in the total body of beliefs. There is, however, no belief which is so well-entrenched that we would under no circumstances choose to dispose of it rather than others. In his own words:

> The totality of our so-called knowledge or beliefs, from the most casual matters of geography and history to the profoundest laws of atomic physics or even of pure mathematics and logic, is a man-made fabric which impinges on experience only along the edges . . . A conflict with experience at the periphery occasions readjustments in the interior.[28]

And, he insists, no statement is immune from revision:

Revision even of the logical law of the excluded middle has been proposed as a means of simplifying quantum mechanics . . . [But] highly theoretical statements of physics or logic or ontology . . . may be thought of as relatively centrally located within the total network, meaning merely that little preferential connection with any particular sense data obtrudes itself.[29]

Quine's position on these issues has been questioned in a number of ways. Grice and Strawson, for example, have argued persuasively[30] that the criteria which Quine expects an account of synonymy to fulfil are unfairly demanding, and that the association between Quine's two 'dogmas' is one which can easily be severed. It looks, indeed, quite likely that a number of strands in Quine's argument can be separated and assessed independently.

In particular, the second 'dogma' seems to many philosophers of science quite wrong, and Quine can be praised for his insistence on the organic nature of our belief systems. In so far as that dogma was based this century on the positivists' theory of meaning as the method of verifying a statement, Quine can be said to have brought out an unacceptable consequence of that theory too. He seems to be correct, also, in his thesis that we (as scientists, or as 'ordinary men in the street') have preferences for our more general and abstract beliefs when it comes to the need to readjust our systems. None of this, however, implies that *every* statement could be revised, that *every* belief is dispensible.

If it can be argued that some proposition is immune from revision, a need would thereby be established for a special class of propositions, which might then be taken to extend to the truths of language, mathematics and logic discussed in the chapter. And there is one proposition which, we have argued above, cannot be disposed of – the law of non-contradiction. This law provides a condition without which, we argued, it would be impossible to say, think, or believe anything whatsoever. Not only would a body of beliefs fail to be a *system* without it, it would not even be a body of *beliefs*. What is more, it would seem that Quine's general account of our system of beliefs presupposes that very law itself, for in its absence there could be no such thing as a *conflict* between the system and experience. The very notion of a 'recalcitrant experience' presupposes the law of non-contradiction.

CHAPTER VII

TRUTH

It is easy to see that the problem of truth is central to the theory of knowledge. The topics that we have considered so far all presuppose that we understand what we mean by 'truth' and 'true' and their negations. Knowledge is commonly understood as justified true belief, and beliefs themselves are valuable only if they are true. The force of the arguments for scepticism depends upon the difficulty of reaching true beliefs and of knowing that a particular belief is in fact true. Memories are valuable only to the extent that they preserve in some way truths about the past. So there is no difficulty in appreciating that the problem of truth is an important element in the problems about knowledge. But what is the problem of truth and why should truth present any problems at all?

After all, we use words like 'true' and 'false' in everyday discourse and have no difficulty in understanding them when they are used by others. We are all taught at our mother's knee to speak the truth and not tell lies. And how could children understand these moral maxims if they did not clearly appreciate the meanings of 'true' and 'false'? The answer is, of course, that there is a big difference between understanding a term well enough to use it in everyday discourse and understanding the concept for which the term stands. We have seen exactly the same distinction in the case of terms like 'knowledge', 'belief' and 'memory'.

But even in its everyday use, the word 'true' is not unambiguous. Statements can be true in different sorts of ways and it is necessary, before we look more closely at the concept of truth, to decide which of these sub-meanings we are going to attend to. Perhaps the simplest way of showing that the word 'truth' is ambiguous is to notice the different ways in which statements can be verified, that is, can be shown to be true. Consider the following examples:

(A)   There are alligators in Florida.
(B)   Smoking is a cause of cancer.
(C)   1913 is a prime number.
(D)   There are an infinite number of primes.
(E)   Abortion is morally wrong.

We try to verify these in very different ways (A) is a simple case of checking by observation. (B) is empirical, but needs very complex experimental investigation. (C) and (D) are proved by mathematical methods, though in different ways, and they are instances of statements which, if true, are true *a priori*. We have already seen some of the problems raised by *a priori* knowledge. (E) is the most controversial of all because there are no agreed and established ways of proving that types of human conduct are morally right or wrong. We shall confine our attention to examples of type (A), that is, to simple observational statements. As we shall see, they raise problems enough.

If we are to answer the question: 'What do we mean by the terms "truth" and "falsehood"?,' it is useful to have in mind some conditions which our answer has to fulfil. These conditions are really set by the nature of the concepts that we are trying to elucidate. (1) The account that we give must allow for the possibility of falsehood and error. (2) Truth and falsehood must be properties of something in a world of conscious beings since a world without consciousness would have no place for truth or error. Obvious candidates for the predicate 'true' and 'false' under this condition would be beliefs or their expressions in language. We can call such entities 'truth bearers'. (3) Such truth bearers must be true in virtue of their relation to something other than themselves and not simply in virtue of their own properties. We do not call a belief true on account of its apparent clarity or the certainty with which it is held but in virtue of its relation to something else. This 'something else' is usually thought of as *the facts*. (4) If a belief or a statement is true at a particular time, it is true once and for all. It cannot change its truth value in the course of time. This condition raises some questions about statements like 'It is raining' or 'I am hungry' which seems at first sight to have different truth values on different occasions.

These conditions are just attempts to clarify and make precise the concept that we are trying to analyse. The first three were first explicitly laid down by Russell in an early version of what is known as the 'Correspondence Theory' of truth.[1] All of them would be quite widely accepted as reasonable. It is the mark of any question that is precisely phrased that it has a clear range of possible answers. If this were not so, we would never know when a purported answer was relevant to the question. Conditions (1) to (4) enable us to know which answers to the question: 'What is truth?' are candidates for serious consideration and which are not.

We can, of course, get a rough answer to questions about the meanings of words by consulting a dictionary. The *Oxford English Dictionary* gives us as an important meaning of 'truth': 'conformity with fact; agreement with reality'. But this does not leave us much wiser. What is meant here by the words 'fact', 'reality', 'conformity', and 'agreement'? Their meanings are no more transparent than the meaning of the word 'truth' itself. But such definitions do suggest a rough approximation to an answer to the question: 'What is truth?' They suggest that truth is some kind of a relation between facts or reality or the world on the one hand, and truth bearers (beliefs, statements etc.) on the other. And this at least suggests a line of enquiry by raising three more specific questions: (1) What are facts? (2) What are truth bearers? (3) What is the relation of 'conformity' or 'agreement' between them?

Theories of Truth

Before we start to take the question further in this way, it must be said that in doing this, we are presuming that a particular theory of truth, the so-called Correspondence Theory, is the right one. But there have been two important rivals to the Correspondence Theory in the earlier part of the present century, and at least one in more recent years. The best known of the earlier rivals was the Coherence Theory, associated principally with the idealist philosophers influenced by Hegel, but also adopted for other reasons by some logical positivists. This theory claims that truth is a relation between beliefs or, as the idealists preferred to call them, *judgements*. And by 'judgement' they meant not *acts* of judging that so-and-so is the case but the *content* of the judgement. If I judge that this stone is an amethyst, the content of my judgement is the proposition 'This stone is an amethyst'. So the coherence account of truth claims that truth consists in a relation of coherence between the contents of acts of judgement, or, as we may call them, propositions. (We can look more closely at the notions of proposition later.)

What is this relation of coherence? A minimum condition for two or more propositions being coherent, in the required sense, is that they should be consistent. However, even this minimum condition is hard to state in a sense which will meet the requirements of the theory. We would ordinarily say that two or more propositions are consistent if any one of them cannot be false if the rest are true. But here we have introduced the notions of truth and falsity that the Coherence Theory is supposed to explain.

Moreover, consistency, though a necessary condition for coherence, is certainly not a sufficient one. But it is left unclear by proponents of the Coherence Theory exactly what the further conditions are that would turn a mutually consistent set of propositions into a coherent one in the required sense. Most advocates of the theory have made it clear that, in practical terms, coherence is necessarily an unrealised ideal because of the limitations of human experience. However, the larger the coherent system of knowledge, the nearer we are to the unattainable ideal of truth. And truth therefore becomes a matter of degree: those propositions are true which cohere with the largest organised system of consistent propositions. It is as if reality is being thought of as an enormous jigsaw puzzle whose individual pieces, the propositions, are true in so far as they fit somewhere into the completed puzzle. Such talk is of course metaphorical, but clear statements of the theory are hard to find among its advocates.

The most natural examples that occur to anyone who is trying to make sense of the theory are mathematical or logical systems – let us say, a consistent system of geometry. Yet such examples are inappropriate, for what we are concerned with are *factual* truths and not the *a priori* truths of logic and mathematics. In any case, even these unsuitable examples do not quite meet the standards set by the Coherence Theory. For the propositions of any formal theory do not mutually entail one another, but follow from the axioms of the system. Moreover, the steps by which they are proved have to be in accordance with the rules of inference of the system.

What coherence theorists have done is to confuse an important criterion for *testing* truth with a definition of the nature of truth. No one would deny that consistency, a minimal condition for coherence, is a reliable negative test of truth. Law courts have always compared the testimony of witnesses and rejected inconsistent testimony as unreliable. And historians have always used the coherence of their evidence as a basic touchstone of its reliability. But though coherence of a body of propositions may be *prima facie* evidence for their truth, it is perfectly possible, as Russell pointed out,[2] to have an indefinite number of equally extensive systems of coherent statements. What is more, if we rely merely on coherence as a test of truth we can canonise any statement we like as true by embedding it in a sufficiently large system of mutually consistent statements. Many good novels would offer examples of this. So coherence is not even a conclusive test of truth, let alone a satisfactory description of its nature.

A similar criticism may be offered of a second well known account of truth, the Pragmatist Theory. In its best known form, this theory was a vulgarisation by the American psychologist and philosopher, William James, of the subtle and important theory of knowledge of his friend, Charles Peirce: a true statement is one which is useful; a true theory is one which works in practice. Much turns here on the exact meaning of phrases like 'works in practice' and 'is useful', but it would be generally agreed that in many straightforward cases, the practical utility of statements and theories is a reliable (though not infallible) criterion of truth. The general truth of electro-magnetic theory is strongly supported by the practical utility and efficiency of our electrical systems and gadgets. There are, on the other hand, many true statements (in the everyday sense of 'true') which have no obvious, or indeed unobvious utility – for example: 'I am now typing this sentence.' And there are well known cases of false scientific theories that have been useful in the development of science – for example, the Ptolemaic theory of the solar system. So utility is *a* criterion of truth but not a unique or a conclusive one. And, like coherence, it is, at best, only a test of truth and not an account of its nature.

The third serious alternative to the Correspondence Theory of Truth is the so-called Redundancy Theory. This has been advocated in various forms since it was first proposed by Frank Ramsey in 1927.[3] As the Redundancy Theory can be considered to be the most important rival to a Correspondence Theory, it will be considered after we have seen what can be said for and against correspondence as an account of the nature of truth.

Correspondence as the Nature of Truth

We have seen above, in order to make clear what we are claiming when we say that a true statement corresponds to the facts, we have first to determine the nature of truth bearers, the entities, whatever they may be, which can be described by the predicates 'true' and 'false'. Then we have to say what we mean by 'facts' in this context. Lastly, we must give a clear account of the nature of the relation of correspondence which links truth bearer to fact. The order in which we deal with these three questions is not important, though we must remember that a particular answer to one of these questions will determine, to some extent, the nature of the answers that we can consistently give to the others.

We can speak of beliefs being true and false, and we can speak similarly of judgements, statements, sentences, utterances and propositions. Can they all be said to be truth bearers in the same sense? We may notice some obvious differences between them. Whereas beliefs and judgements may be expressed in words, they need not be. But sentences, statements and utterances all require the existence of a language in which they are expressed. Creatures without language, such as dogs or infants, may evince by their behaviour that they have some beliefs; and we can show some, at least, of our beliefs in the same way. I evince my belief that something is edible by eating it, and I can display my judgement in the course of a game of chess that the best move is bishop to king's knight five by making that move. In neither case do I have to say anything, even to myself. So some truth bearers are essentially linguistic and some need not be.

However, it is clear that the use of language is very important in expressing our beliefs. Whereas I can express my belief that there is cheese in the pantry simply by going to get it, I cannot express my belief in Pythagoras' theorem, or that the earth is an oblate spheroid, without some language or some symbolic substitute for it. Language enables us to make our beliefs detailed and precise; it also puts them into a permanent and stable form which unexpressed beliefs tend to lack.

There is a second important distinction to be noted. Beliefs may, as we saw earlier, be abiding states, or they may occur in the form of bits of behaviour, linguistic or otherwise. My belief that there is cheese in the pantry is shown by my going to the pantry to get it. But I would not do so unless I had a semi-permanent tendency to act in this way, unless, that is to say, I had that belief as a belief state. Not all of our beliefs need be stored in this form. When I am driving a car, my belief that the lights are changing from green to red is based on an immediate perception. Judgements may be said to be occurrent beliefs so that we need not consider judgements as a separate class of potential truth bearers. But what is it that is common to both an occurrent belief that P (that is, an affirmation in some concrete form that I believe P) and an abiding belief state that P? It seems that what is common is just P, the proposition that is believed. But what is a proposition?

We come to the same question by examining the linguistic candidates for the title of truth bearer. We talk naturally of statements being true or false; and, as statements are embodied in sentences, we can talk of true or false sentences, though this is a less natural way of talking. What then is the difference between a sentence and a statement? And what bearing has this difference on their respective status as truth bearers? The answer to the first question seems to be that a statement is an affirmation by someone of a particular state of affairs using a sentence which describes that state of affairs. In other words, a sentence is true by being a correct linguistic description of a certain state of affairs. The sentence both *describes* the facts it is referring to and also, when it is used as a statement, *refers to* the facts which it correctly describes. Thus, if I say,

There is a piece of green stone on the table

then the sentence (let us call it S for short) describes a particular state of affairs and the use of S in this particular situation is a true statement.

Now it is perfectly possible to use S for other purposes, as a grammatical example in an English language lesson for example, or as a translation of 'Il y a un morceau de pierre verte sur la table'. Here the sentence is not a true sentence, except in the weak sense of correctly describing any situation in which there is a piece of green stone on the table. It becomes true by its being used to make the statement in the appropriate circumstances. And the truth of the statement derives jointly from the fact that S is a correct description (according to the rules of English) of the state of affairs, and from the fact that it is used to make a reference to that state of affairs. Thus truth in linguistic truth bearers has, so to speak, two levels. A particular sentence must have a correct descriptive content appropriate to a particular state of affairs; and it must be correctly assigned to that state of affairs in a context of utterance. And, of course, the first level precedes the second: a sentence can express an accurate description of a certain state of affairs even if it is never uttered in the appropriate circumstances.

So far, perhaps, so good. But there are complications. Suppose that there is a piece of green stone on the table and I utter S. Now suppose that a Frenchman says: 'Il y a un morceau de pierre verte sur la table', and a German says: 'Es gibt ein Stück grüner Stein auf dem Tisch'. We have all made true statements which could be multiplied in other languages, *ad nauseam*, by a sufficiently international gathering. In virtue of what common feature of our utterances have we all made true statements, or, in other words, have we all said the same thing?

It is no good answering this question by saying: 'Any of the sentences uttered is a correct translation of any of the others.' This merely restates the problem. In virtue of what are they correct translations? Nor is it any use to reply: 'In virtue of the lexical and grammatical rules of the languages used to make the statement,' for the same question arises within a given language. Suppose I utter S on two different occasions when there is a piece of green stone before me. Here are two utterances of the same sentence or, as is usually said in such cases, two sentence-tokens of the same sentence-type. What do the two sentence-tokens have in common? Clearly, in addition to their similar structure, they have their *meaning* in common. But what is this meaning? It is questions of this kind that have led to another candidate for the function of truth bearer – the proposition.

We may regard a proposition as the cognitive content of a sentence. It may be supposed to be non-material, unlike sentences or the statements in which sentences are embodied which are noises or marks on paper. There are persuasive reasons for postulating such objects. (1) Since knowledge, beliefs and opinions can be communicated and so shared, they must have some objective and inter-personal content. (2) Just as we can express the same meanings in different sentences in our own language, so we can translate one sentence into other languages. There must therefore be a common content to synonymous sentences. (3) Since truth is believed to be a property independent of human minds, that is, something that we discover rather than create, truth bearers must also exist independently of human minds. (4) The same proposition can be thought of at different times by the same person and by different persons without changing its truth-value. (5) Whether my state of consciousness is one of believing, knowing, remembering, wishing or fearing, it characteristically has an object to which it is directed. Such an object may not exist in the real world as when I suppose or imagine or fear some non-existent state of affairs. Such objects of our states of consciousness we call propositions.

If we accept these reasons for supposing that there are propositions, we are accepting the existence of entities with the following properties: (1) they are immaterial and not located in space or time though they can make appearances at particular places and times, embodied in words; (2) they are independent of particular minds, or of minds in general, although they are public objects which can be contemplated by any minds; (3) they are neutral between languages although, when expressed in words, they must be formulated in some particular natural language. Such entities may seem strange, though if the arguments for them are good ones, they must be accepted. They are indeed rather like Plato's Forms or Ideas, though supported by better arguments.

What are the objections to postulating propositions? It is probably not possible to find a conclusive refutation of such a metaphysical assertion but the following considerations may make it look less plausible. (1) Are we to suppose that propositions are true and false in themselves or are they, like sentences, true or false only in their use in making assertions? If we are not to be involved in a regress, we must suppose that they are true or false in themselves. They carry in their own natures an implicit reference to those features of the world that make them true (when they *are* true).

But what if they are false? We must suppose that false propositions are possible; for any hypothesis that we invoke to account for truth must also account for falsehood. (This is one of Russell's conditions for a theory of truth, mentioned on page 165). But if this is so, then for every true proposition there will be an uncountable multitude of false ones. There will, first of all, be the *negation* of the proposition in question. (Call it not-P.) And then there will be all the innumerable propositions expressing states of affairs *inconsistent* with P. These propositions will fit states of affairs that do *not* now exist at the particular point of time and space that we are referring to. And there are an indefinitely large number of these. But such swarming multitudes of propositions have no function except to satisfy the logical demands of the theory that requires them. Although this is not a conclusive reason for saying that propositions do not exist, it is a very good reason for not supposing that they do.

(2) A second objection arises from the nature of language. It is an essential feature of natural languages that their descriptive words are general and so any particular descriptive sentence would correctly fit a very large number of possible situations. Sentence S which we used above would correctly describe an enormous variety of facts. Were we to modify it by specifying the exact time and place and the shape and weight of the stone referred to, we would still have a sentence which would be compatible with a large number of facts. So the relation of proposition to sentence becomes not a one-one relation (for a particular language) but a many-one relation. For, by hypothesis, a given proposition can be true of only *one* state of affairs, whereas a given sentence must be true of many possible such states. So propositions cannot be simply the cognitive content of declarative sentences. Propositions, as truth bearers, can fit only one fact each; sentences must, by their nature, fit many.

So we have a dilemma: if a proposition is to be the cognitive content of a declarative sentence, it cannot be a truth bearer; but if a proposition does have a truth-value independent of any linguistic instantiation that it may be given, it is hard to see the difference a proposition and a possible state of affairs. And indeed some philosophers have so defined it.[4] But if this is so, propositions can have no value for the Correspondence Theory of truth. For propositions which are supposed to correspond to fact now *become* facts (if they are true) and possible facts (if they are false).

Now that we have looked at the problems raised by truth bearers, we can look more briefly at truth donors or, as Russell put it[5] 'those features of the constitution of the world that make our assertions true (if they are true) and false (if they are false)'. But what are 'those features of the constitution of the world'? We have already seen, in talking about perception, that the features of the world that we, as human beings, can be familiar with are a small selection of what the world has to offer. And that selection is transformed by our particular human senses and moulded by the concepts through which we learn to interpret our reality. What we recognise as 'fact' must depend almost as much on our own cognitive apparatus, sensory and conceptual, as it does on the constitution of the world independent of ourselves. So the facts that we require as truth donors to match our truth bearers, whatever they may be, are only in a limited sense 'objective' or independent of our own ways of thinking and perceiving. Just as we have seen the truth bearers, in the guise of propositions, tend to merge into facts, so too facts, when carefully scrutinised, tend to become hard to distinguish from our own ways of viewing the world. We seem to have no clear cut terms to match in our required relation of correspondence.

What then of correspondence itself? In its ordinary sense, correspondence is a relation of a particular *structural* kind between two terms where the important features of term T_1 are mirrored by features of term T_2, and the relations between the features of T_1 are mirrored by the relations between the features of T_2. For example: a map corresponds to the terrain which it maps in this sense; a translation corresponds to the text of which it is a translation; a performance of a symphony corresponds to the score; and so on. From examples of this sort, it is clear that we need a structure or form in both original and representation and some specifiable kind of similarity between both. But from what we have seen of both truth bearers and truth donors, it seems doubtful whether (a) they can be seen as sufficiently distinct from one another to serve as terms in such a relation, and (b) whether they do have the kind of structure needed by a relation of this sort. Linguistic truth bearers do indeed have a structure conferred by grammar and syntax. But there are strong arguments to show that linguistic structure does not correspond in any clear way to the structure of fact, whatever that may be.[6] But in the case of the more plausible kinds of truth bearers, beliefs and propositions, it is hard to outline a structure which is not the structure resulting from their expression in language.

This examination of the Correspondence Theory of Truth has necessarily been brief. But even on a brief scrutiny, the theory seems to lose the clear common sense aspects that it has when unexamined, that beliefs or propositions are one thing, that facts are another, and that they fit together to give us truth. Clearly, the matter is a lot more complex than that.

The Semantic Theory

It has been seen that the traditional Correspondence Theory of Truth is both vague and imprecise. The nature of truth bearers, of facts, and of the relation between them, is not clear enough for us to be able to understand exactly what the theory is supposed to claim. However, there is a modern version of the Correspondence Theory, proposed in 1931 by the Polish-American logician Alfred Tarski, which does attempt to be clear, precise and systematic.[7] Tarski starts by laying down conditions which a satisfactory account of truth must meet: it must be both 'materially adequate' and 'formally correct'. To satisfy the first condition, Tarski says that his theory must aim 'to catch hold of the actual meaning of an old notion' and must not merely propose some arbitrary account of truth that makes it a restricted technical notion like 'force' or 'work' in physics. The second condition will be satisfied if there is no flaw in the logical processes used to set out the theory.

The truth bearers in Tarski's Semantic Theory are *sentences*. By 'sentences' he means 'not individual inscriptions but classes of inscriptions of similar form'[8] or, in our terminology, type-sentences and not token-sentences. Now let us take an ordinary sentence expressing a familiar empirical truth:

   (1) Snow is white.

If we ask under what conditions we accept this sentence as true, we can express the condition as follows:

   (2) The sentence 'snow is white' is true if and only if snow is white.

In (2) the sentence 'snow is white' occurs twice; first in quotation marks, and then without them. This is because the first occurrence of (1) in (2) is the *name* of the sentence and the second is the sentence itself. (It is important in modern logic to distinguish between *using* a linguistic expression and *mentioning* it in just this way.) We use the sentence to say something about the world; but we mention the sentence, that is, we use its name, in saying that it is true. Tarski now proceeds to generalise the procedure exemplified in (2). He replaces the sentence which is a candidate for a truth-value by the letter p – and replaces the name of this sentence by X. The relation between the two sentence-forms 'X is true' and p, is that they are logically equivalent and so we have:

(3) X is true if, and only if, p.

Now replace p in (3) by any sentence and X by its name and we have what Tarski calls 'an equivalence of the form (T)'. (2) is such an equivalence. Other examples are:

(4) 'Blood is red' is true if, and only if, blood is red
(5) 'The earth is spherical' is true if, and only if, the earth is spherical

and so on.

Although (3) is not itself a definition of truth, nor are its substitution instances, (2), (4), (5) and the like, they can, however, be considered 'partial definitions' of truth. Tarski considers it to be a criterion of the material adequacy of his proposed definition if all equivalences of the form (T) follow from that definition.

Up to now we have talked as if Tarski is trying to make clear and specific the common sense notion of truth that we use in everyday language, the pre-analytic version of a Correspondence Theory. And indeed, he has said that this is his intention. But at this point he raises a difficulty. Any natural language can be shown to be capable of generating antinomies or contradictions. For example:

(6) The sentence on this page prefixed by (6) is false.

Clearly (6) refers to itself, and says of itself that it is false. But if so, then what it says is not true. But if it is false and says of itself that it is not true, it must really be true. But if it *is* true, then it must be false. Whichever truth-value we assign to it, we are forced to conclude that it has the other. Since we have both:

(7) If (6) is true, then (6) is not true

(8) If (6) is not true, then (6) is true

and we may conclude by standard rules of logic:

(9) (6) is true if and only if (6) is not true

which is a clear contradiction.

Any language which can generate a contradiction like this (and all natural languages can do so) is unacceptable to a logician. Among other things, any statement whatever can be shown to be provable in an inconsistent language. For this and other reasons, Tarski concludes that 'The problem of the definition of truth obtains a precise meaning and can be solved in a rigorous way only for those languages whose structure has been exactly specified.'[9]

Why has this contradiction arisen? It has done so because of two features of natural languages that are so familiar that we take them for granted without comment: (i) that our language contains not only expressions but also the names of such expressions, as well as terms like 'true' and 'false'; (ii) that every indicative sentence in our language is either true or false. In fact, as we have already seen, it is possible to use indicative sentences which are perfectly meaningful, but which are not true or false in the full sense. (For example, when we use a sentence as a grammatical example without using it to make a statement.) However, Tarski assumes that (i) and (ii) both apply to natural languages. Using this doubtful assumption, he rejects what he calls 'semantically closed' languages, that is, natural languages conforming to conditions (i) and (ii), as unsuitable vehicles for a clear and rigorous theory of truth. It must be said, however, that any developed natural languages are bound to have the first of these features. Indeed without it, they could hardly be used for the ordinary purposes of communication.

Tarski's rejection of 'semantically closed languages' (that is, any natural languages) as a basis for his account of truth has the consequence that he needs an artificial formal language in order to formulate his Semantic Theory of Truth. He uses the algebra of classes of standard logic but we need not consider here the details of his argument which is long and complex;[10] it will be sufficient to look at two of his basic concepts.

The first is the notion of an *open sentence* (or a *sentential function* to use Tarski's phrase). 'Milk is white' is a sentence; '*x* is white' is an open sentence derived by replacing the subject term of 'milk is white' by the variable '*x*'. Similarly, 'John loves Mary' is a sentence; '*x* loves *y*' is an open sentence. It is clear that whereas sentences can be true or false, open sentences can be neither. The second basic concept is that of *satisfaction*. Tarski explains[11] that *a* satisfies the sentential function '*x* is white' if and only if *a* is white. Or, as Quine writes: 'The open sentence "*x* walks" is satisfied by each walker and by nothing else. The open sentence "x > y" is satisfied by each descending pair of numbers and by no other pairs.'[12] Thus satisfaction is explained by reference to the concept of open sentences.

At the end of his long and technical explanation of truth in his formal language, Tarski comes to his definition: '*S is a true sentence if and only if it is satisfied by every infinite sequence of classes*.'[13] (And, correspondingly, a sentence is false if it is satisfied by no sequence at all.)

We may consider just a few of the objections that have been made to the Semantic Theory of Truth, and, in particular, those that have a bearing on the claim that the Semantic Theory is a clear and accurate account of the essential features of the Correspondence Theory.

(1) How do we know that snow satisfies '*x* is white' unless we *already* know that the sentence 'snow is white' is true? How do we know that blood or soot do *not* satisfy '*x* is white' without knowing that the sentences 'blood is white' or 'soot is white' are false? Indeed, it is obvious that we cannot identify the individuals that satisfy an open sentence without knowing the truth-values of the closed sentences resulting from substituting the names of the individuals for the variable in the open sentence. If this is so, is not an explanation of truth and falsity in terms of satisfaction plainly circular?

(2) It is an essential feature of natural languages that they are, in Tarski's phrase, 'semantically closed', with the result that logical contradictions can be expressed in them without contravening the rules of the language. Tarski makes it plain that his theory cannot be expressed otherwise than in a carefully constructed artificial language. But Tarski's language is one which would be quite inadequate for ordinary communication. It is therefore

hard to believe that his account of truth has any relation to the concept that we employ to characterise some of the statements in our own unregenerate natural languages.

(3) The nature of truth bearers in the Semantic Theory is quite different from truth bearers in natural languages. Tarski is clear that *sentences* are truth bearers in his theory. But when we ask the question: Does he mean token-sentences or type-sentences? we do not get a clear answer. In one place[14] he says: 'For our present purposes, it is somewhat more convenient to understand by "expressions", "sentences" etc., not individual inscriptions but classes of inscriptions of similar form.' But elsewhere he says: 'Sentences are treated here as linguistic objects, as certain strings of sounds or written signs.'[15] This is a point at which the precision and formality of the Semantic Theory masks an underlying vagueness. But in any case, whether he means type or token here, we have seen that *sentences*, unless used to make *statements*, are not convincing candidates for the status of truth bearer. It is easy to produce well-formed indicative sentences which are neither true nor false in the sense required by the Correspondence Theory.[16]

But even if Tarski does mean sentence-types to be his truth bearers, he construes 'type-sentence' in such a way that they cannot serve the purpose for which the Correspondence Theory needs them. There are two ways of constructing types out of tokens. We may say that the type is what the tokens have in common in respect of their *meaning*. Or we may say with Tarski, that we are referring to *classes* of inscriptions of similar form. This is the extensional view, characteristic of formal logicians who find it easier to deal with classes than with meanings. Suppose now that we ask: what is the property in virtue of which sentences $s_1, s_2, s_3,$ ... s_n are all held to be tokens of the sentence-type S? Is it the common meaning load of the sentences, or their similar physical qualities? Tarski accepts the second of these alternatives. In his language, 'the syntactical rules should be purely formal, that is, they should refer exclusively to the form (the shape) of expressions; the function and meaning of an expression should depend exclusively on its form'.[17] But in natural languages, two precisely similar expressions may have entirely different meanings; and conversely, two expressions with the same meaning may be wildly different in form. (Consider the same sentence printed, written in handwriting, written in shorthand, and spoken.) The 'function and meaning' of a linguistic expression are totally different in nature in formal and in natural languages. And since meaning is closely bound up with truth, it is clear that formal theories of meaning, like Tarski's, can have little relevance to the problem of truth in natural languages.

(4) The move from the open sentence which has no truth-value to the closed sentence which does, is an essential move in the construction of Tarski's theory. And since the concept of satisfaction is crucial to the theory, Tarski has to find a means of applying this notion to closed sentences after he has explained and illustrated it for open sentences. Unless he does this, he cannot arrive at this definition of a true sentence as a sentence which is satisfied by all sequences. Tarski adopts the following device. An open sentence with *two* unbound variables may be satisfied, as we have seen, by sequences of ordered *pairs*. An open sentence with a single unbound variable, such as 'x is white', can be satisfied by sequences of objects. And a *sentence* is just to be regarded as a sentential function with *no* unbound variables and so as a *zero-placed* sentential function. Tarski thus tries to bring sentences which are capable of bearing truth-values into the class of sentential functions which are capable of being satisfied by suitable sequences of objects. But we may reasonably ask what sense can be put on the notion of satisfaction for a zero-valued function when it has been defined and illustrated only for functions whose values are one or more? The nearest Tarski gets to an explanation of this logical 'trick' (as one of his expositors calls it[18]) is to say: 'Once the general definition of satisfaction is obtained, we notice that it applies automatically also to those special sentential functions which contain no free variables, i.e., sentences. It turns out that for a sentence only two cases are possible: a sentence is either satisfied by all objects or by no objects.'[19] The phrases 'automatically', 'we notice that' and 'it turns out that' all call for elucidation. But the only other help that Tarski gives is to comment, in his earlier paper: 'In the extreme case, where the function is a sentence and so contains no free variables, . . . the satisfaction of a function by a sequence does not depend on the properties of the sequence at all.'[20]

It has been necessary to give a fairly extended account of the Semantic Theory both because it is of considerable contemporary importance and because it has to be explained in some detail in order for its point to be made clear. But it should be said that the four lines of criticism outlined above are only a small selection of the objections that can be raised against the Semantic Theory, considered as a logical reconstruction of the Correspondence Theory of Truth. Whatever its value for formal semantics, it must be doubted whether Tarski's claim that his theory 'does conform to a very considerable extent with commonsense usage'[21] can be plausibly sustained.

Redundancy Theories

In an influential paper published in 1927,[22] the Cambridge mathematician and philosopher, F. P. Ramsey, sketched an account of truth which has offered a basis for persuasive alternatives to more traditional approaches. 'It is evident that "It is true that Caesar was murdered" means no more than that Caesar was murdered, and "It is false that Caesar was murdered" means that Caesar was not murdered.'[23] So to add the predicates 'is true' or 'is false' to sentences adds no information. We are therefore not *describing* the sentence by these predicates. To suppose that there is a separate problem of truth is merely, according to Ramsey, 'a linguistic muddle'.[24] It is a linguistic muddle because we are misunderstanding the function of phrases like 'is true' and 'is false'. Although they have the grammatical form of predicates like 'is red' or 'is sweet' which do describe their subjects, and do convey information about them, 'is true' and 'is false' are no more than 'phrases that we sometimes use for emphasis or for stylistic reasons'. The proper force of 'is true' and 'is false' on this account is at best that of emphatic adverbs like 'certainly', 'really', 'assuredly' and the like. Thus if ' "Caesar was murdered" is true' means any more than 'Caesar was murdered' it can mean, at most, 'Caesar really was murdered'.

This point of view is persuasive for several reasons. In the first place, the difficulty of finding a clear, positive account of the nature of truth makes it tempting to suppose that we are seeking for something that does not exist. And it does not exist because the adjectives 'true' and 'false' have no descriptive content, being adjectives only in form and not in function. But, secondly, there is a logical point to be made for the Redundancy Theory. The truth-value of any proposition, P, is exactly the same as the truth-value of the proposition 'P is true'. Similarly, the truth values of not-P and 'P is false' must be identical, whatever proposition we substitute for P. And this identity of truth value is very often a sign of identity of meaning. For example:

(A) John is a bachelor

is identical in meaning with:

(B) John is an unmarried man

and whatever truth-value attaches to (A) will also be the truth-value of (B), and vice versa. And similarly with:

(C) That flower is a scarlet pimpernel
and (D) That flower is a specimen of *Anagallis arvenis*.

The list of such examples could be extended indefinitely.

However, these considerations are not conclusive. The fact that no one has yet proposed a completely satisfactory analysis of the concept of empirical truth does not mean that no such analysis is possible. And the argument from identity of truth-values to identity of meaning is flawed with exceptions. No doubt it is true that two propositions must be logically equivalent in this way *if* they are to be identical in meaning. But we may not conclude from this that if any two propositions are logically equivalent then they *are* identical in meaning.

(E) This figure is a circle
and (F) This figure is the locus of all points equidistant from a given point

are hardly equivalent in meaning, but they are certainly logically equivalent. And the same applies to:

(G) Hilary is female
and (H) Hilary's cells carry XX chromosomes.

In any case, as we have seen earlier,[25] the whole concept of identity of meaning or synonymy is a controversial one.

Some so-called 'blind' uses of 'true' seem to present difficulties for Ramsey's redundancy analysis of truth. We may sometimes apply the terms 'true' and 'false' to statements without knowing what the statements are. If someone says:

(J) Everything that the witness tells you will be true

he may well not know exactly what the witness will say, but nevertheless is prepared to endorse his statements in advance on the ground that he knows him to be a completely trustworthy man. We could re-phrase (J) to read:

(K) For all p, if the witness says p, then p is true

or, on Ramsey's account:

(L) For all p, if the witness says p, then p.

Whether Ramsey's account can be accepted depends on whether it is possible to read 'p is true' as equivalent in meaning to 'p' in all contexts. And it is hard to see how a sentence such as:

Cardinal Bellarmine was uncertain whether Galileo's theory was true or false

can be given a Ramseyan interpretation.

An updated version of Ramsey's theory by Strawson combines the assertion that 'true' and 'false' are not descriptive words with an explanation of what their proper function really is. Austin has shown[26] how many words in natural languages have important ways of working other than, or in addition to, their descriptive functions. If I say 'I promise to lend you the money' my use of the word 'promise' in this context is itself the making of a promise. By saying 'I promise', I have actually made the promise. Such uses of language, Austin called 'performatory', and Strawson makes a plausible case for the thesis that many uses of 'true' and 'false' are performatory in this way, or that they evince similar language uses. They may be used to make concessions or to express conviction or some other attitude. For example, 'That's true' often functions as equivalent to 'I agree', or 'I grant you that point'. And these are performatory uses of 'agree' or 'grant' although there is, at the same time, a reference to the statement which is being agreed to or conceded. Strawson is here agreeing with what Ramsey says about truth, but denying that it is the whole story. Ramsey was 'right in asserting that to say that a statement is true is not to make a further statement; but wrong in suggesting that to say that a statement is true is not to do something different from, or additional to, just making the statement'.[27] The crucial addition is the performatory or concessive element in the use of the word 'true'. (And, of course, there are analogous elements in the use of 'false'.)

What can be said in criticism of Strawson's revision of the Redundancy Theory? There are two main points.[28] (1) It is clear that he is right in claiming that phrases like 'That's true' can be used in the performatory or concessive ways that he describes. But we may raise the question whether this is just a linguistic peculiarity of English and perhaps some other languages, or whether it is a philosophical truth that holds in all languages, for if it is a truth of philosophy then it must hold in all languages. Professor Stegmüller[29] has objected that German-speaking philosophers find that Strawson's suggestion about the way 'That's true' works in English is not perfectly mirrored by the way 'Das ist wahr' works in German. In many contexts, the German phrase would sound unacceptably dramatic or unusual if used as an equivalent for 'Ja' or 'Genau'. So we can regard Strawson's suggestion as a testable empirical hypothesis, and ask a large and varied selection of native speakers of different languages whether their equivalents of 'true' and 'false' have the same functions that Strawson says they have in English. This would involve a large-scale investigation in the psychology of language which has not so far been made. For what it is worth, a small pilot survey of twenty languages was not uniformly favourable to Strawson's thesis, although the favourable cases, especially in the Indo-European family, outweigh the counter-examples.[30]

(2) And there is a more serious objection. Let us suppose that Strawson is right in claiming that 'true' functions in English as what he calls 'an abbreviatory statement device' which is used to indicate our endorsement of an assertion. (And similarly, 'false' works analogously to signify our rejection of an assertion.) We have then to ask: In virtue of what supposed properties do we endorse or reject statements? For it is clear that we do so for reasons, and not at random. If we accept Strawson's view, we may no longer say that we endorse statements that seem to us to be *true* and reject those which seem to be *false*. For these words have been assigned by Strawson to other duties. Nevertheless, any rational person has to ask why we endorse some statements and reject others. It is this very question that raises the 'problem of truth' as

it has traditionally been conceived. And we have not disposed of *this* problem by Ramsey's or Strawson's methods. We still have to ask: What are the rational criteria by which we distinguish those statements which are worthy of endorsement from those which are not?

CONCLUDING REMARKS

This book purports to offer an introduction to the theory of knowledge. To end we shall consider briefly what we have been able to do, and in what sense we have offered a 'theory' of knowledge. There are, of course, many ways in which human knowledge can be made the subject of a rational investigation but not all of them would be philosophical enquiries. For example, the history of science is, in a pre-eminent degree, the study of the development of human knowledge. But though it is a pre-requisite for many philosophical discussions, it is not in itself a philosophical enquiry. So, too, psychologists study many of the topics that we have discussed in the previous chapters. Perception, memory, and belief are all subjects on which psychology has a good deal to offer philosophers. But the questions that psychologists ask about these topics are not those which philosophers ask. A psychologist may, for example, investigate the causal origins of beliefs or, at least, of certain types of belief. But he does not concern himself with the question: Are such-and-such beliefs well-founded or rational? The answers to questions of that sort are given partly by the experts in the field to which the belief relates, and partly by the philosopher. For example, the mathematician will concern himself with the proof of propositions like 'There are an infinite number of primes' or 'The square root of two is an irrational number', but the philosopher deals with the general nature of *a priori* propositions and their varieties and mutual relations. The physicist devotes himself, for example, to questions about the structure of the atom; the philosopher deals with general issues about empirical knowledge. It may be said, in summary, that though the philosopher's questions about knowledge are often questions about *justification*, they are *general* questions about types of knowledge and not questions

186

about the truth or falsity of specific beliefs. And the same applies to any questions that philosophers may raise about theories in history, geology, economics or any other field of enquiry.

But in what sense, it may be asked, do these philosophical discussions amount to a genuine theory? The terms 'theory of knowledge' and its equivalent 'epistemology' suggest that the various phenomena of cognition can be organised into an explanatory framework in the way that the phenomena of electricity have been organised into a theory of electro-magnetism: but no philosopher has yet achieved this and it is very improbable that anyone ever will. Theories in philosophy are only loosely analogous to theories in mathematics or in natural science. But they do aim at some of the advantages of scientific theories – to replace vagueness with precision, to show the relations between different parts of the subject and to explain problems and apparent paradoxes that may arise in their field.

As with any theory, constraints may be put upon the theory of knowledge in various ways. Sometimes, the advance of the sciences, whether formal or empirical, will present us with new information about knowledge and its possible limits that has to be accommodated within any epistemology. For example, developments in logic have shown that there can be true but unprovable propositions. And developments in physics have shown that certain kinds of natural knowledge must always remain unavailable. For example, we cannot determine simultaneously the position and momentum of certain sub-atomic particles. These are external constraints imposed by the advance of scientific knowledge. And, of course, there are internal constraints as well. Our epistemology has to be consistent in that what follows from one part of our theory may not contradict what follows from another part. It is a standard way of refuting any philosophical 'theory to show that it results in inconsistency. And it is desirable that in a properly developed theory of knowledge the various parts shall be related together by some relation rather more powerful than simple consistency. This is, after all, what usually happens in a developed science where each historical stage leads to further theories which embody and develop the earlier ones.

So far, this kind of constructive development in philosophy has been limited. Progress in philosophy has rather resembled the exploration of some enormous labyrinth in which we are all imprisoned and whose overall plan we do not know. We can find the way out only by identifying and marking the blind alleys. Once we have marked them all, the paths that remain, if any, will take us out of the maze. Certainly the history of philosophy up to the present has followed this pattern of advancement. We know what solutions will not work; but we do not know of any which certainly will.

We have discussed some varieties of scepticism earlier in the book and we have seen that there is little reason to be convinced by them. If indeed we wish to insist on an unconditionally justified certainty with respect to any proposition whatever, we are asking for something which can never be provided. But if we are content with a reliable confidence in the items of our range of belief, such confidence is well within our grasp. We have argued, indeed, that a form of certainty (beyond all reasonable doubt) frequently characterises the propositions which concern the world we experience, as judged in terms of the relevant criteria of certainty, and warrants our acceptance of the truth of those propositions. As for the rest, all we have to do is to adjust the degree of our belief in any given proposition to the evidence available for it. This, in fact, is the prescription for rationality given by both Hume and Russell.[1] And no one has yet offered a better recipe, for this is simply the procedure by which we regulate both our common sense adjustments to the world and the more complex insights into nature given by science.

Indeed, it is the success of science that provides the conclusive answer to traditional forms of scepticism. What distinguishes the present century so decisively from all previous periods of the world's history is the control of nature resulting from the growth of scientific knowledge. Modern physics, chemistry and physiology offer just that detailed knowledge about the inner microstructure and workings of things in the world which would have seemed incredible to a seventeenth-century empiricist like John Locke. Locke, indeed, asserted 'that there is no discoverable connection between any secondary Quality and those primary Qualities that it depends on'.[2] That is, he was denying those very truths about qualities like colour, sound and warmth that physics has established. But we are in a position to point to natural science as the standard instance of reliable knowledge. It is not, indeed, indubitable, but is far more secure than any other knowledge that we have. And in so far as any form of scepticism professes to find reliable knowledge impossible, it stands refuted by this example.

However, there is at least one important limitation to human knowledge that should be remarked. Whether we call this a source of genuine scepticism is a matter of convention. One part of this limitation has already been briefly noticed at the end of our discussion of perception (pp. 114–15 above). The basic materials of our knowledge come to us through the senses. And whatever limitations the senses may have will be reflected in the scope and detail of whatever knowledge we may come to possess. It may, perhaps, seem unjustified to talk of the 'limitations' of our senses. With respect to what ideal are they supposed to be limited? Surely it is misleading, to say the least, to say of someone whose eyes, ears and the rest of his sensory apparatus are in perfect working order that his senses are subject to any limitations. But it is possible to put a perfectly good sense on this use of language and, moreover, one that has a bearing on the issue of scepticism as a theory about the limits of human knowledge.

As we have seen, the range of our senses is restricted in two ways. Each sense organ is responsive to specific forms of energy, but only to certain ranges of those forms of energy. Thus electro-magnetic radiation, as physicists are familiar with it, forms a spectrum ranging from long-wave radio waves whose wave-length is of the order of 10,000 metres down to X-rays and gamma-rays with a wave-length from 10^{-9} to 10^{-10} metres (that is, from a millionth of a millimetre down to a ten millionth of a millimetre). The type of radiation that we call 'light' occupies a tiny part of this enormous range, from a wave-length of about 760 millionths of a millimetre for red light, to 380 millionths for violet light. Our eyes are not sensitive to radiation outside this range, though the eyes of many other animals have different ranges of sensitivity. The same is true for the other forms of energy that stimulate our senses. Human sensitivity to sound and to smells is notoriously restricted compared to that of many other creatures.

The second way in which our senses are restricted is that there are forms of energy to which none of our senses respond specifically. Such are electrical or magnetic fields, gamma-rays or X-rays and many forms of chemical energy. Again, the sense organs of other animals show sensitivities to forms of energy to which human sense organs are quite indifferent. Thus human sense organs respond to only a tiny fraction of the total energy at large in the universe. The importance of this lies in the fact that energy carries information. And though it is true that only a small part of the energy at large in the universe does carry information, for it has to be structured in a certain way in order to do so, nevertheless all the information that does come to us through the senses has to be carried by energy: it is our only information source. And the wider the range of energy to which our senses give us access, the greater the raw materials of our knowledge. Scientists have indeed been able to detect and measure many forms of energy to which our senses are blind. Devices like electroscopes, galvanometers, cloud chambers, Geiger counters and the like translate such forms of energy into forms that our senses can handle. But for this fact, we would probably not even suspect that there was information at large in the world which was beyond our ken.

So much for the limitations of our sense organs. But there is still another way in which we are limited in the possible range of our knowledge. To have an efficient sensory apparatus is a necessary condition for knowledge, but not a sufficient condition. We have to store information and to *process* our sensory input so that sense fields become perceptual fields, and perceptual fields in their turn provide the information which is interpreted first as common sense knowledge, and then as science. For this we need another level of our cognitive apparatus which will enable us to form concepts and make inferences. The brain which is the organ through which we perform all these tasks is an integrated mass of some 10^{10} (ten thousand million) nerve cells. Creatures with smaller brains composed of smaller numbers of neurons have markedly less capacity for concept formation and inference than we have. And there is good reason to suppose that creatures with substantially greater numbers of neurons than we have (10^{11} or 10^{12} perhaps) would have powers of concept formation and inference far greater than our own. It may be that such creatures do not exist, or that they exist in some other part of the universe. But whether they exist or not, it is clear that were we to have more powerful brains than we do have, there would be ranges of knowledge and intellectual achievement open to us which are at present far beyond us. So it is reasonable to suppose that the possibility of human knowledge is contingently limited by the capacity of the human brain as well as by the range of human senses. We might perhaps call this hypothesis 'functional scepticism'. A full justification of it would need a more extended argument than the sketch that we have offered here. But it does seem to be a variety of scepticism that is grounded in the nature of things.

NOTES

Chapter I: Scepticism and Certainty

1 This will be discussed at length in Chapter III.

2 A good short account of the history of scepticism is R.H. Popkin's article 'Scepticism', in the *Encyclopedia of Philosophy* edited by P. Edwards.

3 This sentence is curiously omitted from the otherwise recommendable translation of Descartes' works (and from which all other quotations are taken) by Anscombe and Geach, *Descartes: Philosophical Writings*, Thomas Nelson and Sons, London, 1954.

4 A classic discussion of Descartes' primary truth is J. Hintikka's paper 'Cogito Ergo Sum: Inference or Performance?', *The Philosophical Review*, Vol. LXXI, 1962.

5 See, for example, A.J. Ayer, *The Problem of Knowledge*, Macmillan, London, 1956, Chapter 2.

6 This fails for just the same reason as 'I know that P but perhaps not-P' in that 'seeing clearly and distinctly' in *this* sense implies knowledge.

7 D. Hume, *Enquiry Concerning Human Understanding*, Section XII, Part III.

8 D. Hume, *Treatise of Human Nature*, Book I, Part IV, Section I.

9 Hume's *Enquiry* IV, I.

10 Hume's *Enquiry* IV, I.

11 Hume's *Treatise* I, III, VI.

12 Hume's *Treatise* I, III, II and *Enquiry* IV, I.

13 Hume's *Enquiry* IV, II.

14 Hume's *Enquiry* V, I.

15 Contrast D.C. Stove, *Probability and Hume's Inductive Scepticism*, Clarendon Press, Oxford, 1973. Stove considers 'deductivism', as he calls it, the thesis that an argument is reasonable only if deductive, to be the *basis* of Hume's charge: on the contrary, it is the *result* of Hume's argument.

16 N. Malcolm 'The Verification Argument', in M. Black (ed.), *Philosophical Analysis*, Cornell University Press, 1950. Reprinted in his collection *Knowledge and Certainty*, Cornell University Press, 1963.

17 G.E. Moore, *Philosophical Papers*, Allen & Unwin, London, 1959. (Originally published in 1925 in J.H. Muirhead (ed.), *Contemporary British Philosophy*, Allen & Unwin, London.) There is a systematic

description of Moore's criteria for Common Sense in A.R. White, *G.E. Moore*, Basil Blackwell, Oxford, 1959.

18 G.E. Moore, *Philosophical Papers*, pp. 44–5.
19 The term 'epistemic' has achieved general philosophical currency as a convenient adjective fulfilling a role for which 'epistemological' is ill-fitted. Whereas this latter term connotes the *inquiry* of epistemology itself, 'epistemic' is applied to the terms, concepts, judgements and situations forming the subject matter of that inquiry. In its most usual application (and in the present text) it describes those terms such as 'know', 'certain', and 'possible', which essentially concern the evidential status of a proposition.
20 J.O. Urmson 'Some Questions Concerning Validity', *Revue Internationale de Philosophie*, No. 25, 1953. Reprinted in R. Swinburne (ed.), *The Justification of Induction*, Oxford University Press, 1974; references are to this latter text.
21 J.O. Urmson, *loc. cit.*, p. 80.
22 J.O. Urmson, *loc. cit.*, p. 80.
23 P.F. Strawson, *Introduction to Logical Theory*, Methuen, London, 1952, p. 257. The designations 'A' and 'B' do not appear in the original text.
24 Apart from the objective certainty here discussed there is another use of 'It is certain that P' where certainty is being ascribed to an event rather than a proposition, and no covert reference is made to the available evidence. In that use what is meant is that circumstances are such that the event described in P cannot fail to occur.
25 N. Malcolm 'Knowledge and Belief', *Mind*, Vol. 61, 1952, pp. 178–89. Reprinted in a revised form in N. Malcolm, *Knowledge and Certainty*. References are to this reprinted version.
26 See the last footnote to Malcolm's paper, as well as the account given by Malcolm of these conversations on pp. 87–92 of *Ludwig Wittgenstein: A Memoir*, Oxford University Press, 1962.
27 N. Malcolm, *Knowledge and Certainty*, p. 62.
28 N. Malcolm, *loc. cit.*, p. 64.
29 L. Wittgenstein, *On Certainty*, Blackwell, Oxford, 1969 – see Section 10 for example.
30 N. Malcolm, *loc. cit.*, p. 67.
31 N. Malcolm, *loc. cit.*, p. 69.
32 N. Malcolm, *loc. cit.*, p. 69.
33 L. Wittgenstein, *On Certainty*, Section 343.
34 H.A. Prichard, *Knowledge and Perception*, Clarendon Press, Oxford, 1950, p. 86.
35 See the exchange between Malcolm and R. Taylor in *Analysis*, Vols. 13 and 14, 1952–3 and 1953–4.
36 L. Wittgenstein, *On Certainty*, Section 83.
37 L. Wittgenstein, *loc. cit.*, Sections 341 and 342.
38 Hume's *Enquiry*, IV, I. The empiricists of the Vienna Circle – the logical empiricists or logical positivists – gave a great deal of attention to the nature of basic beliefs, for their content provides the sense of, as well as the evidence, for non-basic beliefs according to the ver-

ificationist theory of meaning to which they subscribed. See the introduction to A.J. Ayer's collection *Logical Positivism*, Glencoe, Ill., 1960, as well as various papers included there.

39 See A.J. Ayer, 'Basic Propositions,' in M. Black (ed.), *Philosophical Analysis*, Cornell University Press, 1950. Reprinted in A.J. Ayer, *Philosophical Essays*, Macmillan, London, 1969.

40 A.J. Ayer, 'Basic Propositions', *loc. cit.*, p. 120.

41 A.J. Ayer 'Knowledge, Belief, and Evidence', *Metaphysics and Common Sense* Macmillan, London, 1967, p. 121. (This paper originally appeared in *The Danish Yearbook of Philosophy*, Vol. 1, 1964.)

42 See for example the 'Replies to Objections to the *Meditations*', by Arnauld, where Descartes insists that 'the fact that nothing can exist in the mind, in so far as it is a thinking thing, of which it is not conscious, seems to me self-evident'. E.S. Haldane and G.R.T. Ross (trans. and eds.), *The Philosophical Works of Descartes*, Vol. II, Dover, New York, 1911, p. 115.

Chapter II: Belief

1 L. Wittgenstein, *Philosophical Investigations*, Basil Blackwell, Oxford, 1963. It is Wittgenstein's contention that any language is necessarily shared, for language is a rule-governed activity and the possibility must exist for the correction of mistakes in applying the rules. The possession and application of concepts is likewise a rule-governed activity, and concepts are necessarily shared. Does this leave room for new concepts to be introduced into a language by an individual? A collection of papers devoted to the general thesis is O.R. Jones (ed.), *The Private Language Argument*, Macmillan, London, 1971.

2 H.H. Price, 'Some Considerations about Belief', *Proceedings of the Aristotelian Society*, Vol. 35, 1934–5. This is reprinted in A. Phillips Griffiths (ed.), *Knowledge and Belief*, Oxford University Press, 1967, and it is to this reprinted edition that references are made. J. Cook Wilson's version of this theory is contained in the posthumous collection *Statement and Inference*, Clarendon Press, Oxford, 1926.

3 H.H. Price, *loc. cit.*, p. 45.

4 H.H. Price, *loc. cit.*, p. 58.

5 H.H. Price, *Belief*, George Allen and Unwin, London, 1969.

6 H.H. Price, *Belief*, p. 201.

7 Hume's *Treatise*, p. 629 (Selby-Bigge edition).

8 R.B. Braithwaite, 'The Nature of Believing', *Proceedings of the Aristotelian Society*, Vol. 33, 1932–3. This is reprinted in A. Phillips Griffiths (ed.), *Knowledge and Belief*, Oxford University Press, 1967, to which all references are made.

9 G. Ryle, *The Concept of Mind*, Penguin edition, 1963, Chapter V. (Originally published by Hutchinson, London, 1949.)

10 R.B. Braithwaite, *loc. cit.*, p. 37.

11 R. Carnap, *Meaning and Necessity*, University of Chicago Press, 1947, Sections 13–15.
12 Compare the revised account of belief given by Braithwaite in 'Belief and Action', *Proceedings of the Aristotelian Society*, Supplementary Vol. XX, 1946.
13 R.B. Braithwaite, 'The Nature of Believing', *loc. cit.*, p. 31.
14 R.B. Braithwaite, *loc. cit.*, pp. 31–2.
15 R.B. Braithwaite, *loc. cit.*, p. 31.
16 R.B. Braithwaite, *loc. cit.*, p. 32.
17 Cf. R.M. Chisholm, 'Sentences about Believing', *Proceedings of the Aristotelian Society*, Vol. 56, 1955–6.
18 G. Ryle, *The Concept of Mind*, Penguin edition, pp. 43–4.
19 Cf. S.G. Langford, *Human Action*, Macmillan, London, 1972, pp. 89–90.
20 We shall assume that there is no problem about the freedom of choice of our beliefs: Descartes thought we had such freedom, Hume that we did not.
21 F.P. Ramsey, *The Foundations of Mathematics*, R.B. Braithwaite (ed.), Routledge and Kegan Paul, London, 1931. A recent version of this collection, with a number of changes, has been edited by D.H. Mellor, *Foundations*, Routledge and Kegan Paul, London, 1978. The map analogy occurs on p. 134 of this new edition.
22 D.M. Armstrong, *Belief, Truth and Knowledge*, Cambridge University Press, 1973.

Chapter III: The Analysis of Knowledge

1 Relevant works include Plato's *Theaetetus*, translated and edited with substantial commentary by F.M. Cornford in *Plato's Theory of Knowledge*, Routledge and Kegan Paul, London, 1935; *Locke's Essay Concerning Human Understanding*, 1690; Hume's *Treatise of Human Nature*, 1739; and Kant's *Critique of Pure Reason*, 1781 (2nd edition 1787).
2 Cf. L. Wittgenstein's comments on games in *Philosophical Investigations*, Basil Blackwell, Oxford, 1963, Sections 65–78.
3 G. Ryle, *The Concept of Mind*, Penguin edition, 1963, Chapter II.
4 B. Russell, *The Problems of Philosophy*, Oxford University Press, 1912, Chapter 5.
5 F.M. Cornford, *Plato's Theory of Knowledge*, p. 142. Cornford translates the Greek word 'logos' as 'account' or 'explanation'.
6 A.J. Ayer, *The Problem of Knowledge*, Penguin edition, p. 35.
7 R.M. Chisholm, *Perceiving: a Philosophical Study*, Cornell University Press, Ithaca, New York, 1957, p. 16. Chisholm rejects this definition on p. 6 of his later *Theory of Knowledge*, Prentice-Hall, Englewood Cliffs, N.J., 1966; but he does offer a further variation on the Platonic analysis on p. 23 of that work, claiming that knowledge is true belief where the proposition involved is 'evident' for the believer.

8 J. Cook Wilson, *Statement and Inference*, Clarendon Press, Oxford, 1926. An extract from this work, concerning the unanalysability of knowing, is included in A. Phillips Griffiths (ed.), *Knowledge and Belief*.

9 J.L. Austin, 'Other Minds', *Proceedings of the Aristotelian Society*, Supplementary Volume XX, 1946. This paper is reprinted in Austin's *Philosophical Papers*, Clarendon Press, Oxford, 1961, and references are made to this text.

10 J.L. Austin, *loc. cit.*, p. 99.

11 Cf. J.R. Searle, *Speech Acts*, Cambridge University Press, 1969, pp. 136–41.

12 J.L. Austin, *How to Do Things with Words*, Clarendon Press, Oxford, 1962.

13 P.T. Geach, 'Assertion', *Philosophical Review*, Vol. 74, 1965.

14 B.S. Benjamin, 'Remembering', *Mind*, Vol. LXV, 1956. Reprinted in D.F. Gustafson (ed.), *Essays in Philosophical Psychology*, Macmillan, London, 1967. References given are to this latter text.

15 B.S. Benjamin, *loc. cit.*, p. 188.

16 I. Scheffler, *Conditions of Knowing*, Scott, Foresman & Co., Glenview, Illinois, 1965, Chapter 2.

17 E.g. G.E. Moore in P.A. Schilpp (ed.), *The Philosophy of G.E. Moore*, Evanston, Illinois, 1942, pp. 542–3.

18 The paradox is discussed by Max Black in 'Saying and Disbelieving', *Analysis*, Vol. 13, 1952, reprinted in Black's *Problems of Analysis*, Routledge and Kegan Paul, London, 1954; and by A.D. Woozley in 'Knowing and not Knowing,' *Proceedings of the Aristotelian Society*, Vol. 53, 1952–3, reprinted in A. Phillips Griffiths (ed.) *Knowledge and Belief*.

19 See note (8) above.

20 A. Phillips Griffiths (ed.), *Knowledge and Belief*, p. 10.

21 D.W. Hamlyn describes the form of the example, without the detail, in *The Theory of Knowledge*, Macmillan, London, 1971, pp. 84–5.

22 C. Radford, 'Knowledge by Examples', *Analysis*, Vol. 27, 1966–7.

23 D. Armstrong, 'Does Knowledge entail Belief?', *Proceedings of the Aristotelian Society*, Vol. 69, 1969–70.

24 L. Wittgenstein, *Philosophical Investigations*, Sections 68–78.

25 A version of this idea, adapted to include an Austinian connection between knowing and giving one's authority to the truth of P, is offered by D.W. Hamlyn in *The Theory of Knowledge*, pp. 101–2.

26 A.J. Ayer, *The Problem of Knowledge*, Penguin edition, p. 35.

27 See note (18) above.

28 E.g. by D.W. Hamlyn, *The Theory of Knowledge*, p. 81.

29 See, e.g. J. Hintikka, *Knowledge and Belief*, Cornell University Press, Ithaca, N.Y., 1962; Hintikka quotes Schopenhauer as another proponent of this view.

30 A.C. Danto, *Analytical Philosophy of Knowledge*, Cambridge University Press, 1968.

31 G. Ryle, *The Concept of Mind*, Introduction.

32 L. Wittgenstein, *On Certainty*, Blackwell, Oxford, 1969.

33 Cf. P.F. Strawson's review of L. Wittgenstein's *Philosophical Investigations* in *Mind*, Vol. LXIII, 1954.

34 J. Hintikka, *Models for Modalities*, Reidel, Dordrecht, 1969.

35 J. Hintikka, *op. cit.*, p. 5.

36 A relatively short account of N. Chomsky's views is his *Language and Mind*, Harcourt, Brace & World, New York, 1968.

37 Edmund L. Gettier, 'Is Justified True Belief Knowledge?', *Analysis*, Vol. 23, 1963; reprinted in A. Phillips Griffiths (ed.), *Knowledge and Belief*. Cf. B. Russell, *The Problems of Philosophy*, Ch. XIII.

38 For some such papers see the recent collection edited by G.S. Pappas and M. Swain, *Essays on Knowledge and Justification*, Cornell University Press, 1978.

39 E.L. Gettier, *loc. cit.*

40 E.L. Gettier, *loc. cit.* One philosopher who has questioned this latter assumption, and consequently questioned whether Gettier has produced cases of justified true belief after all, is I. Thalberg in 'In Defence of Justified True Belief,' *Journal of Philosophy*, Vol. 66, 1969.

41 A variant of this is *indefeasible* justified true belief – see below.

42 Cf. W.D. Ross, *The Right and the Good*, Oxford University Press, 1930, p. 18.

43 Cf. R.M. Chisholm, 'The Ethics of Requirement', *American Philosophical Quarterly*, Vol. 1, 1964.

44 This is the approach followed by M. Swain in 'Epistemic Defeasibility', *American Philosophical Quarterly*, Vol. 11, 1974. Lehrer and Paxson (see note 45 below), though using an 'undefeated' definition, seem to have the notion of indefeasibility in mind; for a defeating proposition, on their account, need not be known by the believer, or even believed by him.

45 K. Lehrer and T. Paxson, 'Knowledge: Undefeated Justified True Belief', *The Journal of Philosophy*, Vol. LXVI, 1969. (This article, and that by Swain, mentioned in note 44 above, are reprinted in the Pappas and Swain collection *Essays on Knowledge and Justification*.) Criticisms of the Lehrer and Paxson analysis can be found in M. Swain's paper, and in E. Sosa, 'Two Conceptions of Knowledge', *Journal of Philosophy*, Vol. 67, 1970.

46 For Lehrer and Paxson 'undefeated justified true belief' is equivalent to 'indefeasible justified true belief' on our usage; see note 44 above.

47 M. Swain, *op. cit.*

48 One reason why we say 'might be taken' here is that it ignores such cases as the volcano one below.

49 A.I. Goldman, 'A Causal Theory of Knowing', *Journal of Philosophy*, Vol. 64, 1967. This paper is reprinted in the Pappas and Swain collection *Essays on Knowledge and Justification*, but references are to the original paper.

50 A.I. Goldman, *loc. cit.*, p. 369.

51 A.I. Goldman, *loc. cit.*, p. 361.

52 A.I. Goldman, *loc. cit.*, p. 363.

53 A.I. Goldman, *loc. cit.*, p. 362.
54 Actually Goldman's claim is that such inferential steps are links in causal chains, but not causal connections themselves. This is enough, nevertheless, to constitute a major departure from our ordinary notion of a causal chain.
55 A.I. Goldman, *loc. cit.*, p. 368.

Chapter IV: Perception

1 J.L. Austin, *Sense and Sensibilia*, Oxford University Press, 1962, p. 8.
2 H.H. Price, *Perception*, Methuen, London, 1932, p. 145.
3 J. Locke, *Essay Concerning Human Understanding*, 1st edition 1690, 5th edition 1706, Book II, Chapter IV, Section 1.
4 Various versions of this 'argument from illusion' have been used by philosophers over the years, and can be found in the works of Locke, Berkeley, Russell, Price, and Ayer mentioned in the present chapter.
5 J. Locke, *op. cit.*, II, VIII, 21; and G. Berkeley, *Three Dialogues between Hylas and Philonous*, 1713, Everyman edition, Dent, London, 1910, p. 208.
6 H.H. Price, 'The Argument from Illusion', in H.D. Lewis (ed.), *Contemporary British Philosophy*, Third Series, Allen and Unwin, London, 1956, p. 396.
7 J. Hospers, *An Introduction to Philosophical Analysis*, Routledge and Kegan Paul, London, 1967, p. 561. Hospers is here stating a position with which he does not necessarily agree. But this view has been held by influential contemporary philosophers.
8 The first appearance of the term 'sense datum' was in B. Russell's *Problems of Philosophy*, published in 1912 by Home University Library, Oxford University Press. Extensive discussions of the problems of perception are contained in G.E. Moore's *Philosophical Studies*, Routledge and Kegan Paul, London, 1922.
9 J.S. Mill, *An Examination of Sir William Hamilton's Philosophy*, 1865, Chapters 11 and 12.
10 The phrase was introduced by the American philosopher, R.B. Perry.
11 G. Berkeley, *A Treatise Concerning the Principles of Human Knowledge*, 1710, Section 29.
12 Locke, *op. cit.*, II, VIII, 8.
13 Locke, *op. cit.*, II, VIII, 9.
14 Locke, *op. cit.*, II, VIII, 13.
15 A.N. Whitehead, *Science and the Modern World*, Cambridge University Press, 1926, p. 55.
16 Berkeley, *op. cit.*, Section 18.
17 A.J. Ayer, *Foundations of Empirical Knowledge*, Macmillan, London, 1940, p. 220.
18 Representatives of the factual approach are Berkeley and Mill, in the works cited above. The linguistic approach was favoured by the

logical positivists of the 1920s and 1930s, and is defended in A.J. Ayer's *Foundations of Empirical Knowledge*. A later paper of Ayer's, representing a change of position, is 'Phenomenalism', *Proceedings of the Aristotelian Society*, 1946–7.

19 See note 1 above.
20 A.J. Ayer, 'Has Austin Refuted the Sense Datum Theory?', *Synthese*, Vol. 17, 1967; reprinted in Ayer's *Metaphysics and Commonsense*, Macmillan, London, 1967.
21 D.W. Hamlyn, *The Theory of Knowledge*, Macmillan, London, 1970, p. 161.
22 L. Wittgenstein, *Philosophical Investigations*, Basil Blackwell, Oxford, 1963, Sections 242ff, 293ff.
23 L. Wittgenstein, *op. cit.*, Section 580.
24 L. Wittgenstein, *op. cit.*, Section 164.
25 J.S. Bruner, *Beyond the Information Given*, New York, 1972, p. 162.
26 G. Ryle, *The Concept of Mind*, Hutchinson, London, 1949, p. 213.
27 M. Von Senden, *Space and Time* (translated by P.L. Heath), Methuen, London, 1960.
28 R.L. Gregory, *Eye and Brain*, Weidenfeld, London, 1966, p. 193.
29 L. Kaufman, *Perception: The World Transformed*, Oxford University Press, New York, 1979.

Chapter V: Memory

1 E. Tulving, in Tulving and Donaldson, *The Organisation of Memory*, Academic Press, New York, 1972.
2 H. Bergson, *Matière et Memoire*, Alcan, Paris, 1908. (English translation, *Matter and Memory*, Allen and Unwin, London, 1912.)
3 B. Russell, *The Analysis of Mind*, Allen and Unwin, London, 1921, pp. 167–8.
4 C.D. Broad, *The Mind and its Place in Nature*, Routledge and Kegan Paul, London, 1925.
5 C.D. Broad, *loc. cit.*
6 Aristotle, *de Memoria*, 450a 13.
7 Aristotle, *de Memoria*, 450b 13.
8 The term was introduced by R.F. Holland in his paper 'The Empiricist Theory of Memory', *Mind*, Vol. 63, 1954.
9 D. Hume, *Treatise of Human Nature*, I, I, III.
10 B. Russell, *Analysis of Mind*, p. 163.
11 B. Russell, *Analysis of Mind*, p. 162.
12 T. Reid, *Essays on the Intellectual Powers of Man*, Bell, Edinburgh, 1785, (Facsimile reprint, Menston, Scolar Press, 1971) p. 349.
13 T. Reid, *loc. cit.*
14 T. Reid, *op. cit.*, p. 163.
15 T. Reid, *op. cit.*, p. 349.
16 T. Reid, *op. cit.*, p. 306.
17 T. Reid, *op. cit.*, p. 342.

18 See, for example, Alan Richardson, *Mental Imagery*, Routledge and Kegan Paul, London, 1969.

19 F. Galton, *op. cit.*, Everyman Library Edition, Dent, London, p. 58.

20 The realist theory of memory was defended by H. Bergson in *Matter and Memory*; by J. Laird in *Studies in Realism*, Cambridge University Press, 1920, Chapter 3; S. Alexander in *Space, Time and Deity*, Macmillan, London, 1920, Chapter 4; and by G.H. Stout in *Mind and Matter*, Cambridge University Press, 1931, Book III, Chapter 5.

21 G. Ryle, *The Concept of Mind*, Penguin, Harmondsworth, 1963, p. 257. This work was originally published by Hutchinson, London, 1949.

22 B. Russell, *Analysis of Mind*, pp. 159–60.

23 Cf. H.H. Price, 'Memory-Knowledge', Proceedings of the Aristotelian Society Supplementary Vol. XV, 1946, for a Humean argument along such lines.

24 R.F. Holland, 'Memory', *Mind*, Vol. 51, 1942.

25 R.F. Holland, *loc. cit.*, p. 476.

26 J.T. Saunders, 'Scepticism and Memory', *Philosophical Review*, Vol. 72, 1963, p. 477.

27 J.T. Saunders, *loc. cit.*, p. 479.

28 J.O. Nelson, 'The Validation of Memory and our Conception of a Past', *Philosophical Review*, Vol. 72, 1963.

29 Cf. N. Malcolm, Section IV of 'Memory and the Past', in *Knowledge and Certainty*, Cornell University Press, 1963.

30 S. Shoemaker, *Self-Knowledge and Self-Identity*, Cornell University Press, 1963, especially pp. 229–36. A very similar thesis, but limited to memory, is defended by N. Malcolm in 'Memory and the Past'.

31 S. Shoemaker, *op. cit.*, p. 229.

32 S. Shoemaker, *op. cit.*, p. 231.

33 S. Shoemaker, *op. cit.*, p. 232.

34 S. Shoemaker, *op. cit.*, pp. 232–3.

35 Don Locke, *Memory*, Macmillan, London, 1971, p. 123.

36 S. Shoemaker, *op. cit.*, pp. 233–4.

37 S. Shoemaker, *op. cit.*, p. 234.

38 I. Kant, *Critique of Pure Reason*, The Transcendental Aesthetic, 1781.

39 S. Alexander, *Space, Time and Deity*, Vol. I, p. 113.

40 C.D. Broad, *The Mind and its Place in Nature*, p. 266.

41 W. James, *Principles of Psychology*, Macmillan, London, 1890, Vol. I, p. 609.

42 D.O. Hebb, *A Textbook of Psychology* (Second Edition), Saunders, Philadelphia, 1966, p. 333.

Chapter VI: *A Priori* **Knowledge**

1 Kant would have denied that we can know 'All bachelors are unmarried' empirically, because this proposition (like all *a priori* propositions) is necessarily true. It seems better, however, to distinguish between this proposition and the related proposition 'Necessarily all

bachelors are unmarried', which is also true and is *not* knowable empirically.

2 I. Kant, *Critique of Pure Reason*, 1781 (Second Edition 1787) translated by N. Kemp Smith, Macmillan, London, 1929, p. 43.

3 Kant, *op. cit.*, p. 48.

4 Kant, *op. cit.*, p. 52.

5 Locke, *Essay Concerning Human Understanding*, IV, II.

6 Locke, *op. cit.*, IV, VIII.

7 E.g. G.W. Leibniz, *Monadology*, 1714, reprinted in *Leibniz: Philosophical Writings*, edited by G.H.R. Parkinson, Dent, London, 1973.

8 Cf. Leibniz, 'Necessary and Contingent Truths', in the Parkinson collection (see note 20), p. 96.

9 Hume, *Enquiry*, IV.

10 Hume, *Treatise*, I, III, 1.

11 Locke, *op. cit.*, I, II, 1.

12 See, e.g. Plato's *Meno*.

13 Aristotle, *Posterior Analytics*, 100a–100b.

14 Locke, *op. cit.*, IV, I, 2.

15 B. Russell, *The Problems of Philosophy*, Chapter X.

16 This programme was pursued in G. Frege, *Die Grundlagen der Arithmetik*, 1884.

17 F. Waismann, 'Analytic-Synthetic', *Analysis*, Vols. 10ff., 1949–52.

18 A.J. Ayer, *Language, Truth and Logic*, 1936 (Second edition 1946) Gollancz, London, p. 16.

19 Ayer, *op. cit.*, p. 79.

20 Ayer, *op. cit.*, pp. 16–17.

21 Ayer, *op. cit.*, p. 17.

22 Aristotle, *Metaphysics* IV, 4.

23 P.F. Strawson, 'Referring', *Mind*, Vol. 59, 1950.

24 J.S. Mill, *System of Logic*, 1843, Book II, Chapter VI.

25 Hume, *Treatise*, I, IV, 1.

26 See next section.

27 Some important papers are W.V.O. Quine, 'Two Dogmas of Empiricism', *Philosophical Review*, Vol. 60, 1951; a reply to that paper by H.P. Grice and P.F. Strawson, 'In Defence of a Dogma', *Philosophical Review*, Vol. 65, 1956; and N. Goodman, 'On Likeness of Meaning', *Analysis*, Vol. X, 1949–50. Quine's views were developed further in his *Word and Object*, M.I.T. Press, Cambridge, Mass., 1960. References are given to the reprint of the original Quine paper in a useful collection, edited by L.W. Sumner and J. Woods, *Necessary Truth*, Random House, New York, 1969.

28 Quine, 'Two Dogmas of Empiricism', *loc. cit.*, p. 136.

29 Quine, *op. cit.*, pp. 137–8.

30 See note 27.

Chapter VII: Truth

1 B. Russell, *The Problems of Philosophy*, Oxford University Press, 1912, pp. 120–1.

2 B. Russell, *Philosophical Essays*, Allen & Unwin, London, 1910, p. 156.

3 Reprinted in F.P. Ramsey, *The Foundations of Mathematics*, R.B. Braithwaite (ed.), Routledge and Kegan Paul, London, 1931, pp. 138ff.

4 E.g. R. Carnap, *Meaning and Necessity*, Chicago University Press, (First edition 1947) Second Edition 1951, pp. 27ff; and H. Leonard, *The Principles of Reasoning*, Dover, New York, 1967, p. 47.

5 B. Russell, *Logic and Knowledge*, edited by R.C. Marsh, Allen & Unwin, London, 1956, p. 285.

6 See, e.g. E. Sapir, *Language*, Harcourt, Brace, New York, 1921; and B.L. Whorf, *Language, Thought and Reality*, J.B. Carroll (ed.), M.I.T. Press, Cambridge, Mass., 1956.

7 The theory was set out in a long and very technical paper in 1931, and explained briefly in a popular and more readable version in 1944 (in *Philosophy and Phenomenological Research*, Vol. 4). But the second paper gives a very cursory account of the technical notion of *satisfaction* which is basic to the theory. The 1931 paper is reprinted as 'The Concept of Truth in Formalised Languages', in *Logic, Semantics and Metamathematics*, translated by J. Woodger, Oxford University Press, 1956, pp. 152–278. The 1944 paper, 'The Semantic Concept of Truth', is reprinted in Feigl and Sellars, *Readings in Philosophical Analysis*, Appleton-Century, New York, 1949.

8 A. Tarski, *op. cit.* 1944, 1949, p. 50.

9 A. Tarski, *op. cit.* 1944, 1949, p. 58.

10 A simplified account of the formal aspects of Tarski's theory is given in D.J. O'Connor, *The Correspondence Theory of Truth*, Hutchinson University Library, London, 1975, pp. 91–111.

11 A. Tarski, *op. cit.* 1956, p. 190.

12 W.V.O. Quine, *The Philosophy of Logic*, Prentice-Hall, 1970, p. 36.

13 A. Tarski, 1956, p. 195.

14 A. Tarski, 1944, p. 80.

15 A. Tarski, 'Truth and Proof', *Scientific American*, June 1969.

16 E.g. see p. 170.

17 A. Tarski, 'Truth and Proof', 1969.

18 W. Stegmuller, *Das Wahrheitsproblem und die Idee der Semantik*, Springer-Verlag, Vienna, 1957.

19 A. Tarski, *op. cit.* 1944, 1949, p. 63.

20 A. Tarski, *op. cit.* 1956, p. 194.

21 A. Tarski, *op. cit.* 1944, 1948, p. 65.

22 See note 3 above.

23 F.P. Ramsey, *op. cit.*, p. 142.

24 F.P. Ramsey, *loc. cit.*

25 See pp. 162–3 above.

26 J.L. Austin, *How to do Things with Words*, Oxford University Press, 1962, pp. 6ff.

27 P.F. Strawson, 'Truth', *Analysis*, Vol. 9, No. 6, 1949.

28 See our discussion of Austin's treatment of the words 'I know' in Chapter III, pp. 65–8.

29 W. Stegmuller, *op. cit.*, p. 229.

30 See D.J. O'Connor, *The Correspondence Theory of Truth*, Hutchinson University Library, London, 1975, p. 127.

Concluding Remarks

1 B. Russell, *Human Knowledge: Its Scope and Limits*, Allen & Unwin, London, 1948, p. 415.

2 Locke, *Essay Concerning Human Understanding*, IV, III, 12.

BIBLIOGRAPHY

The following is a selective bibliography only. It includes the more important works referred to in the text and notes, together with some works of interest which have not been mentioned so far. Starred items (*) are those with which the newcomer to the theory of knowledge might begin.

*R.J. Ackermann, *Belief and Knowledge*, Macmillan, London 1972.
G.E.M. Anscombe and P.T. Geach (eds.), *Descartes: Philosophical Writings*, Thomas Nelson, London 1954.
Aristotle, *de Memoria, Metaphysics, Posterior Analytics*.
D.M. Armstrong, *Belief, Truth and Knowledge*, Cambridge University Press, 1973.
*D.M. Armstrong, 'Does knowledge entail Belief?', *Proceedings of the Aristotelian Society* Vol. 69, 1969–70.
D.M. Armstrong, *Perception and the Physical World*, Routledge and Kegan Paul, London, 1961.
R.F. Atkinson, *Knowledge and Explanation in History*, Macmillan, London, 1978.
St. Augustine, *Contra Academicos*, 386 AD.
J.L. Austin, *Philosophical Papers*, Clarendon Press, Oxford, 1961.
J.L. Austin, *Sense and Sensibilia*, Oxford University Press, 1962.
*A.J. Ayer, 'Basic Propositions', in M. Black (ed.), *Philosophical Analysis*, Cornell University Press, Ithaca, New York, 1950; reprinted in A.J. Ayer, *Philosophical Essays*, Macmillan, London, 1954.
*A.J. Ayer, *Language, Truth and Logic*, Gollancz, London, 1936 (Second edition 1946).
A.J. Ayer, *Metaphysics and Common Sense*, Macmillan, London, 1967.
*A.J. Ayer, *Problem of Knowledge*, Macmillan, London, 1956; Penguin edition, Harmondsworth, 1963.
F. Bacon, *Novum Organum*, 1620.
P. Bayle, *Dictionnaire historique et critique*, 1697.
H. Bergson, *Matière et Memoire*, Alcan, Paris, 1908; English translation, *Matter and Memory*, Allen & Unwin, London 1912.
*G. Berkeley, *Three Dialogues between Hylas and Philonous*, 1713; Everyman edition, Dent, London, 1910.

G. Berkeley, *Treatise Concerning the Principles of Human Knowledge*, 1710.

*R.B. Braithwaite, 'The Nature of Believing', *Proceedings of the Aristotelian Society*, Vol. 33, 1932–3; reprinted in Griffiths' *Knowledge and Belief*.

C.D. Broad, *Mind and its Place in Nature*, Routledge and Kegan Paul, London, 1925.

R. Carnap, *Meaning and Necessity*, University of Chicago Press, 1947.

R.M. Chisholm and R.J. Swartz (eds.), *Empirical Knowledge*, Prentice-Hall, Englewood Cliffs, New Jersey, 1973.

R.M. Chisholm, *Perceiving: a Philosophical Study*, Cornell University Press, Ithaca, New York, 1957.

*R.M. Chisholm, *Theory of Knowledge*, Prentice-Hall, Englewood Cliffs, New Jersey, 1966.

N. Chomsky, *Language and Mind*, Harcourt, Brace and World, New York, 1968.

J. Cook Wilson, *Statement and Inference*, Clarendon Press, Oxford, 1926.

*F.M. Cornford *Plato's Theory of Knowledge*, Routledge and Kegan Paul, London, 1935.

A.C. Danto, *Analytical Philosophy of Knowledge*, Cambridge University Press, 1968.

R. Descartes, *Discourse on Method*, 1637; included in Anscombe and Geach collection, and in Haldane and Ross collection.

*R. Descartes, *Meditations on First Philosophy*, 1641; included in Anscombe and Geach collection, and in Haldane and Ross collection.

R. Descartes, *Principles of Philosophy*, 1644; included in Anscombe and Geach collection, and in Haldane and Ross collection.

F. Dretske, *Seeing and Knowing*, Routledge and Kegan Paul, London, 1969.

*P. Edwards (ed.), *Encyclopedia of Philosophy*, Macmillan, New York, 1967.

D. Erasmus, *De Libero Arbitrio*, 1524.

P.T. Geach, 'Assertion', *Philosophical Review*, Vol. 74, 1965; reprinted in P.T. Geach, *Logic Matters*, Basil Blackwell, Oxford, 1972.

P.T. Geach, *Mental Acts*, Routledge and Kegan Paul, London, 1957.

*E.L. Gettier, 'Is Justified True Belief Knowledge?', *Analysis*, Vol. 23, 1963; reprinted in Griffiths' *Knowledge and Belief*.

*H.P. Grice and P.F. Strawson, 'In Defence of a Dogma', *Philosophical Review*, Vol. 65, 1956; reprinted in Sumner and Woods' *Necessary Truth*.

*A. Phillips Griffiths (ed.), *Knowledge and Belief*, Oxford University Press, 1967.

D.F. Gustafson (ed.), *Essays in Philosophical Psychology*, Macmillan, London, 1967.

E.S. Haldane and G.R.T. Ross (eds.), *Philosophical Works of Descartes*, (2 volumes) Dover, New York, 1911.

D.W. Hamlyn, *Sensation and Perception*, Routledge and Kegan Paul, London, 1961.

*D.W. Hamlyn, *Theory of Knowledge*, Macmillan, London, 1971.

C.G. Hempel, *Aspects of Scientific Explanation*, Macmillan, New York, 1965.

*J. Hintikka, 'Epistemic Logic and the Methods of Philosophical Analysis', in J. Hintikka, *Models for Modalities*, D. Reidel, Dordrecht, Holland, 1969.

J. Hintikka, *Knowledge and Belief*, Cornell University Press, Ithaca, New York, 1962.

R.F. Holland, 'The Empiricist Theory of Memory', *Mind*, Vol. 63, 1954.

*J. Hospers, *Introduction to Philosophical Analysis*, Routledge and Kegan Paul, London, 1967.

*D. Hume, *Enquiry Concerning Human Understanding*, 1748; edited, with an Analytical Index, by L.A. Selby-Bigge, 3rd edition: revised by P.H. Nidditch, Oxford University Press, 1975.

*D. Hume, *Treatise of Human Nature*, 1739–40; edited, with an Analytical Index, by L.A. Selby-Bigge, Oxford University Press, 1888.

I. Kant, *Critique of Pure Reason*, 1781 (Second edition 1787); translated and edited by N. Kemp Smith, Macmillan, London, 1929.

*I. Kant, *Prolegomena to Any Future Metaphysics*, 1783; translated and edited with notes by P.G. Lucas, Manchester University Press, 1953.

*A.R. Lacey, *Dictionary of Philosophy*, Routledge and Kegan Paul, London, 1976.

*S.G. Langford, *Human Action*, Macmillan, London, 1972.

K. Lehrer, *Knowledge*, Clarendon Press, Oxford, 1974.

G.W. Leibniz, *Monadology*, 1714; included in Parkinson collection.

G.W. Leibniz, 'Necessary and Contingent Truths', c.1686; included in Parkinson collection.

G.W. Leibniz, *New Essays on the Human Understanding*, c.1704; included in Parkinson collection.

I. Levi, *Gambling with Truth*, Routledge and Kegan Paul, London, 1967.

*D. Locke, *Memory*, Macmillan, London, 1971.

D. Locke, *Perception and our Knowledge of the External World*, Allen & Unwin, London, 1967.

*J. Locke, *Essay Concerning Human Understanding*, 1690 (Fifth edition 1706); edited by P.H. Nidditch, Oxford University Press, 1975.

M. Luther, *De Servo Arbitrio*, 1525.

*N. Malcolm, 'Knowledge and Belief', *Mind*, Vol. 61, 1952; reprinted in Malcolm's *Knowledge and Certainty*; and in Griffiths' *Knowledge and Belief*.

N. Malcolm, *Knowledge and Certainty*, Cornell University Press, Ithaca, New York, 1963.

*N. Malcolm, 'Memory and the Past', in Malcolm's *Knowledge and Certainty*.

J.S. Mill, *Examination of Sir William Hamilton's Philosophy*, 1865.

J.S. Mill, *System of Logic*, 1843.

M.E. de Montaigne, 'Apology for Raimond Sebond', 1580.

G.E. Moore, *Philosophical Papers*, Allen & Unwin, London, 1959.

G.E. Moore, *Philosophical Studies*, Routledge and Kegan Paul, London, 1922.

*D.J. O'Connor, *Correspondence Theory of Truth*, Hutchinson University Library, London, 1975.

*D.J. O'Connor (ed.), *Critical History of Western Philosophy*, Free Press, Glencoe, Illinois, 1964.

Pan Dictionary of Philosophy (ed. A.G.N. Flew), Pan, London, 1979.

A. Pap, *Semantics and Necessary Truth*, Yale University Press, 1958.

G.S. Pappas and M. Swain, *Essays on Knowledge and Justification*, Cornell University Press, Ithaca, New York, 1978.

G.H.R. Parkinson (ed.), *Leibniz: Philosophical Writings*, Dent, London, 1973.

J. Passmore, *Hundred Years of Philosophy*, Duckworth, London, 1957; Penguin edition, Harmondsworth, 1968.

*Plato, *Meno, Phaedo, Theaetetus*.

J.L. Pollock,*Knowledge and Justification*, Princeton University Press, 1974.

K. Popper, *Conjectures and Refutations*, Routledge and Kegan Paul, London, 1963.

K. Popper, *Objective Knowledge*, Oxford University Press, 1972.

G. Pitcher (ed.), *Truth*, Prentice-Hall, Englewood Cliffs, New Jersey, 1964.

H.H. Price, *Belief*, Allen & Unwin, London, 1969.

H.H. Price, Hume's *Theory of the External World*, Clarendon Press, Oxford, 1948.

H.H. Price, *Perception*, Methuen, London, 1932.

*H.H. Price, 'Some Considerations about Belief', *Proceedings of the Aristotelian Society*, Vol. 35, 1934–5; reprinted in Griffiths' *Knowledge and Belief*.

H.H. Price, *Thinking and Experience*, Hutchinson University Library, London, 1953.

H.A. Prichard,*Knowledge and Perception*, Clarendon Press, Oxford, 1950.

W.V.O. Quine,*Philosophy of Logic*, Prentice-Hall, Englewood Cliffs, New Jersey, 1970.

*W.V.O. Quine, 'Two Dogmas of Empiricism',*Philosophical Review*, Vol. 60, 1951; reprinted in Sumner and Woods' *Necessary Truth*.

W.V.O. Quine, *Word and Object*, M.I.T. Press, Cambridge, Mass., 1960.

F.P. Ramsey, *Foundations of Mathematics* (ed. R.B. Braithwaite), Routledge and Kegan Paul, London, 1931; new edition edited by D.H. Mellor under the title *Foundations*, Routledge and Kegan Paul, London, 1978.

T. Reid, *Essays on the Intellectual Powers of Man*, Bell, Edinburgh, 1785; facsimile reprint, Scolar Press, 1971.

B. Russell, *Analysis of Mind*, Allen & Unwin, London, 1921.

B. Russell, *Human Knowledge: Its Scope and Limits*, Allen & Unwin, London, 1948.

B. Russell,*Inquiry into Meaning and Truth*, Allen & Unwin, London, 1940; Penguin edition, Harmondsworth, 1962.

B. Russell, *Our Knowledge of the External World*, Allen & Unwin, London, 1914.

B. Russell, *Problems of Philosophy*, Oxford University Press, 1912.

G. Ryle, *Concepts of Mind*, Hutchinson, London, 1949; Penguin edition, Harmondsworth, 1963.

*J.T. Saunders, 'Scepticism and Memory', *Philosophical Review*, Vol. 72, 1963.

*I. Scheffler, *Conditions of Knowledge*, Scott, Foresman, Glenview, Illinois, 1965.

P.A. Schilpp (ed.), *Philosophy of G.E. Moore*, Evanston, Illinois, 1942.

S. Shoemaker, *Self-Knowledge and Self-Identity*, Cornell University Press, Ithaca, New York, 1963.

B. Spinoza, *Ethics*, 1677; included in Wild collection.

B. Spinoza, *On the Improvement of the Understanding*, 1677; included in Wild collection.

G.H. Stout, *Mind and Matter*, Cambridge University Press, 1931.

D.C. Stove, *Probability and Hume's Inductive Scepticism*, Clarendon Press, Oxford, 1973.

P.F. Strawson, *Introduction to Logical Theory*, Methuen, London, 1952.

*P.F. Strawson, review of Wittgenstein's *Philosophical Investigations* in *Mind*, Vol. LXIII, 1954.

L.W. Sumner and J. Woods, *Necessary Truth*, Random House, New York, 1969.

M. Swain (ed.), *Induction, Acceptance and Rational Belief*, D. Reidel, Dordrecht, Holland, 1970.

*R.J. Swartz (ed.), *Perceiving, Sensing and Knowing*, Doubleday, New York, 1965.

R. Swinburne (ed.), *Justification of Induction*, Oxford University Press, 1974.

W. von Leyden, *Remembering*, Duckworth, London, 1951.

*A.R. White, *Truth*, Macmillan, London, 1971.

J. Wild (ed.), *Spinoza Selections*, Scribners, New York, 1930.

C.J.F. Williams, *What is Truth?*, Cambridge University Press, 1976.

*L. Wittgenstein, *On Certainty*, Basil Blackwell, Oxford, 1969.

L. Wittgenstein, *Philosophical Investigations*, Basil Blackwell, Oxford, 1963.

*A.D. Woozley, *Theory of Knowledge*, Hutchinson, London, 1949.

INDEX